Diplomacy

Also by G. R. Berridge

BRITISH DIPLOMACY IN TURKEY, 1583 TO THE PRESENT: A Study in the Evolution of the Resident Embassy

A DICTIONARY OF DIPLOMACY: Second Edition (*with Alan James*)

DIPLOMACY AT THE UN (*co-editor with A. Jennings*)

DIPLOMATIC THEORY FROM MACHIAVELLI TO KISSINGER (*with Maurice Keens-Soper and T. G. Otte*)

DIPLOMATIC CLASSIC: Selected Texts from Commynes to Vattel

ECONOMIC POWER IN ANGLO-SOUTH AFRICAN DIPLOMACY: Simonstown, Sharpeville and After

GERALD FITZMAURICE (1865–1939), CHIEF DRAGOMAN OF THE BRITISH EMBASSY IN TURKEY

INTERNATIONAL POLITICS: States, Power and Conflict since 1945, Third Edition

AN INTRODUCTION TO INTERNATIONAL RELATIONS (*with D. Heater*)

THE POLITICS OF THE SOUTH AFRICA RUN: European Shipping and Pretoria

RETURN TO THE UN: UN Diplomacy in Regional Conflicts

SOUTH AFRICA, THE COLONIAL POWERS AND 'AFRICAN DEFENCE': The Rise and Fall of the White Entente, 1948–60

TALKING TO THE ENEMY: How States without 'Diplomatic Relations' Communicate

Diplomacy

Theory and Practice

Fourth Edition

G. R. Berridge
Emeritus Professor of International Politics,
University of Leicester, UK
and
Senior Fellow, DiploFoundation

palgrave
macmillan

First published 2010 by
PALGRAVE MACMILLAN

Palgrave Macmillan in the UK is an imprint of Macmillan Publishers Limited, registered in England, company number 785998, of Houndmills, Basingstoke, Hampshire RG21 6XS.

Palgrave Macmillan in the US is a division of St Martin's Press LLC, 175 Fifth Avenue, New York, NY 10010.

Palgrave Macmillan is the global academic imprint of the above companies and has companies and representatives throughout the world.

Palgrave® and Macmillan® are registered trademarks in the United States, the United Kingdom, Europe and other countries.

ISBN: 978-0-230-22959-4 hardback
ISBN: 978-0-230-22960-0 paperback

This book is printed on paper suitable for recycling and made from fully managed and sustained forest sources. Logging, pulping and manufacturing processes are expected to conform to the environmental regulations of the country of origin.

A catalogue record for this book is available from the British Library.

A catalog record for this book is available from the Library of Congress.

6
11

Printed and bound in Great Britain by
CPI Antony Rowe, Chippenham and Eastbourne

For Brian Barder

Contents

Part III Diplomacy without Diplomatic Relations

Boxes

Preface

This edition of *Diplomacy* has not only been updated but also reorganized and expanded. I have added a new part on diplomacy without diplomatic relations, inspired in part by my earlier book *Talking to the Enemy* (Macmillan, 1994), and new chapters on following up agreements, consulates, public diplomacy, and special missions.

In the interests of economy and clarity, I have cut out footnotes and all but the most necessary citations. In 'Further reading' and 'References' I have indicated an internet source simply by '[www]', partly because URLs are so long and frequently either change or disappear altogether, and partly because it is easy enough to find a source that still exists via a search engine. Unless otherwise stated, any figures given (for example, for consulates in Chapter 8) are those current at the time of writing, March–June 2009.

For critical observations on parts of the text and/or for help in other ways, I am grateful to Stefano Baldi, Keith Hamilton, Alan Henrikson, Larry Pope, Kishan Rana, Arianna Arisi Rota, Malcolm Shaw, Alexandra Webster, John Young, Palgrave's reader and the team at Newgen Imaging Systems, India. I am responsible for all remaining errors of fact or weaknesses of analysis.

I have dedicated this edition of *Diplomacy* to Sir Brian Barder, whose generosity knows no bounds and who has helped me perhaps more than he knows.

G. R. B.
Leicester, June 2009

Online Updating

For each chapter in the book, there is a corresponding page on my website. These pages contain further reflections and details of recent developments on the subject in question. The website also contains resources for students of diplomacy, such as the full catalogue of the Archive of Diplomatic Lists at the University of Leicester and reviews of recent books. It also has suggestions for dissertation topics. Please visit http://grberridge.diplomacy.edu/

Abbreviations used in Text and Citations

ABM	anti-ballistic missile
ASEAN	Association of South-East Asian Nations
ATTC	Anglo-Taiwan Trade Committee
AU	African Union [formerly Organization of African Unity]
CAT	Convention Against Torture and Other Cruel, Inhuman or Degrading Treatment or Punishment
CHOGM	Commonwealth Heads of Government Meeting
CNN	Cable News Network
CPRS	Central Policy Review Staff
DLO	drugs liaison officer
EC	European Community
ECHR	European Convention on Human Rights
EU	European Union
FAC	Foreign Affairs Committee [British House of Commons]
FCO	Foreign and Commonwealth Office
FMLN	*Frente Farabundo Marti para la Liberacrorz Nacional* [coalition of armed insurgent groups in El Salvador]
FO	Foreign Office [British]
FRUS	*Foreign Relations of the United States*
GATT	General Agreement on Tariffs and Trade
IAEA	International Atomic Energy Agency
ICC	International Criminal Court
ICRC	International Committee of the Red Cross
ICT	information and communications technology
ILC	International Law Commission
ILO	immigration liaison officer
IMF	International Monetary Fund
MFA	Ministry of Foreign Affairs
MIRV	multiple independently targetable re-entry vehicle
MOU	memorandum of understanding
NGO	non-governmental organization
NPT	Nuclear Non-Proliferation Treaty
OAS	Organization of American States

OECD	Organisation for Economic Co-operation and Development
OGDs	other government departments
OIG	Office of Inspector General [US State Department]
OSCE	Organization for Security and Co-operation in Europe
P5	Permanent 5 [on the UN Security Council]
PLO	Palestine Liberation Organization
PRC	People's Republic of China
QDF	Qadhafi Development Foundation
ROC	Republic of China
SAARC	South Asian Association for Regional Cooperation
SALT I	Strategic Arms Limitations Talks [first negotiations, 1969–72]
SIAC	Special Immigration Appeals Commission
SIGINT	signals intelligence
SOE	Special Operations Executive
TRNC	Turkish Republic of Northern Cyprus
UNMOVIC	United Nations Monitoring, Verification and Inspection Commission
UNSCOM	United Nations Special Commission
USINT	US Interests Section Cuba
VCCR	Vienna Convention on Consular Relations, 1963
VCDR	Vienna Convention on Diplomatic Relations, 1961
WMD	weapons of mass destruction
WTO	World Trade Organization

Introduction

Diplomacy is an essentially political activity and, well-resourced and skilful, a major ingredient of power. Its chief purpose is to enable states to secure the objectives of their foreign policies without resort to force, propaganda, or law. It follows that diplomacy consists of communication between officials designed to promote foreign policy either by formal agreement or tacit adjustment. Although it also includes such discrete activities as gathering information, clarifying intentions, and engendering goodwill, it is thus not surprising that, until the label 'diplomacy' was affixed to all of these activities by the British parliamentarian Edmund Burke in 1796, it was known most commonly as 'negotiation' – by Cardinal Richelieu, the first minister of Louis XIII, as *négociation continuelle*. Diplomacy is not merely what professional diplomatic agents do. It is carried out by other officials and by private persons under the direction of officials. As we shall see, it is also carried out through many different channels besides the traditional resident mission. Together with the balance of power, which it both reflects and reinforces, diplomacy is the most important institution of our society of states.

Diplomacy in its modern form has its immediate origins in the Italian peninsula in the late fifteenth century AD. Nevertheless, its remote origins are to be found in the relations between the 'Great Kings' of the Near East in the second, or possibly even in the late fourth, millennium BCE (Liverani: introduction; Cohen and Westbrook: 1–12). Its main features in these centuries were the dependence of communications on messengers and merchant caravans, of diplomatic immunity on ordinary codes of hospitality, and of treaty observance on terror of the gods under whose gaze they were confirmed. However, although apparently adequate to the times, diplomacy during these centuries

1

remained rudimentary. In the main, this would seem to be because it was not called on very often and because communications were slow, laborious, unpredictable, and insecure.

In the Greek city state system of the fourth and fifth centuries BC, however, conditions both demanded and favoured a more sophisticated diplomacy. Diplomatic immunity, even of the herald in war, became a more entrenched norm, and resident missions began to emerge, although employing a local citizen. Such a person was known as a *proxenos*. In medieval Europe, the development of diplomacy was led first by Byzantium (the eastern Roman Empire) and then, especially, by Venice, which set new standards of honesty and technical proficiency. However, diplomacy remained chiefly in the hands of special envoys, limited by time and task.

It was in the Italian city states system in the late fifteenth century, when conditions were especially favourable to the further development of diplomacy, that the recognizably modern system first made its appearance. The hyper-insecurity of the rich but poorly defended Italian states induced by the repeated invasions of their peninsula by the ultramontane powers after 1494, made essential a diplomacy that was both continuous and conducted with less fanfare. Fortunately, no barriers were presented by language or religion and, although communications still depended on horsed messengers, the relatively short distances between city states made this less important. It is not surprising, therefore, that it was this period that saw the birth of the genuine resident embassy; that is to say, a resident mission headed by a citizen of the prince or republic whose interests it served. This Italian system, the spirit and methods of which are captured so well in the despatches of Niccolò Machiavelli, evolved shortly into the French system that, in the middle of the twentieth century, was praised so highly by the British scholar-diplomat, Harold Nicolson (Nicolson, 1954). This was the first fully-developed system of diplomacy and the basis of the modern – essentially bilateral – system (see Chapter 7).

In the early twentieth century, the French system was modified but not, as some hoped and others feared, transformed. The 'open diplomacy' of *ad hoc* and permanent conferences (notably the League of Nations) was simply grafted onto the existing network of bilateral communications. As for the anti-diplomacy of the Communist regimes in Soviet Russia and subsequently in China, this was relatively short-lived. Why did diplomacy survive these assaults and continue to develop to such a degree and in such an inventive manner that, at the beginning of the twenty-first century, we can speak with some confidence of a world diplomatic system of unprecedented strength? The reason is that the conditions that first encouraged the development of diplomacy have, for some decades, obtained perhaps more fully than ever before. These are a balance of power between a plurality of states, mutually impinging interests of an unusually urgent kind, efficient and secure international communication, and relative cultural toleration – the rise of radical Islam notwithstanding.

As already noted, diplomacy is an important means by which states pursue their foreign policies, and these policies are still framed in significant degree in many states in a ministry of foreign affairs. Such ministries also have the major responsibility for a state's diplomats serving abroad and for dealing (formally, at any rate) with foreign diplomats at home. It is for this reason that this book begins with a detailed examination of the origins and the current position of the ministry of foreign affairs. Following this, it is divided into three parts. Part I is devoted to a consideration of the art of negotiation, the most important activity undertaken in the world diplomatic system *as a whole*. Part II examines the different channels through which negotiations, together with the other functions of diplomacy, are pursued when states enjoy normal diplomatic relations. Part III examines some of the most important ways in which these are pursued when they do not.

Further reading

Adcock, F. and D. J. Mosley, *Diplomacy in Ancient Greece* (Thames & Hudson: London, 1975): pt 2.

Anderson, M. S., *The Rise of Modern Diplomacy* (Longman: London, 1993).

Berridge, G. R. (ed.), *Diplomatic Classics: Selected texts from Commynes to Vattel* (Palgrave Macmillan: Basingstoke/New York; Peking University Press: Beijing, 2004).

Berridge, G. R., M. Keens-Soper and T. G. Otte (eds), *Diplomatic Theory from Machiavelli to Kissinger* (Palgrave Macmillan: Basingstoke/New York, 2001).

Bozeman, Adda B., *Politics and Culture in International History*, 2nd edn (Transaction: New Brunswick/London, 1994): 324–56, 457–504.

Bull, Hedley and Adam Watson (eds), *The Expansion of International Society* (Clarendon Press: Oxford; Oxford University Press: New York, 1984).

Cohen, Raymond and Raymond Westbrook (eds), *Amarna Diplomacy: The beginnings of international relations* (Johns Hopkins University Press: Baltimore/London, 2000).

Dictionary of the Middle Ages, Volume 4 (Scribner's: New York, 1984): chs by Queller and Wozniak.

Hamilton, Keith and Richard Langhorne, *The Practice of Diplomacy* (Routledge: London, 1995): chs 1–4.

Jones, Raymond A., *The British Diplomatic Service, 1815–1914* (Colin Smythe: Gerrards Cross, Bucks., 1983).

Lachs, Phyllis S., *The Diplomatic Corps under Charles II and James II* (Rutgers University Press: New Brunswick, NJ, 1965).

Liverani, Mario, *International Relations in the Ancient Near East* (Palgrave: Basingstoke, 2001), intro. and ch. 10.

Mattingly, G., *Renaissance Diplomacy* (Penguin: Harmondsworth, 1965).

Meier, S. A., *The Messenger in the Ancient Semitic World* (Scholars Press: Atlanta, GA, 1988).

Mösslang, M. and T. Riotte (eds), *The Diplomats' World: A cultural history of diplomacy, 1815–1914* (Oxford University Press: Oxford, 2008)

Munn-Rankin, J. M., 'Diplomacy in Western Asia in the early second millennium B.C.', *Iraq*, 1956, Spring, 18(1).

Sharp, Paul and Geoffrey Wiseman (eds), *The Diplomatic Corps as an Institution of International Society* (Palgrave Macmillan: Basingstoke/New York, 2007).

Queller, D. E., *The Office of Ambassador in the Middle Ages* (Princeton University Press: Princeton, NJ, 1967).

Yurdusev, A. Nuri (ed.), *Ottoman Diplomacy: Conventional or unconventional?* (Palgrave Macmillan: Basingstoke/New York, 2004).

1
The Ministry of Foreign Affairs

It is difficult to find a state today that does not have, in addition to a diplomatic service, a ministry dedicated to directing and administering it. This is usually known as the ministry of foreign affairs (MFA) or, for short, foreign ministry. It is easy to forget that this was not always the case and that the MFA came relatively late onto the scene. In fact, as commonly defined, its appearance in Europe post-dated the arrival of the resident diplomatic mission by between two and three centuries. This chapter will begin by looking briefly at the origins and development of the foreign ministry, and then examine its different roles. These include staffing and supporting missions abroad, policy advice and implementation, policy coordination, dealing with foreign diplomats at home, and building domestic support.

The origins and growth of the MFA

Until the sixteenth century, the individual states of Europe did not concentrate responsibility for foreign policy and the diplomatic machine in one administrative unit but allocated it between different, infant bureaucracies on a geographical basis. Some of these offices were also responsible for certain domestic matters. This picture began to change under the combined pressure of the multiplying international relationships and thickening networks of resident embassies that were a feature of the early modern period. The first trend increased the possibilities of inconsistency in the formulation and execution of foreign policy, and this demanded more unified direction and better preserved archives. The second trend – foreign policy execution by means of resident missions – brought a vast increase in the quantity of correspondence flowing home. This meant the need for attention to methods of communication with the missions, including the composition and renewal of their ciphers. It also meant attention to their staffing and, especially, their financing – including that of their secret intelligence activities, because separate secret service agencies did not appear until very much later. All of this demanded better preserved archives as well, not to mention more clerks, cipher clerks, and messengers. In sum, the rapid increase abroad in what was called 'continuous negotiation' by Cardinal Richelieu, the legendary chief minister of the French king, Louis XIII, required not only continuous organization at home but also one bureaucracy, rather than several in competition.

It has often been assumed that it was in France that the first foreign ministry began to emerge when, in 1589, Henry III gave sole responsibility for foreign affairs to one of his secretaries of state, Louis de Revol, an administrative innovation that – after some regression – was confirmed by Richelieu in 1626. But there might well be other candidates, within and beyond Europe, for the title of first foreign ministry. Moreover, the office of the French secretary of state for foreign affairs in Richelieu's time was little more than a personal staff: it was not even an outline version of a modern foreign ministry, with an organized archive and defined bureaucratic structure. This had to wait until the last years of the reign of Louis XIV at the beginning of the eighteenth century (Picavet: 39–40).

Indeed, it was only during the eighteenth century that a recognizably modern ministry of foreign affairs became the general rule in Europe, and even then the administrative separation of foreign and domestic business was by no means watertight (Horn: 1). Britain came late, having to wait until 1782 for the creation of the Foreign Office. The US Department of State was established shortly after this, in 1789 (Box 1.1). It was the middle of the nineteenth century before China, Japan, and Turkey followed suit.

Even in Europe, however, it was well into the nineteenth century before foreign ministries, which remained small, became bureaucratically sophisticated. By this time, they were divided into different administrative units ('departments' or '*bureaux*') on the basis either of specialization in a particular function (for example, protocol or treaties), or a particular geographical region. In addition to the foreign minister, who was the temporary political head of the ministry, the typical MFA had, by this time, also acquired a permanent senior official to oversee its administration. As time wore on, this official (in Britain, the permanent under-secretary; elsewhere, more commonly, the secretary-general

---

Box 1.1   'Department of Foreign Affairs' to 'Department of State'

A Department of Foreign Affairs was established by the Continental Congress on 10 January 1781. This title was also initially employed for the foreign ministry of the United States itself under legislation approved by the House and Senate on 21 July 1789 and signed into law by President Washington six days later. In September, the Department was given certain *domestic* duties as well, which subsequently came to include management of the Mint, fulfilling the role of keeper of the Great Seal of the United States, and the taking of the census. No longer charged solely with *foreign* tasks, it was for this reason that, at the same juncture, the Department's name was changed to 'Department of State'. Despite surrendering most of its domestic duties in the nineteenth century, the Department found itself stuck with the name.

---

or director-general) also acquired influence over policy, sometimes very great. Entry into the foreign ministry increasingly demanded suitable educational qualifications, although the pool from which recruits came was limited to the upper reaches of the social hierarchy until well into the twentieth century.

The foreign ministry still had rivals for influence over the formulation and execution of foreign policy in the nineteenth century. Among these were the monarchs and presidents, chancellors, and prime ministers, who felt that their positions gave them special prerogatives to dabble in this area, as also the war offices with their nascent intelligence services. Nevertheless, if the MFA had a golden age of influence and prestige, this was probably it. It did not last long. Distaste for both commerce and popular meddling in foreign policy was entrenched in most foreign ministries, which were essentially aristocratic in ethos, and this soon put them on the defensive in the following century. World War I itself was also a tremendous blow to their prestige because it seemed to prove the failings of the old diplomacy over which they presided. Much of the burgeoning dissatisfaction with the way ministries such as these were staffed and organized, as well as with the manner in which they conducted their affairs, focused on the administrative (and, in some instances, social) divisions within the bureaucracy of diplomacy.

Despite the intimate link between those in the foreign ministry and the diplomats serving abroad, their work and the social milieux in which they mixed were very different. Persons attracted to one sort were not, as a rule, attracted to the other, and they were usually recruited by different methods. Foreign ministry officials had more in common with the civil servants in other government ministries than with their own, glittering diplomats, whom in any case they rarely met and had good grounds for believing looked on them as social inferiors. They also tended to develop different outlooks. American diplomats, who closed ranks in the face of constant ridicule at home, developed a particularly strong 'fraternal spirit' (Simpson: 3–4). The result was that, except in small states, it became the norm for the two branches of diplomacy – the foreign ministry and its representatives abroad – to be organized separately and have distinct career ladders. Between the two branches there was little, if any, transfer. It was also usual for the representatives abroad to be divided into separate services, the diplomatic and the consular – and, sometimes, the commercial as well.

These traditional bureaucratic divisions institutionalized the prejudices of their members and impeded not only desirable personnel transfers, but also cooperation between them. However, resistance to change remained strong, and it came only slowly. In Britain, the staffs of the Foreign Office and the Diplomatic Service were merged immediately after World War I, although they retained their separate identities until 1943, when, along with the Consular Service, they became part of the new, unified Foreign Service (restyled 'Diplomatic Service' in 1964). However, it was not until the 1950s that, following the Wriston Report of 1954, the US Foreign Service absorbed the personnel of the hitherto separate Department of State.

The gradual unification during the twentieth century of the bureaucracy of diplomacy, including that of the diplomatic and consular services (on which, see Chapter 8), no doubt played its part in enabling the MFA to resist the next challenge to its position, which came in the century's last decades, chiefly from 'direct dial diplomacy' (discussed later in this chapter). Freedom from the conservative reflexes likely to have been produced by close relationships with powerful domestic interests also assisted the foreign ministry by making it easier to adapt to changing circumstances (Hocking and Spence: 6). There is no doubt, however, that it is the continuing importance of the tasks discharged by the MFA that has ensured its survival as a prominent department of central government (Berridge 2005; Box 1.2). The staff of most MFAs is also now significantly larger relative to that of the body of diplomats in their missions abroad than it was in the nineteenth century, and there is a common view that 'for every two diplomats posted abroad, there should be at least one official at Headquarters' (Rana 2000: 255). What are the tasks that have contributed to the survival of such a relatively large ministry of foreign affairs?

Box 1.2   MFAs: formal titles making a point, and some metonyms

Most MFAs are formally described as the 'Ministry of Foreign Affairs', but a few add some words in order to advertise a priority or make some other point. For example, since the last edition of this book appeared in 2005, both the Austrian and French ministries have added 'European' to their titles, in order to stress that they do not regard other EU members as foreigners; and the Senegalese ministry has added 'African Union'. Some additions seem unnecessary, and possibly unwise: 'Cooperation', for example, and, even more so, 'International Cooperation', a choice of language that makes the ministries concerned appear either verbose or anxious to make up for an *un*cooperative past. Some MFAs are often referred to by the names of buildings or streets with which they are associated (metonyms). The following list illustrates the variety of titles given to foreign ministries, together with some metonyms:

Australia:	*Department of Foreign Affairs and Trade*
Austria:	*Federal Ministry for European and International Affairs*
Belgium:	*Ministry of Foreign Affairs, Foreign Trade, and Development Aid*
Benin:	*Ministry of Foreign Affairs and African Integration*
Botswana:	*Ministry of Foreign Affairs and International Cooperation*
Brazil:	*Ministry of External Relations ('Itamaraty')*
Croatia:	*Ministry of Foreign Affairs and European Integration*
France:	*Ministry of Foreign and European Affairs ('Quai d'Orsay')*
India:	*Ministry of External Affairs ('South Block')*
Italy:	*Ministry of Foreign Affairs ('Farnesina')*
Japan:	*Ministry of Foreign Affairs ('Gaimusho')*
Malaysia:	*Ministry of Foreign Affairs ('Wisma Putra')*
PRC:	*Ministry of Foreign Affairs*
Senegal:	*Ministry of Foreign Affairs, the African Union, and Senegalese Abroad*
South Africa:	*Department of International Relations and Cooperation*
Spain:	*Ministry of Foreign Affairs and Cooperation*
United Kingdom:	*Foreign and Commonwealth Office ('Foreign Office' or 'FCO')*
United States:	*Department of State ('Foggy Bottom')*

Staffing and supporting missions abroad

An important task for the MFA is providing the personnel for the state's diplomatic and consular missions abroad, including posts at the permanent headquarters of international organizations. This means not only their recruitment and training (sometimes in a fully-fledged diplomatic academy such as the Rio Branco Institute in Brazil), but also the sensitive job of selecting the right persons for particular posts. It also means supporting the diplomats and their families, especially when they find themselves in hardship posts or in the midst of an emergency. Because of the murderous attacks on its embassies in recent decades, the US Department of State has had to devote considerable energy and resources to giving them greater protection, and now even has to have an Office of Casualty Assistance. Among other things, this engages in contingency planning and oversees a number of crisis support teams.

The foreign ministry also has to provide the physical fabric of the missions abroad, which means renting or erecting suitable buildings, and then providing them with equipment and furnishings, regular maintenance, guards, and secure communications with home. The efficiency of the *administrative* departments that carry out the tasks mentioned in this and the preceding paragraph is particularly important in the MFAs of states where the diplomatic career has tended to lose its glitter and the loss of experienced staff in mid-career is consequently a serious risk.

A less popular task now undertaken by many MFAs as part of their general support for missions abroad is their periodic inspection. The reports that follow visits need to praise good work, as well as draw attention to embassy failings. This is the more important since inspectors are also usually required to advise on cost-cutting measures. Inspections must be handled with sensitivity and conducted by persons who command professional respect. The *Semiannual Reports* of the Department of State's Office of Inspector General are available on the world wide web. These are unclassified summaries of detailed individual reports of inspections. However, some of the latter are also available. They are all instructive.

Policy-making and implementation

As well as posting diplomats and consuls abroad, officials in the foreign ministry are responsible for advising on the policies they should be required to implement, issuing the appropriate instructions, and ensuring that they are carried out. They also have the task of digesting the information the missions send home. This is where what are sometimes known as the 'political departments' come in, and most of these are arranged partly along geographical and partly along functional lines, although in an acute crisis a special section within the ministry might take over (see Box 1.3). *Geographical* departments normally concentrate on regions or individual states of particular importance to the country concerned, while *functional* departments deal typically with high

---

Box 1.3   Crisis management

The foreign ministries of states that have to deal regularly with crises with national security implications tend to have a crisis section that is permanently operational. In the Israeli MFA, for example, this is called the 'Situation Room'; and, in the US Department of State, its name is the 'Operations Center'. Significantly, both are located within the office with overall coordinating functions within their ministry, the Coordination Bureau and the Executive Secretariat, respectively. Most states, however, handle crises of this sort by means of temporary arrangements, for which they have more or less precise plans, although increasing numbers have permanent units ready to respond to consular emergencies abroad.

---

profile general issues such as climate change, drugs and international crime, human rights, energy security, and refugees and migration.

Historically, the geographical departments dominated foreign ministries and so, until relatively recently, had more prestige. Among those in the British Foreign Office, the Eastern Department, which covered the Ottoman Empire and its Russian predator – and, thus, the awesome 'Eastern Question' – was, for many years before World War I, the most prestigious and aristocratic. In the US Department of State, an attempt in the 1950s and 1960s to give more prominence to functional departments at the expense of the geographical ones was made more difficult by personnel distinctions remaining from the pre-Wriston reform era: the functional departments were staffed by civil servants, while the geographical ones were staffed by diplomatic officers (Simpson: 19).

Nevertheless, even issue-oriented functional departments had some historical pedigree. The British Foreign Office's Slave Trade Department, for example, which was its first department of this kind, was created in the early nineteenth century and for many years was actually its largest (FCO Historians: 29). Functional departments concentrate technical expertise and advertise the fact that the MFA is seized with the current international problems of greatest concern. (Hiving off a major function, such as development aid, from the foreign ministry and making it the subject of a separate ministry is an even better way of doing this but can lead to problems of coordination.) Perhaps fostered by the growth of democracy, and certainly more in harmony than geographical departments with the concept of 'globalization', functional departments now tend to be at least as prominent. But it is highly unlikely that they will replace the geographical departments completely and – except in poor states with limited foreign interests (see Box 1.4) – it is a serious

---

Box 1.4   MFA structure in less developed countries

The ministries of very poor states, especially micro-states – which, by and large, have extremely limited networks of diplomats abroad – tend to have few, if any, geographical departments. For example, in 2009 the Ministry of Foreign Affairs and Foreign Trade of Barbados had only one geographical department out of a total of ten, although this was larger than most, with separate desks dealing with the Americas, Europe/Asia/Africa, Caribbean/CARICOM, and Multilateral Affairs. The remaining nine functional departments were described as Human Resources and Administration, Protocol and Conferences, Foreign Trade, Consular, Information Systems, Facilitation Unit for Returning Nationals, Public Affairs, Maritime Delimitation Unit, and Strategic Analysis Unit. Even the foreign ministry of the much larger – although certainly not richer – state of Senegal, in West Africa, had only two geographical departments, one for Africa and Asia, and another for Europe, the Americas, and Oceania, although it had a further one dealing with the African Union (AU).

---

mistake to seek this end. Apart from the fact that the disappearance of geographical departments would weaken the case for a separate MFA (since the international sections of 'Other Government Departments' (OGDs) might be regarded as capable of taking over their functional work), there are two main reasons for this. First, globalization notwithstanding, there remain marked cultural differences between the world's regions, and knowledge of them in functional departments is inevitably limited. Second, the conduct of relations with a state by half a dozen or more functional departments, each with a different global agenda, is hardly likely to be coordinated. Major reforms in the French foreign ministry in 1976/8, which restored administrative divisions on geographical lines after decades of advance by the functional principle, were designed precisely to allay this last anxiety (*France-Diplomatie*). With the rise in importance of international organizations, most MFAs now have *multilateral* departments as well, some of which also have a geographical focus in so far as they deal with regional bodies such as the African Union (AU).

MFAs also have departments known by names such as 'intelligence and research' or 'research and analysis'. These specialize in general background research and in assessing the significance of information obtained by secret intelligence agencies. The MFA is chiefly a consumer of the product of these agencies but – along with other policymakers – it sometimes plays a key role in its assessment in high-level inter-departmental committees, which might enhance its influence – but possibly at the cost of objectivity in threat assessment. In Britain, the FCO also has responsibility for the Secret Intelligence Service (SIS), which must have its approval before launching 'significant operations', and for Government Communications Headquarters (GCHQ), the major eaves-dropping agency.

If policy is to be well-made and implemented properly, the MFA's institutional memory must be in good order. This applies especially to the details of promises made and received in the past, and poten-tial promises that have been long gestating in negotiations. This is why such an important section of even the earliest foreign ministries was their archive (later, registry) of correspondence and treaties, as well as maps, reports, internal memoranda, and other important documents. Before separate foreign ministries were created, such archives were kept by other secretaries of state or palace officials. They even existed in the palaces of the Great Kings of the ancient Near East (Meier: 212). Preserving securely, organizing systematically, and facilitating rapid access to their archives by indexing are key foreign ministry respon-sibilities. A related task is determining carefully what sensitive docu-ments – and parts of sensitive documents – can be released to the public upon application under Freedom of Information legislation. Many for-eign ministries also have a small historians' section that is responsible, among other things, for selecting and publishing hitherto secret docu-ments of historical interest. In America, these appear under the title *Foreign Relations of the United States* (FRUS).

Since foreign policy should be lawful and, sometimes, be pursued by resort to judicial procedures, and since agreements negotiated by exhausted diplomats need to be scrutinized for inconsistencies and sloppy language, legal advice and support is always necessary. In some states, it has been traditional to provide this from a law min-istry (or ministry of justice) serving all government departments. Nevertheless, the predominant pattern is now for the MFA to have its own legal (or treaties) division, headed by an officer usually known as the 'legal adviser' or, in French-speaking states, '*directeur des affaires juridiques*'. It is also now more usual for the members of this division to be lawyers specializing in this work and not diplomats with a legal education who are rotated between the legal division and general dip-lomatic work in posts abroad. It is interesting, and perhaps hopeful for the strengthening of international law, that since the end of the 1980s informal meetings of the legal advisers of the foreign ministries of UN member states have been held on a regular basis at UN headquarters in New York.

The MFAs of the developed states, and a few others, also have a policy-planning department. Very much a product of the years following World War II, this was a response to the frequent criticism of unpreparedness when crises erupted and was inspired in part by the planning staffs long-employed by military establishments. It is no accident that the State Department was given its first planning staff when a former soldier, General George C. Marshall, became secretary of state after World War II (Simpson: 23, 79, 85). Planning units appear, in practice, to be chiefly concerned with trying to anticipate future problems and thinking through how they might be met and, in the process, challenging conventional mindsets. The FCO's planners appear not to look much beyond the medium term of about five years, although others are more ambitious. They are given freedom from current operational preoccupations but are not left so remote from them that they become 'too academic' (Coles: 71, 87–8). With such a strategic brief and supposed to provide independent judgements, it is not surprising that the policy planners are usually permitted to work directly under the executive head of the MFA. However, it is often difficult to get busy foreign ministers, who must inevitably give priority to current events, to focus on discussions of even the medium term, while the operational departments might well be obstructive. As a result, the policy planners sometimes feel that they are wasting their time, which was the experience of George Kennan. The first director of the State Department's planning staff, he resigned after Dean Acheson, who had replaced Marshall as secretary of state, began to make him feel like a 'court jester' and the operational units began to insist on policy recommendations going up through the 'line of command' (Kennan: 426–7, 465–6). Today's policy planners probably sometimes feel the same but the value of the political protection they afford to the MFA – which, at least in states with a free and lively press, has to be *seen* to be scanning the horizon – should not be overlooked.

It is inevitable that the policy role of the MFA's permanent officials should sometimes lead them to adopt attitudes that become so fixed as to seem part of the fabric of their departments. To take some examples, the FCO was long associated with pro-Arab sentiment although, when the issue of departmental attitudes is raised today, it is normally its pro-European reflexes that are mentioned; the South African Department of External Affairs inherited by the National Party from General Smuts in the fateful election of 1948 was regarded by the new government as hopelessly pro-British, while in the last years of the *apartheid* regime its successor came to be seen as *verligte* (enlightened on race); and according to certain sections of the Indian press, the Indian MFA was, at least until recently, steeped in conservatism, especially in regard to relations with Pakistan.

The foreign ministry's influence on government policy varies from one state to another. In those with both long-established foreign ministries and a constitutional mode of government, as in Britain and France, the ministry tends to remain highly influential, except in wartime. In others, however, it is much weaker. These include states with shorter diplomatic traditions and highly personalized political leadership. The situation also tends to be the same in any state where anxiety over military security has always generated acute neurosis and, thus, given great influence to the defence ministry, as in Israel and – to a lesser degree – the United States. In all countries, however, the influence of the MFA fluctuates over time. This might occur for any number of reasons but the most important is probably the personality and level of interest in foreign affairs of the head of government, now usually great because of the growth of summitry (see Chapter 10). If a leader suspects political hostility in the foreign ministry, or just that it is stuffed with those who are over-sensitive to the interests of foreigners, its position will tend to be worse still. The FCO is widely believed to have suffered from suspicion of the latter fault by Mrs Thatcher when she was prime minister in the 1980s, although it has been persuasively argued that she found it politically expedient to denigrate it publicly while, in private, showing it respect and, in practice, following its advice (Walden: 208–13). Less debateable seems to be the instance of the Malaysian MFA, which was quite eclipsed when the even more autocratic Dr Mahatir became prime minister shortly afterwards (Ahmad: 121–2).

Coordination of foreign relations

Despite the MFA's continuing role in foreign policy advice and implementation, it is rare for it now to have the considerable authority in the direct conduct of foreign relations that it once had. The United States is perhaps unusual in having so many departments and agencies devoted chiefly to foreign affairs that they are referred to collectively as the 'foreign affairs community'. Nevertheless, in all states today the OGDs – commerce, finance, defence, transport, environment, and so on, not forgetting the central bank – engage in *direct* communication not only with their foreign counterparts, but also with quite different agencies abroad, and do so to an unprecedented degree. Indeed, the extent of this 'direct dial diplomacy', as it is sometimes called, is now so great that the OGDs commonly have their own international sections (Rozental: 139–40). As a result, it is no longer practical – or, indeed, advisable – for the MFA to insist that, in order to ensure consistency in foreign policy and prevent foreigners from playing off one ministry against another, it alone should have dealings with them.

The development of direct dial diplomacy was a result of the growing complexity and range of international problems during the twentieth century, the diminishing ability of the generalists in the MFA to master them, and the increasing ease with which domestic ministries could make contact with ministries abroad. But this development was by no means as threatening to the MFA as some observers thought and its enemies hoped. This is because direct dial diplomacy threatened the overall coherence of foreign policy. So, too, did other trends: pursuit of the same or related negotiations through multilateral as well as bilateral channels, unofficial as well as official channels, and backchannels as well as front ones. The chaos in the conduct of foreign relations threatened by all of these trends could only be prevented by some authoritative body charged not with reinstating exclusive responsibility for handling them, but with the more modest brief of *coordinating* the foreign activities of the OGDs: enter the born-again MFA.

It has been noted earlier in this chapter that foreign ministries have had coordination very much in mind in retaining (even reasserting) the geographical principle in their internal administration, but how do they promote coordination beyond their own doors? There are various options here:

- A standard device is to insist on retaining control of all external diplomatic and consular missions, and to require that officials from other ministries attached to them report home via the ambassador
- A second common strategy is to ensure that senior MFA personnel are placed in key positions on any special foreign affairs committee attached to the office of a head of government, often known by some such title as 'cabinet office' or 'prime minister's office', and themselves usually charged with a coordinating role
- A third option, employed in Mexico, is for the MFA to enjoy the legal prerogative of vetting all international treaties entered into by agencies of the government
- A fourth option is a requirement that the MFA must be given prior notice of any proposed official trip abroad by a senior government employee

- A fifth option is the interdepartmental (in the USA, inter-agency) committee, composed usually of senior officials of the departments with an interest in a particular aspect of foreign policy, and preferably chaired by an MFA representative. (Analogous to this is the informal network of private secretaries to ministers, which might well be even more effective.)
- A sixth option is the temporary exchange of staff between the MFA and other ministries
- And, finally, the most radical solution is to house key functions under the same ministerial roof. The favoured, although still minority, option here is to merge the MFA with the ministry dealing with trade, and perhaps with development aid (some examples are mentioned in Box 1.2), although this does not solve the problem of coordinating the foreign activities of the remaining OGDs. This particular variant has not yet been favoured in the United States, although in 1999 the Clinton administration oversaw the integration of three previously separate foreign affairs agencies into the Department of State (the 'lead foreign affairs agency'): the Arms Control and Disarmament Agency, the US Information Agency, and the US Agency for International Development.

Dealing with foreign diplomats at home

Senior officials of the MFA periodically find themselves having to respond to a *démarche* on a particular subject made by the head of a foreign mission in the capital and, occasionally, the foreign minister will summon a head of mission to listen to a protest of his own. When something of this nature occurs, the MFA is engaged in a function that has already been discussed; namely, policy implementation. It should not be forgotten, however, that it has other responsibilities relative to the resident diplomatic corps (Sharp and Wiseman).

Well aware of the capacity for intrigue and the information-gathering role of diplomats, governments have treated their official guests with commensurate suspicion since the inception of resident missions in the second half of the fifteenth century. In some states, as in China in the second half of the nineteenth century, foreign missions were actually confined to a particular quarter of the capital (Legation Quarter), the better to keep their activities under close scrutiny. Today, although this custom is not entirely dead (a purpose-built Diplomatic Quarter was created near the Saudi capital of Riyadh in the mid-1980s), the majority of states are more relaxed about the political activities of the diplomatic corps in their capital cities.

There remains, nevertheless, a concern about the abuse by diplomats of their immunities from the criminal and civil law. Indeed, this concern has grown since the 1950s, chiefly because the increase in the number of states has greatly increased the size of the diplomatic corps. The number of visiting dignitaries has also increased vastly (see Chapter 14). It is not surprising, therefore, that all MFAs should have either a separate protocol department or one that embraces protocol together with a closely related function. Such departments contain experts in diplomatic and consular law and ceremonial. Among other things, they serve in effect as mediators between the diplomatic corps and the local community, and oversee the arrangements for visiting dignitaries. The Chinese government still takes a particularly close interest in the activities of the diplomatic corps, with a Diplomatic Service Bureau (DSB) affiliated to the MFA, as well as a Protocol Department. Among other things, the Bureau provides service staff for the diplomatic and consular missions in Beijing. Old habits also die hard in Russia, where an analogous organization – the Main Administration for Service to the Diplomatic Corps (*GlavUpDK*) – still survives. In some states, too, the MFA is charged with assisting in both the physical protection of certain visiting dignitaries and foreign missions. In the United States, for example, special agents in the Protective Liaison Division of the State Department's Bureau of Diplomatic Security are charged with coordinating the protection of all foreign officials and their missions across the country.

Building support at home

For much of the period following World War II, foreign ministries and their diplomatic services were frequently targets of attack from politicians and commissions of inquiry, and persistently sniped at by the tabloid press. It is not difficult to see why: they had acquired reputations for social exclusiveness in recruitment and high living abroad, and faced a growing challenge to their very *raison d'être*. It was, thus, an acute weakness that they had no domestic political base on which to fall back for support. Education ministries had teachers, agriculture ministries had farmers, defence ministries had the armed forces – but foreign ministries had only foreigners, a political base worse than useless. The foreign ministries in many countries have responded to this situation with predictable resourcefulness, and have had some success.

MFAs now nurture the national media at least as carefully as they cosset foreign correspondents in the capital. They also cultivate popular approval directly, especially via their websites. These often provide up-to-date information on foreign travel destinations, including advice on personal safety. Websites also highlight the consular services that are available to their nationals, should they find themselves in need of assistance abroad. The Italian foreign ministry, for example, now goes so far as to say on its website that lending assistance via its Crisis Unit to Italian nationals caught up in emergencies abroad (telephone number in large, bold font) is its 'primary commitment'. A logical bureaucratic extension of arrangements of this sort, also much hyped up, is a separate department devoted to the more routine welfare needs of nationals permanently resident abroad, including the facilitation of their return, as in the case of the Barbados MFA. Foreign ministries also take every opportunity to impress on exporters and agencies seeking inward investment the value of the commercial diplomacy of their overseas missions. And, in the small number of cases where foreign ministries have actually merged with trade ministries, they have not only promoted coordination, but also moved directly to capture a key political constituency; namely, businessmen. Finally, MFAs in the West now fling open their doors to the representatives of NGOs (even attaching them to conference delegations), academics, and others, not only in order to benefit from their specialist advice, but also to recruit them as domestic allies. In short, it is now widely recognized that it is as important for the MFA to engage in 'outreach' at home as it is for its missions to engage in this abroad.

Summary

In most states today, the foreign ministry must formally share influence over the making of foreign policy with other ministries and executive agencies. Nevertheless, in many of them it retains significant influence via its geographical expertise, control of the diplomatic service abroad, investment in public diplomacy (discussed in Chapter 11), nurturing of domestic allies, and growing acceptance by outsiders that it is well positioned to make a major contribution to the coordination of the state's multidimensional international relationships. Most of these relationships issue, from time to time, in the activity of negotiation, which – even narrowly conceived – represents the most important function of diplomacy. It is therefore appropriate to turn next to this subject.

Further reading

Albright, Madeleine, *Madam Secretary: A memoir* (Macmillan: London, 2003).

Anderson, M. S., *The Rise of Modern Diplomacy, 1450–1919* (Longman: London/ New York, 1993): 73–80, 110–19.

Burke, Shannon, 'Office of the Chief of Protocol: Following protocol is this office's charter', *State Magazine*, January, 1999 [www].

FCO Historians, 'Slavery in Diplomacy: The Foreign Office and the suppression of the transatlantic slave trade', *History Note*, 17 [www].

Fitzmaurice, Gerald G., 'Legal advisers and foreign affairs', *American Journal of International Law*, 59, 1965: 72–86.

Fitzmaurice, Gerald G., 'Legal advisers and international organizations', *American Journal of International Law*, 62, 1968: 114–27.

Hennessy, Peter, *Whitehall* (Fontana: London, 1990), index refs. to 'Foreign (and Commonwealth) Office'.

Herman, Michael, 'Diplomacy and intelligence', *Diplomacy & Statecraft*, 9(2), July 1998: 1–22.

Hocking, Brian (ed.), *Foreign Ministries: Change and adaptation* (Macmillan – now Palgrave: Basingstoke, 1999).

Hocking, Brian and David Spence (eds), *Foreign Ministries in the European Union: Integrating diplomats* (Palgrave Macmillan: Basingstoke, 2002).

Jones, Ray, *The Nineteenth-Century Foreign Office: An administrative history* (Weidenfeld & Nicolson: London, 1971).

Kennan, George F., *Memoirs, 1925–1950* (Hutchinson: London, 1967): 325–7, 426–7, 465–6, on formation of policy planning staff in the State Department.

Kissinger, Henry A., *Years of Upheaval* (Weidenfeld & Nicolson/Michael Joseph: London, 1982): 432–49, on the Department of State and the Foreign Service.

Kurbalija, Jovan (ed.), *Knowledge and Diplomacy* (DiploFoundation: Malta, 1999): ch. by Keith Hamilton.

Lauterpacht, Elihu, 'Hurst, Sir Cecil James Barrington (1870–1963)' [FO Legal Adviser], rev., *Oxford Dictionary of National Biography* (Oxford University Press: Oxford, 2004).

Loeffler, Jane C., *The Architecture of Diplomacy: Building America's embassies* (Princeton Architectural Press: New York, 1998).

Neilson, Keith and T. G. Otte, *The Permanent Under-Secretary for Foreign Affairs, 1854–1946* (Routledge: New York/Abingdon, Oxon., 2009).

Office of Inspector General, US Department of State [www].

Prados, John, *Keepers of the Keys: A history of the National Security Council from Truman to Bush* (Morrow: New York, 1991).

Rana, Kishan S., *Inside Diplomacy* (Manas: New Delhi, 2000): ch. 11, on the Indian MFA.

Rana, Kishan S., *Asian Diplomacy: The foreign ministries of China, India, Japan, Singapore and Thailand* (DiploFoundation: Malta/Geneva, 2007).

Rothstein, R. L., *Planning, Prediction, and Policymaking in Foreign Affairs: Theory and practice* (Little, Brown: Boston, 1972).

Simpson, Smith, *Anatomy of the State Department* (Houghton Mifflin: Boston, 1967).

Steiner, Zara, *The Foreign Office and Foreign Policy, 1898–1914* (Cambridge University Press: Cambridge, 1969).

Steiner, Zara (ed.), *The Times Survey of Foreign Ministries of the World* (Times Books: London, 1982).

Urban, Mark, *UK Eyes Alpha: The inside story of British Intelligence* (Faber & Faber: London/Boston, 1996).

Walden, George, *Lucky George: Memoirs of an anti-politician* (Allen Lane/Penguin Press: London, 1999): 172–214, on the role of the principal private secretary to the Foreign Secretary.

Many foreign ministries have their own websites, most of which provide at least a list of the different departments (sometimes even an 'organigram'), while a few go so far as to give a detailed history of the ministry. In the last regard, the website of the Canadian MFA is outstanding. The back copies of *State Magazine*, available via the US State Department's website, are also useful.

Part I
The Art of Negotiation

Introduction to Part I

In international politics, negotiation consists of discussion between officially designated representatives that is designed to achieve the formal agreement of their governments to a way forward on an issue that has come up in their relations. Negotiation, as noted in the Introduction to this book, is only one of the functions of diplomacy and, in some situations, not the most urgent; in traditional diplomacy via resident missions, neither is it the activity to which most time is now generally devoted. (Although when diplomats 'lobby' some agency of the state to which they are accredited, as they have always spent much of their time doing, the only differences from negotiation are that the dialogue is configured differently and any successes are not formally registered.) Nevertheless, negotiation remains the most important function of diplomacy. This is, in part, because the diplomatic system now encompasses considerably more than the work of resident missions, and negotiation becomes more and more its operational focus as we move into the realms of multilateral diplomacy, summitry, and that other growth sector of the world diplomatic system – mediation. Furthermore, it hardly needs labouring that it is the process of negotiation that grapples directly with the most threatening problems, whether they be economic dislocation, environmental catastrophe, war, or – as at the time of writing – global financial meltdown. It is because negotiation is the most important function of diplomacy that the first Part of this book is devoted to this.

Students of negotiations, notably Zartman and Berman, divide them into three distinct stages: those concerned with prenegotiations, formula, and details. The first two chapters of Part I hinge on these distinctions, Chapter 2 dealing with prenegotiations and Chapter 3 with the formula and details stages together – 'around-the-table' negotiations

(Saunders). The characteristics of each stage are analyzed, including their characteristic difficulties. However, two cautions must at once be registered. First, the concept of sequential stages of negotiation is an analytical construct: in reality, not only do the stages usually overlap but, sometimes, the difficulties of a particular stage are so acute that return to an earlier stage is unavoidable ('back-tracking'). Second, the notion of three-stage negotiations has developed principally out of analysis of talks on issues where the stakes are high, typically between previously or still warring parties; in negotiations between friendly states on matters of relatively low importance, the prenegotiations stage will often present few problems and might barely be noticeable at all.

Following discussion of the stages of negotiations, Chapter 4 considers the various devices whereby their momentum might be preserved or – if lost – regained. In Chapter 5, an examination will be found of the different ways in which negotiated agreements might be presented to the world, and why different situations demand that agreements be differently 'packaged'. Part I concludes with Chapter 6, which deals with the question of how agreements are best followed up in order to ensure that their provisions are actually implemented without the need for recourse to law or force.

Since high-stakes negotiations are of greatest interest and, by definition, most consequential, it is these that are principally in mind throughout this Part of the book.

2
Prenegotiations

Prenegotiations, despite their misleading name, are the first stage of negotiations. Perhaps more readily understood by the term 'talks about talks', their job is to establish that substantive, around-the-table negotiations are worthwhile, and then to agree the agenda and the necessary procedures for tackling it. In bilateral relationships, these discussions are usually informal and well out of the public gaze. However, in multilateral diplomacy, where the parties are more numerous and procedure more complex, a good part of the prenegotiations might be both formal and well-advertised. For example, the substantive stage of the Conference on Security and Cooperation in Europe, which had 35 participating states and culminated in the Helsinki Final Act in 1975, was preceded by nine months of 'Multilateral Preparatory Talks' that produced a 'Blue Book' containing their recommendations (Alexander: 29–34).

Whether formal or informal, public or well-hidden, prenegotiations – or, as they are also sometimes innocently described, 'preliminaries' – are often far more important and far more difficult than is usually supposed. This is especially true in tense relationships, where prenegotiations are always fragile; but, even in friendly relationships, they are far from trivial and can cause problems requiring lengthy discussion. This chapter considers, in turn, each of the chief tasks confronting the negotiators in this stage.

Agreeing the need to negotiate

It should never be forgotten that states sometimes engage in prenegotiations, and even substantive negotiations, merely in order to buy time or obtain a good press for being considered accommodating.

Procrastinating – or, as the British government used to call it, 'playing it long' – has an extended history in diplomacy. There is a widespread view in the United States that this has been the Iranian approach to negotiations over its nuclear programme ever since 2003. But, sometimes, even an unfriendly state may feel compelled to give serious thought to serious negotiations.

Having said this, it is an unusual situation in which the parties to a conflict – whether it is principally military, economic, or waged by means of propaganda – are *equally* convinced that a stalemate exists or, in other words, that each has a veto over the outcome preferred by the other. It is also an unusual situation in which, even if there is widespread acceptance of a stalemate, all are *equally* agreed that negotiation is the only way forward. One party might believe that time is on its side. This might be because of some anticipated technical or scientific development that it hopes will tip the balance of military power in its favour, or because it looks forward to the possibility that more dovish politicians might take over the leadership of its rival. Even if there is widespread agreement that the time is ripe for a negotiated settlement, it is also an unusual situation in which all are *equally* prepared to acknowledge this – suing for peace, after all, is usually a sign of weakness – or, if they are so prepared, *equally* able to devote the time and resources needed to launch a negotiation.

It should not be surprising, therefore, that establishing that negotiations are worthwhile is often a complicated and delicate matter, 'in many cases...more complicated, time-consuming, and difficult than reaching agreement once negotiations have begun' (Saunders: 249). For instance, because establishing the need for negotiations rests fundamentally on gaining acceptance of the fact that a stalemate exists, any party to whom suspicions of weakness attach might feel the need to raise the temperature of the conflict while simultaneously putting out feelers for negotiations. Third parties might be calling for gestures of goodwill, but stepping up the pressure will safeguard the balance and offer protection against domestic hard-liners. If, on the other hand, powerful third parties are positioning themselves to act as mediators, they might be able – for example, by regulating the flow of arms to the rivals – to engineer a stalemate.

In bitter conflicts where the stakes are high – for example, between the Arabs and the Israelis over the old mandate of Palestine, the Americans and the Iranians over the latter's nuclear programme, and the Indians and the Pakistanis over Kashmir – acceptance of a stalemate nearly always takes a considerable time. When the issues concern core values, and perhaps even survival itself, it is obvious that there will be enormous reluctance to accept that another party has the ability to block achievement of one's aspirations or permanently threaten an otherwise satisfactory *status quo*. Acceptance of a stalemate in such circumstances requires repeated demonstrations of power and resolve by both parties. In the Arab–Israeli conflict, it took four wars (five, including the War of Attrition from 1967 until 1970) before Egypt made peace with Israel, in 1979 – and even then it required the assistance of sustained top-level American mediation and the application of heavy pressure on both sides. It was a further 14 years before the Palestine Liberation Organization (PLO) and Israel reached out for the olive branch. Acceptance of a stalemate might also require each party to lobby the allies of the other for, if these powers concede that there is a stalemate, this is more likely to be accepted by the parties themselves.

If, ultimately, existence of a stalemate is accepted, the parties next have to acknowledge the possibility that a negotiated settlement (although not *any* negotiated settlement) might be better for all concerned than continuing with the current situation. This is, perhaps, the true beginning of prenegotiations. Through direct or indirect contacts between rivals, and through propaganda directed at allies and domestic constituencies, this generally means conveying three messages:

- that the parties have important common interests – for example, avoiding nuclear war – as well as interests that divide them
- that disaster will be inescapable if negotiations are not grasped, and
- that there is a possible solution. This might involve the suggestion that negotiation of the dispute in question be linked to another in which the parties are also on opposite sides, thus increasing the scope for trade-offs.

Indeed, encouraging the belief that negotiations are worth a try means floating a formula or framework for a settlement. This will have to give something to both sides and, at the least, suggest that enlisting intelligence, imagination, and empathy – that is to say, diplomacy – might be able to produce a solution. It will also have to be fairly vague because a vague formula avoids giving hostages to fortune in a world in which circumstances are constantly changing. Such a formula is also meat and drink to the ubiquitous wishful thinker, and, at this early stage, when nothing that will help to launch the negotiations can be spurned, the wishful thinker is the negotiator's ally.

When parties to a conflict start to explore the possibility of a negotiated settlement, they do not do this in a political vacuum. A variety of circumstances, at home and abroad, will affect the likelihood that negotiations will be launched successfully. To begin with, it is necessary for the leadership on both sides to be domestically secure. This will give them the confidence that they will be able to ride out any charge that they are proposing to 'sell out' to the enemy. In democracies, this consideration argues for rapid movement after elections, when a new government has the opportunity to take unpopular action in the reasonable expectation that the voters will either have forgotten or secured compensating blessings by the time they are next able to express a view. Thus, the American president, Jimmy Carter, moved as fast as possible on the Arab–Israeli front after his inauguration in January 1977 because he knew that the kind of settlement that he had in mind would cause some anguish to the powerful pro-Israel lobby in the United States (Quandt: ch. 2). In autocracies, domestic hard-line opponents have to be dealt with in some other way before negotiations – at least, substantive negotiations – can be launched. Lin Piao, the pro-Soviet minister of defence in the People's Republic of China (PRC) who appears to have opposed any *rapprochement* between Peking and Washington, died in a mysterious air crash in early 1972 (Macmillan: 202–3).

It is a further advantage to the leadership of parties contemplating negotiations if they have a record of hostility towards the other side. With such track records, they are well-placed to defend themselves against any charge that they are moved by secret sympathies for the enemy or an inadequate grasp of their own national or ideological priorities; and they are suitably positioned to hold their own conservatives in line. So it was that the reputation of US President Richard Nixon for fierce anti-Communism was a great asset to him in the early 1970s. This was because he had come to the conclusion that it was necessary to restore normal relations with the PRC, improve relations with the Soviet Union, return Okinawa to Japan, and dump South Vietnam – all policies that were anathema to American conservatives (Safire: 366–7). Another leader whose superhawk reputation stood him in good stead when it came to making peace with his enemy was the Israeli prime minister Menachem Begin. Begin, who headed the Likud coalition that triumphed in the elections in mid-1977, was a former leader of the Jewish underground movement, the Irgun, and the leader of its political successor, the Herut Party. Herut had a reputation for extremism and Begin's name was traditionally linked to the policy of absolute refusal to surrender territory to the Arabs – 'not one inch' (Weizman: 36–7).

This reputation helped him to carry the Israeli parliament, the Knesset, through the negotiations from 1977 to early 1979 that produced the surrender of Sinai to Egypt and an agreement on the West Bank that to many Israeli hardliners appeared to be the thin end of the wedge of a future Palestinian state.

Finally, it is worth noting that prenegotiations are most likely to make progress if incidents that cause public alarm are avoided. A tragic recent example is provided by the terrorist attacks on Mumbai on 26 November 2008, which were blamed by India on groups operating in Pakistan and brought talks on improving relations between the weak governments of the two countries to a tense halt. Such occurrences can wreck any stage of negotiations, but prenegotiations are most vulnerable to them. In this stage, relatively little prestige has been tied to a successful outcome, and retreat from negotiations does not generally carry a high price (Stein: 482–3). A high premium attaches, therefore, not only to preventing terrorist outrages such as the one in Mumbai, but also the avoidance of exchanges of fire along any ceasefire line, and the discouragement of hostile popular demonstrations and virulent press campaigns. Such incidents put pressure on leaders to increase their demands; they also give them a pretext, if they want one, to avoid or break off initial contacts with the other party.

Agreeing the agenda

If the need for negotiations is recognized and conditions are propitious, it becomes possible to discuss an agenda for talks. This means not only agreeing what will be discussed, but also the order in which the agreed items will be taken. Unless one of the parties is indifferent to these points on the complacent assumption that it is merely entering a dialogue rather than a negotiation (De Soto: 362), this often creates more difficulties than might be imagined. In an adversarial relationship, in particular, a proposed agenda might be 'prejudicial' rather than 'neutral' (Young 1968: 378–80).

There are three main reasons why agenda *content* might be prejudicial. The first is that it might indicate that one party has already conceded a vital point of substance. A perfect example of this is provided by the argument over the agenda when the government of El Salvador and the coalition of insurgent groups (FMLN) with which it was faced began to edge towards negotiations at the end of the 1980s. Not surprisingly, the FMLN wanted El Salvador's existing armed forces abolished. As a result, the wording it proposed for the armed forces item on the agenda was 'the future' of the armed forces. By contrast, the government insisted on discussing their 'restructuring' or, even better, 'modernization'. Acceptance of the latter wording by the FMLN clearly indicated their acceptance that the armed forces could not be abolished, and had provoked 'serious controversy' (De Soto: 363).

The second reason why agenda content might be prejudicial is that it could hand a propaganda victory to one side. This is possible because, while the cut and thrust of negotiations usually remains secret, the broad agenda is invariably leaked if not publicly acknowledged. This being so, the parties to a potential negotiation can suggest agenda items that they know will never produce concessions from the other side in order, at a minimum, to advertise their own priorities. If, for some reason, the victims of this treatment feel bound to permit the inclusion of these items on the agenda, they will not only have magnified the effects of their rival's propaganda, but perhaps also created all manner of trouble for themselves with friends and allies. This is why the United States resisted the suggestion of Saddam Hussein that the Palestinian question, as well as Iraqi occupation of Kuwait, should be on the agenda of their talks in late 1990 and early 1991. Had this proposal been accepted, Washington would not only have fuelled Saddam's implausible campaign to present himself as the sword of Palestine, but also have conceded the principle that his aggression entitled him to some reward, thereby completely compromising the American policy of persuading Israel to maintain a low profile in the crisis.

The third reason why agenda content might be prejudicial is that it can, in practice, permit formal discussion of an issue despite the fact that one party might have initially refused to countenance it. This possibility is always present if an agenda is left too vague. It is, therefore, precisely for an agenda of this nature that a party will be likely to press, if faced with obstinate resistance to specific inclusion of an item in which it is particularly interested (De Soto: 363; Webster: 62).

The *order* of the agenda can also create difficulties. This is because the parties to any negotiation generally approach them in the expectation that they will have to give concessions on some items and receive them on others. It is also natural for them to demand that the latter should be taken first. This creates the impression of strength and avoids trouble at home; it might also lead the other side to be generous with its concessions in the hope that this will be reciprocated further down the agenda. Calculations of this sort were evident during important negotiations between the South African government and the shipping companies in the Europe–South Africa trade in late 1965 and early

1966. Until the very end of three series of negotiations covering 33 formal meetings, the government managed to delay discussion of the issue of an increase in freight rates, which was the major item on which it expected to have to *make* concessions to the companies. In the meanwhile, the government won concession after concession on other items, such as the shipment of arms in national flag vessels (Berridge 1987: 102–8). In a more recent example, Syria demanded that the return of the Golan Heights (seized from them in 1967) should be settled in negotiations with Israel before any other matters could be considered. In this case, though, the other party refused to go along and – despite the best efforts of President Clinton in his last days before leaving office – the negotiations failed to make progress (*Guardian* 2000).

The significance of the order in which agenda items are taken is reduced if it is possible to make the grant of early concessions conditional on receipt of later ones; this often happens. On the other hand, conditionality cannot obscure the fact that the party concerned is willing, in principle, to make these concessions, or entirely erase the image of weakness created by their early granting. Indeed, the party that agrees to permit early consideration of items on which it expects to have to give most concessions has already conceded a point – or missed a trick. Furthermore, since the principal beneficiary of negotiations on the first items will generally maintain that it has made some concessions on these points as well, it might not always be easy to secure payment later – and, if conditionality is evoked too forcefully, might lead to a charge of bad faith. In general, then, the order or sequence in which agenda items are taken is unlikely to be a matter of indifference.

Agreeing procedure

With the agenda agreed, although sometimes every last detail does not need to be ironed out, the final task of the prenegotiations stage is agreement on procedure. Here, there are four main questions to resolve: format, venue, delegations (if necessary), and timing.

Format

Will the negotiations be direct or indirect? It is axiomatic that direct, or 'face-to-face', talks will be employed when the parties have normal relations, and in routine matters it might readily be agreed that an embassy will play a leading role. Direct talks between enemies also have many practical advantages. If negotiations between bitter rivals nevertheless need to be indirect, perhaps because of problems of recognition or worries over loss of prestige, who will be the intermediary? Will it have to be a genuine mediator, or will provision of good offices by a third party be sufficient? (On mediation and good offices, see Chapter 15.) Whatever the role of the third party, can the negotiations be made somewhat easier by taking the form of proximity talks, as in the case of the discussions held in Turkey between Israel and Syria that began in 2007? In such talks, an intermediary is employed but the delegations of the principal parties are prepared to base themselves in more or less close proximity to each other, ideally in the same hotel or conference centre. This makes the mediator's job easier.

If more than two parties are to be involved in the talks, as is often the case, will they be conducted by a series of parallel bilateral discussions, a multilateral conference, or some combination of both? Bilateral discussions have in their favour maximum flexibility, speed, and secrecy. On the other hand, they are likely to inspire suspicion among allies that one or other among their number is seeking a separate deal with the rival; they also lack the propaganda value of a big conference. If a combination of bilateral discussion and multilateral conference is preferred, what powers shall the multilateral plenary conference have relative to decisions made in its bilateral subcommittees? Do the latter merely report to the former as a matter of courtesy, or do they give it a veto? If a key player fears it might be in a minority in the plenary, it is highly unlikely that it will agree to the latter course. Apart from established conventions, choice of format is thus influenced by the degree of urgency attending a negotiation, the state of relations among allies, and the determination of the most powerful or most resolute among the parties as to which format will best suit its own interests. Weaker states generally prefer to negotiate with those that are more powerful in a multilateral forum, since the environment is more regulated and their chances of forming coalitions are greater. In early 2009, questions of this nature were very much alive in discussions of the method of 'engaging' Iran and North Korea, where the American preference appeared to be bilateral talks under the 'umbrella' of a multilateral framework of regional players (Haass and Indyk: 51). These were an echo of the serious and complicated problems they presented for the Middle East diplomacy of US president, Jimmy Carter, in the late 1970s, which are still worth recalling.

With the drastic decline in Soviet influence in Egypt that had preceded the Yom Kippur War of 1973, the United States was firmly in the driving seat as far as negotiations to resolve the Arab–Israeli conflict were concerned. And Washington's view was that, while secret bilateral diplomacy was the only format that would be likely to achieve any real breakthrough, this would only happen if the Geneva Conference format (Box 2.1) was to be employed in some way. Among other things, this would symbolize trends toward making peace and put pressure on the radicals to moderate their demands, minimize the chances of the Soviet Union disrupting the process out of pique at being excluded and, above all, legitimize direct Arab–Israeli contact. In each of these regards, the Geneva Conference had had some degree of success. However, by the time that Carter inherited the mantle of Middle East brokerage in 1977, circumstances had changed.

Carter's reasons for initially supporting a reconvening of Geneva, albeit after some progress in bilateral talks were essentially the same as those of former secretary of state, Henry A. Kissinger. These reasons were: protecting the flank of the moderate Arab states on the Palestinian question (there would be 'Palestinian' representation of some kind at Geneva, as well as representation of all Arab states), advertising the peace process, and limiting the potential of the Soviet Union for trouble-making (Quandt: 118–21, 137–43). However, Egypt had moved much further away from the Soviet Union by 1977 and was worried about the influence that the Geneva format might give it over a settlement. This format, especially if it involved a unified Arab delegation, would also

---

Box 2.1   The Geneva Conference format for Middle East peace negotiations

This had its immediate origins in the aftermath of the Yom Kippur War, when the UN Security Council called (in Resolution 338) for immediate talks between the Arabs and the Israelis 'aimed at establishing a just and durable peace in the Middle East'. A conference was duly held in Geneva in late December 1973. It had six notable features: it was held under UN auspices (the venue was the UN's European headquarters, and the secretary-general issued the invitations and presided in the conference's opening phase); it was co-chaired by the United States and the Soviet Union; all interested parties were invited (which meant the Israelis sitting down with the Arabs); it consisted chiefly of 'a battery of public speeches', rather than serious secret negotiation (Kissinger 1982: ch. 17); neither superpower would be present in negotiations at the sub-committee level (Quandt: 143); and the plenary conference was to have no right of veto over decisions taken in any subsequent bilateral negotiations. This conference was in direct line of descent from earlier multilateral conferences on regional questions chaired by major powers from opposite sides of the Cold War, and, for that matter, also held in Geneva. These included the Geneva Conference on South-East Asia (1954), which was co-chaired by Britain and the Soviet Union, and reconvened in 1961–62 in order to discuss Laos.

reduce its flexibility in negotiations with Israel. These considerations were now the more important for Egypt, since the relatively easy steps of military disengagement had by now been achieved, and what was left were the big questions: sovereignty over Sinai and the future of the West Bank, in that order. Geneva might help Egypt but, as it was shaping up, it was more likely to prove a trap. In the event, the delay in reconvening Geneva – caused, in part, by the enormous difficulty of agreeing on how the Palestinians should be represented – gave Sadat the pretext for sabotaging this route by making his spectacular journey to Jerusalem in November 1977. After this, the Geneva format was a dead letter, despite the fact that much of the top-level and time-consuming diplomacy of 1977 had been concerned with preparing for it.

Venue

In a friendly relationship, especially when issues of relatively low importance are coming up for negotiation and the lead is left to an embassy or a special mission supported by an embassy, the choice of venue might well present little or no problem in prenegotiations. The choice is limited – home or away – and a tradition might even have been established as to which capital should be employed. For example, as with many governments with confidence in their own embassies, Britain has normally preferred to negotiate through them rather than through a foreign embassy in London. This gives the British government greater assurance that its messages to the foreign government are delivered quickly and securely to the right people, and are not distorted *en route*. In its negotiations with Turkey, which in any case did not have resident embassies abroad on a regular basis until the early nineteenth century, Anglo–Turkish negotiations were almost always conducted in Constantinople, later in Ankara (Berridge 2009: 34, 210–11, App. 9). In more difficult relationships, however, particularly when the stakes are high, attitudes to venue tend to be quite different.

In such circumstances, choice of the format of negotiations sometimes goes a long way towards dictating where they will take place. For example, had the Arab–Israeli talks of the Carter years followed the Geneva Conference format, it is likely that they would have taken place in Geneva. Indeed, the American proposal was that, as in 1973, the UN secretary-general should once more issue the invitations, and there is no suggestion in the public record of the discussions at the time that an alternative venue was ever seriously considered. It was likely, then, that the talks would have taken place in Geneva – but not inevitable. When the next international conference on the Middle East – co-chaired by the superpowers and, in most essentials, resembling the 1973 Geneva Conference – actually took place, in the aftermath of the Gulf War in November 1991, it did not convene in Geneva but in Madrid. Why is venue often an important matter in prenegotiations between bitter rivals and why, as a result, does it often cause considerable difficulties?

The venue of negotiations is important because, if a state is able to persuade its rival to send a delegation to its own shores, this will be of great practical convenience to it. For this reason, it will also suggest very strongly that it is the more powerful. In consequence, the travellers will have suffered a loss of face. It is hardly surprising, therefore, in light of the speed and efficiency with which images and other kinds of information can be flashed across the world, that this happens only rarely, and that alternative solutions are the subject of discussion in the prenegotiations stage. In fact, there are three common strategies for getting over this problem: neutral ground, meeting 'halfway', and alternating home venues (rotating, if there are more than two parties).

Some venues are chosen for negotiations because, either by convention or law, they are neutral ground. This explains the popularity of venues in Switzerland and Austria, both permanently neutral states in international law. Vienna, the capital of Austria, has the added advantage of unique historical association with the development of modern diplomacy, from the Congress of 1815 to the UN Conferences on Diplomatic Intercourse and Immunities (1961) and Consular Relations (1963) (see Chapters 7 and 8, respectively). The Hague, which was chosen as the site of the Iran–United States Claims Tribunal in 1981, provides another example. Although the Netherlands is a NATO member, The Hague is home to the International Court of Justice and also the Permanent Court of Arbitration, which, indeed, provided the Iran–United States Claims Tribunal with its first quarters in the city (Berridge 1994: 124).

Another traditional device for saving face is to choose a venue that is roughly equidistant between the capitals of the rival states. Since compromise is the essence of diplomacy, it is appropriate, as well as face-saving, if the parties agree to meet somewhere that is geographically halfway between their own countries. This was yet another ingredient of the appeal of Vienna during the Cold War, since it is roughly equidistant between Moscow and the capitals of the European members of NATO. And it was the whole of the appeal of Wake Island in the Pacific Ocean as the venue for the highly sensitive and subsequently controversial talks in October 1950 between President Truman and Douglas MacArthur, a particularly troublesome general. MacArthur was virtually the American 'emperor' of Japan and an independent power in his own right. He had not visited the United States since 1938, and Truman had never met him (Miller: 314–20). What is particularly interesting about the convention of meeting halfway, however, is that its appeal is so great that a state might even be content to forgo neutral ground and meet a rival on the territory of the latter's ally – provided it is halfway between them. Thus, when in 1986 the Soviet leader, Mikhail Gorbachev, proposed a US–Soviet summit preparatory to the one already arranged in Washington, he mentioned as possibilities either London or Reykjavik, although both Britain and Iceland were NATO members. However, both were consistent with his other suggestion, which was that he and President Reagan should meet 'somewhere halfway' (Adelman: 25). In the event, they settled on Reykjavik.

Finally, states can avoid any loss of prestige over the issue of venue by agreeing – should there be a need for lengthy negotiations – to alternate between their respective capitals. Since someone has to be the first to travel, however, taking it in turns is a solution that is generally acceptable only after some diplomatic breakthrough and general improvement in relations. There has to be, in other words, reasonable confidence that a sequence will be established, that each will share the benefits of negotiating at home. For example, after the initial superpower summits in the 1950s and early 1960s, which were held on neutral ground (Geneva and Vienna), a rough pattern of alternation was established in the early 1970s. At about the same time, the Americans and the Chinese Communists agreed to meet alternately in their embassies in Warsaw (Berridge 1994: 88). Following the settlement of the Angola/Namibia conflicts in 1988, the venue of the regular meetings of the joint commission created to consolidate the agreement rotated between the capitals of the full members (Berridge 1994: 121). And this is the procedure adopted for summit meetings of the member states of the EU, the European Council.

Venue, however, is not only of symbolic importance because of its implications for prestige; it might also be of symbolic significance because of the ability of a particular venue to assist one or other of the parties in making some point of propaganda. For example, Israel has generally wanted talks with the Arabs to take place in the Middle East itself rather than outside, as was the case with some of the negotiations with Egypt after 1977 and also with the PLO after 1993. One of the reasons for this is that it emphasizes the point that Israel is a legitimate member state of the region, rather than a temporary foreign implant. For a similar reason, among others, South Africa was much more enthusiastic about holding the 1988 talks on Angola and Namibia in Africa rather than in Europe or North America and, in the event, Brazzaville and Cairo were the settings for some rounds of the negotiations. To return to the Middle East, it seems likely that one of the reasons why Madrid, rather than Geneva, was chosen for the 1991 conference on the Middle East was the need to underline, for the benefit of Israel, that this would be in no sense a UN-driven conference. Israel had a general aversion to the UN, which went back to the General Assembly's 'Zionism is a form of racism' resolution of the mid-1970s. But it also disliked the UN's identification with the version of the 'international conference' proposal associated with Saddam Hussein and the PLO at the time of the Gulf War. Madrid was also conveniently placed for the PLO, which was headquartered in Tunis, while the Spanish government was currently enjoying a *rapprochement* with Israel following the establishment of diplomatic relations in 1986 and the constitutional recognition of Judaism in 1990.

Practical considerations, as hinted earlier, are also of first-class importance in influencing preferences for the venue of negotiations. It is generally for these reasons, as well as reasons of prestige, that states prefer their rivals to come to them. In true Middle Kingdom tradition, 'the Chinese unquestionably prefer to negotiate on their own territory as it facilitates their internal communications and decision-making procedures and maximizes their control over the ambiance of a negotiation' (Binnendijk: 9). If states, nevertheless, have to send delegations abroad to negotiate, it is generally an advantage if they do not have to send them too far. Proximity usually makes communication with home easier, and also makes it easier to respond quickly to any sudden developments by flying in more senior personnel or recalling negotiators for consultation. If the venue has to be more remote, it is an advantage if it is in a country where they have a sizeable embassy. This will provide them with local back-up and reliable communication facilities. The force of this point was brought home to the American delegation that accompanied President Reagan to the summit with Gorbachev in Reykjavik in October 1986. The secure room, or 'bubble', in the US embassy was the smallest ever built and could seat only eight people. At one point, this maximum had already been reached when the President himself turned up. Being closest to the door, the US Arms Control Director, Kenneth Adelman, at once surrendered his chair to his chief. 'I then plopped down on the only square foot of unoccupied floor space,' he reports, 'leaning solidly against the President's legs and with nearly everyone's shoes touching my legs' (Adelman: 46).

Some venues also have air services, conference facilities, hotels, entertainment, and security that are vastly superior to those available to others. Some also have better climates. The Mozambique capital, Lourenço Marques (now Maputo), was quite rightly rejected as the venue for a major conference on southern African transport in the early 1950s, partly on the grounds that the weather in the chosen month, February, was intolerably hot and humid.

A final practical implication of venue worth noting is illustrated by the Israeli attitude to the bilateral negotiations on different subjects that it was agreed at Madrid in 1991 should be held between Israel and its various Arab rivals. Different venues were proposed for each by the Israelis in order to make Arab coordination more difficult although, in the event, they failed to achieve this point and all of the 'bilateral tracks' were pursued in Washington (Ashrawi: 153–4).

Delegations

If the agreed format for the forthcoming negotiations requires the appointment of one or more delegations, further points requiring agreement in prenegotiations concern their level, composition, and size. The last aspect is not normally controversial, unless a state proposes to send a delegation that is so small that it implies lack of seriousness of purpose, or so large that difficult problems of accommodation and security are raised. Level and composition of delegations is, however, another matter altogether.

Whether or not talks should be held at ministerial or merely official level has often been an issue in prenegotiations, since, the higher the level, the more priority might reasonably be assumed and the more rapid progress reasonably expected. (This now generally subsumes the question of whether or not the delegation has 'full powers'.) For example, in the 1950s, the South African government, ever anxious to persuade Britain to signal high priority to defence talks on Africa, was constantly urging London to conduct negotiations at senior ministerial level. By contrast, the British government, which did not share the enthusiasm of Pretoria for this subject and which was anxious to avoid over-identification with its racial policies, was generally adamant that they should be 'written down' to the level of officials. In some regimes, the line between 'officials' and 'ministers' never had any meaning and, even in those where it did, the line now seems more blurred. Nevertheless, it remains fairly obvious who is important and who is not. The greater ease of foreign travel has also made it more difficult for states to resist the notion that their most senior people – including heads of state and government themselves – cannot take part in a negotiation abroad on grounds of practical impossibility. One answer to this problem is mixed delegations, which seem increasingly common, including delegations in which ministers participate for short periods. This is often the case with negotiations that it is formally agreed should be held at foreign minister level. If there is a huge disparity in status between the states in question, the issue of level of delegations is less likely to be troublesome. Micro-states know that, as a general rule, matters to which they are happy to have their president attend cannot command the personal attention of the leader of a superpower.

The level of a delegation has an intimate bearing on its composition. Nevertheless, level might be agreed but problems of composition remain. This is especially the case where a multilateral negotiation is proposed but there is hostility to participation by certain parties *at any level*. This is typically because of the non-recognition of one potential participant by another – for example, the non-recognition of the PRC by the United States at the time of the Geneva Conference on South-East Asia in 1954. To take another example, the refusal of Israel to have anything whatever to do with the PLO, together with the Arab insistence that talks on the future of the West Bank and Gaza would be meaningless without it, led to a horrendous wrangle in 1977. As in the case of the issue of the agenda, this illustrated that prenegotiations can, in fact, disguise the most vital points of substance. For, had the Israelis conceded separate Palestinian representation (whether by the PLO or in some other manner), they would have conceded a separate Palestinian identity – and thus, on grounds of national self-determination, the right of the Palestinians to their own state. It was much better from the Israeli point of view, therefore, that, if the so-called 'Palestinians' were to be represented at all, it should be as part of a Jordanian delegation, since it was a widely held view in Israel that the Palestinians were 'really' Jordanians.

Timing

The final procedural question is timing. The issue of whether or not there should be a deadline for concluding the talks – and, if so, what sort it should be – is so important to the question of diplomatic momentum that it is better to leave this discussion until Chapter 4. But when should the negotiations commence? The possibility that favourable circumstances are unlikely to last forever argues for a prompt start, but pressing for this might suggest weakness. Other commitments on the part of key negotiators have to be considered as well, practical arrangements made, and time allowed for the preparation of briefing papers and for appropriate consultations: the greater the number of parties involved and the more sensitive the issues at stake, the longer all of this is likely to take. However, it is unusual today for the timing of the opening of a negotiation to be as difficult as it was for the Congress of Münster and Osnabrück summoned to end the Thirty Years War. This was originally called for 25 March 1642, then put back to the start of July 1643, and did not officially open until 4 December 1644 (Satow: vol. II, 5–6).

The practical difficulties of finding a mutually convenient date for the start of negotiations nevertheless remain considerable in the modern world, even for those that are part of a regular pattern. For example, the General Council of the World Trade Organization (WTO) agreed in January 2001 to accept the invitation of the government of Qatar to hold its next ministerial conference at its capital, Doha, in early November. However, the WTO subsequently found that these dates clashed with a summit meeting in Rome of the Food and Agriculture Organization. The government of Qatar then pointed out that it could not host the meeting after 9 November due to the commencement of Ramadan, which would not end until about 16 December, rather close to Christmas. As for bringing it forward, there was the problem of the summit of the Asia-Pacific Economic Cooperation forum expected to be held in mid-October in China (Raghavan). Because of such difficulties in finding a date that is practicable, it might no longer be normal practice also to want good omens before commencing a negotiation – although it would be surprising if this were not the case in those parts of the world where astrology (which penetrated the White House itself during the Reagan years) is influential. However, dates on the calendar that evoke particularly bitter memories are naturally regarded as inauspicious. 'Bloody Sundays' are avoided with great care in the planning of any negotiations touching on Northern Ireland – and with good reason. For any attempt to relaunch negotiations between Palestinians and Israelis, the anniversary of the creation of the state of Israel, 14 May 1948, falls into the same category.

Summary

In prenegotiations, states first have to agree that it might be in their mutual interests to negotiate at all. Having agreed that negotiating might be better than not negotiating, they then have to agree an agenda and all of the multifarious questions that come up under the heading of 'procedure'. This being so, it might be thought surprising that, in tense relationships, states ever get round to substantive negotiations at all. That they do is testimony not only to the remorseless logic of circumstance, but also to the fact that diplomacy is a professionalized activity.

Further reading

Alexander, Michael, *Managing the Cold War: A view from the front line*, ed. and introduced by Keith Hamilton (RUSI: London, 2005): 29–34.

Ashrawi, Hanan, *This Side of Peace: A personal account* (Simon & Schuster: New York/London, 1995).

Cohen, R., *Negotiating across Cultures*, 2nd edn (US Institute of Peace Press: Washington, 1997): 67–82.

Corbacho, Alejandro Luis, 'Prenegotiation and Mediation: The Anglo-Argentine diplomacy after the Falklands/Malvinas War (1983–1989)', *CEMA Working Papers from Universidad del CEMA*, 269.

Cradock, P., *Experiences of China* (John Murray: London, 1994): chs 16–18.

Gross-Stein, J. (ed.), *Getting to the Table: The process of international pre-negotiation* (Johns Hopkins University Press: Baltimore, 1989).

Hampson, Fen Osler, with Michael Hart, *Multilateral Negotiations: Lessons from arms control, trade and the environment* (Johns Hopkins University Press: Baltimore, 1995).

Kazuo, Ogura, 'How the "inscrutables" negotiate with the "inscrutables": Chinese negotiating tactics vis-à-vis the Japanese', *China Quarterly*, 79, September 1979: 535–7, 541–2, on agendas.

Patten, Chris, *East and West: The last governor of Hong Kong on power, freedom and the future* (Pan Books: London, 1999): 73–4.

Quandt, W. B., *Camp David: Peacemaking and politics* (Brookings Institution: Washington, 1986): chs 3–7.

Saunders, H., 'We need a larger theory of negotiation: the importance of prene-gotiating phases', *Negotiation Journal*, 1, 1985.

Young, Kenneth T., *Negotiating with the Chinese Communists: The United States experience, 1953–1967* (McGraw-Hill: New York, 1968): ch. 15.

Zartman, I. W. and M. Berman, *The Practical Negotiator* (Yale University Press: New Haven/London, 1982): ch. 3.

3
'Around-the-Table' Negotiations

If prenegotiations are successfully concluded, the next task for the negotiators is to move into around-the-table mode. This stage is generally more formal and there is usually more public awareness of what, in broad terms, is going on. After wrapping up any outstanding procedural points, first comes the task of trying to agree on the basic principles of a settlement: the formula stage. If this is achieved, the details then have to be added. This chapter will begin by looking at the formula stage and conclude with an examination of the details stage. The latter is often more difficult, not least because it is the moment of truth for the negotiators.

The formula stage

For the broad principles of a settlement there are many deliberately anodyne synonyms, among the more common of which are 'guidelines', 'framework for agreement', and 'set of ideas'. Zartman and Berman prefer 'formula' and, since it is short and clear, so do I. A classic example of a successful formula was the 'one country [China], two systems [communism and capitalism]' idea for a solution to the relationship between the PRC and the British colony of Hong Kong, the lease from China on the greater part of which was due to expire in 1997. This formula had evolved in the course of Chinese thinking about Taiwan and was originally resisted by the British, who wanted to retain administrative control of Hong Kong after relinquishing sovereignty. However, it became the basis of the Anglo–Chinese Joint Declaration on Hong Kong in 1984. Other instructive examples of agreed formulas include those on Cyprus and the Arab–Israeli conflict. The high-level agreements on Cyprus of 1977 and 1979 provided for a deal in which the

Turks would give up some of the territory seized following their intervention in 1974 provided the Greeks would admit replacement of the unitary constitution of the island state by a federal one, thereby granting Turkish Cypriots sovereignty over some of their affairs in a defined geographical zone: the land for federation formula. As for the Middle East, in UN Security Council Resolution 242 of November 1967, passed following the Six Day War, it was agreed that Israeli forces would withdraw 'from territories [not, famously, from *the* territories] occupied in the recent conflict' provided the Arab states would recognize the state of Israel and end the condition of belligerency with it: the land for peace formula.

The chief characteristics of a good formula are simplicity, comprehensiveness, balance, and flexibility. Simplicity is important because this makes the formula a straightforward guide for the negotiators to follow. It also lends itself to publicity, and it is often the intention of at least one of the parties to broadcast the formula to the world; this rallies supporters, unnerves rivals, and makes it more difficult for the other side to wriggle out of its undertakings. When, in 1939, the British government was desperate to claim progress in constructing an anti-Axis 'peace front' in the Balkans and the Mediterranean but found itself unable to rush a nervous Turkey into signing up, it persuaded Ankara to agree to an early, joint declaration of the *principles* of Anglo–Turkish solidarity. This produced cheers in the House of Commons and relief in the press (see Box 3.1).

The best formula will also be comprehensive; that is, it will promise solutions to all major points of dispute between the parties. However, this is often not practical politics, and a formula is not vitiated if this is impossible. Some issues might be registered but postponed for later consideration, as was the case with Taiwan in the Shanghai Communiqué in February 1972. Other issues might be fudged if simplicity's price in embarrassment is too high, as with the question of a state for the Palestinian Arabs in the Camp David Accords of September 1978, another well-known formula. Others might be omitted altogether, as with multiple independently targetable re-entry vehicles (MIRVs) in the interim agreement on the limitation of offensive arms produced at the end of the Strategic Arms Limitation Talks (SALT I) in May 1972. Whichever strategy is employed will depend on the priorities of the moment and the nature of the external pressure on the parties. It was, for example, unnecessary for the United States and the Soviet Union to fudge, or pretend to have made progress on MIRVs in SALT I since neither party was under overwhelming pressure on this particular score.

Box 3.1   Formula for an Anglo–Turkish Alliance, 12 May 1939

On 12 May 1939, as reported in Hansard, the British prime minister, Neville Chamberlain, said to applause in the House of Commons:

> It is agreed that the two countries will conclude a definitive long-term agreement of a reciprocal character in the interests of their national security. (Cheers.) Pending the completion of the definitive agreement his Majesty's Government and the Turkish Government declare that *in the event of an act of aggression leading to war in the Mediterranean area they would be prepared to cooperate effectively and to lend each other all the aid and assistance in their power* (Cheers.) [emphasis added].

This enabled *The Times* to announce on the following day:

DEFENSIVE AGREEMENT WITH TURKEY

A COMMON DECLARATION

———

MUTUAL UNDERTAKINGS IN THE MEDITERRANEAN

LONG-TERM PACT TO FOLLOW

By contrast, Egyptian leadership of the Arab world turned on whether or not there appeared to be *something* for the Palestinians in the Camp David Accords; in the event, it was not enough.

As for balance in a formula, this means that it must promise roughly equal gains to all parties. Although it must not be as vague as the kind of formula floated in the prenegotiations stage, it must imply sufficient flexibility to permit each side to believe that it might get what it wants in the details stage of the negotiations. How is such a formula obtained?

The nettle of general principle might be grasped immediately by the negotiators once they are seated around the table. This is sometimes described as the 'deductive approach' (Zartman and Berman: 89) and requires little further comment. Going from the general to the particular is the logical way to proceed in negotiations. Alternatively, the nettle of principle might be approached with caution – by stealth, perhaps from its flank, always slowly, and with thickly gloved hands. Sometimes described as the 'inductive approach' (going from the particular to the general), this is more commonly known as 'step-by-step' diplomacy. The most advertised case of this method was the Middle East diplomacy of Henry Kissinger in the years following the Yom Kippur

War of October 1973, but it was not a Kissinger invention. It was, for example, the key tactic of the functionalist – as opposed to the federalist – movement for European integration following the end of World War II (Mitrany).

The step-by-step approach is usually considered appropriate to the negotiation of a dispute characterized by great complexity and pathological mistrust. In such circumstances it normally makes sense to begin the negotiations on an agenda limited in scope and restricted to items that are relatively uncontroversial. This makes the negotiation more manageable, which is especially important if the diplomatic resources of the parties are also limited. Additionally, it permits mistrust to be gradually broken down, builds faith in the efficacy of diplomacy by making early successes more likely, and familiarizes the parties with the procedures involved in dealing with each other ('learning to walk before trying to run'). The idea is that, as confidence builds, the more difficult questions can gradually be broached with a greater prospect of success; they might even turn out to have been implicitly broken down already (Zartman and Berman: 90). If the initial negotiation is predicated on the hope that more recalcitrant parties will be drawn in later, the step-by-step approach also has the advantage of establishing precedents. Thus, it was Kissinger's hope in 1973 – in the event, justified – that having negotiated a limited disengagement agreement between Israel and Egypt, the Syrians would be emboldened to risk a similar step.

The step-by-step approach, however, is not without its problems. It can mislead by suggesting a relative lack of concern over the bigger questions; it carries the danger of 'paying the whole wallet' for just one item (Zartman and Berman: 178); above all, it takes time. Because it takes time, the favourable circumstances that made launching the negotiations possible might change for the worse and the moment might be lost. There might have been no alternative to employing the step-by-step approach, but this is the risk it carries.

If and when a formula is agreed, states often wish to give maximum publicity to the event, as already indicated. However, if the formula is based on 'linkage' – that is, the trading of concessions in unrelated or only remotely connected issues – such a course of action has its drawbacks, and the negotiations might at this point run into difficulties. (This might have happened earlier, if the deal was suspected from the nature of the agreed agenda.) The reason for this is that, while linkage, or negotiating on a broad front, is more likely to break an impasse by increasing the scope for imaginative solutions, it is also offensive to those who believe that issues should be treated on their merits, especially if their interests are harmed in the process without any *quid pro quo* on their own issue. As Hoffmann points out, 'on each issue, a separate constituency develops, which objects to being treated as a pawn in a global log-rolling game' (Hoffmann: 61). This is why Kissinger's problems with members of the anti-defence spending lobby were magnified when it became clear, early in the first Nixon administration, that he was contemplating trading US concessions in arms control negotiations for Soviet help in places such as Damascus and Hanoi. The issue of nuclear weapons, they believed, should be dealt with on its merits. It is also why many members of the OAU (now the African Union) were enraged when it became clear, in the early 1980s, that the Americans and the South Africans were insisting on Cuba's departure from Angola as the price for South Africa's withdrawal from Namibia. Cuban troops were in Angola at the invitation of the recognized government, it was argued, whereas the occupation of Namibia was illegal and South Africa was obliged to get out anyway. Nevertheless, in a formula based on linkage, there are winners as well as losers; this helps.

The details stage

If a formula is agreed by the parties to a negotiation (whether by immediate, head-on talks following prenegotiations, or by the more oblique step-by-step approach, and whether based on linkage or not), the final stage involves fleshing it out – agreeing the details. This is by no means as simple as it sounds. Indeed, insofar as it is possible to generalize about negotiations, the details stage is a strong candidate for the dubious honour of being called the most difficult stage of all.

One aspect of the formula agreed on Cyprus, in the late 1970s, was that the island should have a new constitution. This would be a bi-communal, bi-zonal federation. 'Bi-communal' meant that the composition of the central government and its agencies would have to reflect the division of the population between Turkish Cypriots and Greek Cypriots, which was roughly 2:8. 'Bi-zonality' meant that the island itself (effectively partitioned in 1974) would become a federal state based on two geographical zones, a Turkish zone in the north and a Greek zone in the south. So far so good. But this left a myriad of sensitive details to be agreed, as might be imagined. Not the least among these was where exactly the line would be drawn on the ground between the two zones.

A further example of the difficulties of the details stage is provided by the agreement, in mid-1988, that South Africa would withdraw its forces from Namibia and permit the country to become independent in return for the withdrawal of Cuban troops from Angola: this left a large number of vital issues of detail to resolve on which the interests of the parties were clearly divergent. In the case of the Cuban troops alone, these included: When exactly would the departure commence? When would it terminate? Would the withdrawal be front-loaded, end-loaded, or consist of a uniform stream (the same number of troops leaving in each month)? From which areas of Angola would the first troops be withdrawn? And so on. Why is the details stage often so difficult and why, as a result, do talks often founder here?

Difficulties

The first reason for difficulty in the details stage is that it is, by definition, complicated. It might not be more complicated than prenegotiations – although it usually is – but it is invariably more complicated than the formula stage. In addition to providing a difficulty in itself, complexity also means, as a rule, that larger teams of negotiators are required in the details stage; and this brings in its train much greater scope for disagreement within the negotiating teams. It is, for example, a commonplace of American commentary on the detailed arms control talks between the United States and the Soviet Union in the 1970s that the really tough negotiations took place not in Vienna or Helsinki but, rather, between the various agencies of the administration in Washington.

Second, it is in the details stage that careful thought has to be given to the definition of terms, or to establishing a common language. This is necessary to avoid misunderstanding, but can be extremely problematical because some definitions serve the interests of some parties better than others. Definitions proved to be a nightmare in the US–Soviet arms control negotiations, where wrangles over some terms (chiefly concerning categories of weapon) lasted for years. It was, for example, not until 1986 – 16 years after SALT I began in 1969 – that Soviet negotiators abandoned their insistence that 'strategic weapons' were those capable of reaching the territory of a potential adversary irrespective of their location (Adelman: 52). On such a definition, US forward-based systems such as those in Western Europe would be included in any regime to limit 'strategic weapons', while Soviet missiles targeted at Western Europe but unable to reach the United States would not.

Third, because the details stage of negotiation is complicated and time-consuming, and usually requires the participation of specialists, the negotiating teams are normally composed of individuals of lower authority than those involved – or, at any rate, leading – in the negotiations during the formula stage. This might well cause delays, as they will need to refer back for guidance to their political leaders. The stickiness of the details stage caused by this situation might well be compounded further, since, having returned home, their principals will be under less pressure from the other side and under greater pressure from their own constituencies. This could lead to a reversion to a tougher attitude and cause hard-line instructions to be issued to the negotiators saddled with fleshing out the formula. This is precisely what happened after the Camp David formulas had been agreed in the rarified atmosphere of the American presidential retreat in September 1978. 'Isolating the leaders from the press and their own public opinion', as Quandt notes, 'had no doubt been a prime ingredient in reaching the two framework agreements. Now, however, each leader would have to return to the real world in which domestic constituencies would have their say. As each of the Camp David participants felt compelled to justify what he had done at the summit,' Quandt continues, 'the gap separating them began to widen again' (Quandt: 259). Indeed, it was only after the resumption of top-level participation in the talks, not least by President Carter himself, that at least an Egypt–Israel peace treaty was finally produced five months after the 'framework' had been agreed.

A fourth reason why the details stage is often particularly difficult is that it might well present an opportunity to one or both sides to load the balance of advantage in the agreed formula in their favour. In light of the complexity of this stage, this might occur in a manner not necessarily easy to detect (Zartman and Berman: 149–52). In other words, and especially if trust between the parties is minimal, the atmosphere in the details stage is likely to suffer simply because of the fear that each side might be trying to redraft the formula by massaging the small print.

Finally, the details stage is the last stage: the moment of truth. What is agreed here has to be acted on, so, if the negotiators get it wrong, they will suffer. When the details stage is concluded, it might mean soldiers surrendering positions in defence of which they have lost brothers, settlers giving up land in which they have sunk roots, exporters abandoning prized markets, or workers losing their livelihoods. There should, thus, be no vagueness and no inconsistencies, and the deal should be defensible at home. Magnanimity is generally at a discount in the details stage of negotiations.

Negotiating strategies

Detailed agreements are negotiated by one of two means, or – more usually – by some combination of both. The first method is to compromise on individual issues; for example, by splitting the difference between the opening demands of the parties on the timetable for a troop withdrawal. This is what happened in regard to the Cuban troops in Angola during the American-brokered negotiations in 1988. The South Africans wanted them out as soon as possible, and had in mind a timetable of months. By contrast, the Marxist government of Angola, anxious to retain the protection afforded by Castro's 'internationalist military contingent' for as long as possible, was thinking of a timetable for its withdrawal in terms of three or four years. In the end, they compromised on a timetable of a year and half, which was spelled out in detail in an annex to the agreement.

The second method for making concessions is to give the other side more or less what it wants on one issue in return for satisfaction on a separate one, which is, in principle, the same as linkage (p. 47), except that here the issues, while separate, are of the same species. Described by Zartman and Berman as 'exchanging points', this works best when each party is able to acquire from the other something it considers of greater value than what has to be surrendered in return. This was elaborated by the sociologist George Homans in a work published in 1961, sometimes known as 'Homans's theorem' (Zartman and Berman: 13–14, 66, 175–6). A simple example would be the exchange of a packet of rich biscuits for a piece of lean steak, where the former was held initially by a meat-loving weight-watcher and the latter by a vegetarian with a sweet tooth.

A variant on Homans's theorem is a deal in which one party trades something that it values highly but which it knows it is going to have to surrender anyway, irrespective of whether or not it gets a *quid pro quo* from the other side. In principle, both parties can do this as well. The trick here is to make sure that the other side does not share the same information. This is where liberal democracies are at a severe disadvantage compared with authoritarian regimes, which was a constant lament of Henry Kissinger in the 1970s. Thus, in seeking to trade a US freeze in the deployment of anti-ballistic missiles (ABMs) in return for Soviet limitations on offensive nuclear forces, Kissinger was seriously hampered by the obvious determination of Congress to kill off the ABM programme anyway (Kissinger 1979: 194–210, 534–51). Neither did it help him in his negotiations with the North Vietnamese in Paris that, under even more fierce Congressional pressure, his major trump card – US military power in South Vietnam – was slipping remorselessly from his grasp with every fresh public announcement of further troop with-drawals. When the other party knows that history is on its side, it has little incentive to pay for 'concessions'.

Should negotiators be accommodating or tough in their general approach? Each has advantages and disadvantages, and, since the circumstances of different negotiations vary so enormously, generalization in this area is a risky business. Nevertheless, at the price of inviting the charge of banality, the following might be hazarded:

- First, extremes of flexibility and rigidity are both inconsistent with the logic of negotiation.
- Second, since negotiation involves concessions by both sides (by definition), it is usually best to make them in one fell swoop in order to avoid the impression given by making small concessions incrementally that there are always more for the asking (Zartman and Berman: 171). But this does not mean that major concessions should be made right at the beginning of negotiations. This mistake was made by Turkey during the Mosul negotiations with Britain in 1926. The Turkish negotiator astonished his British counterpart by, at the outset, surrendering the former Ottoman province to the then British-mandated territory of Iraq, when only months before his government had been threatening to go to war over it. This had the momentary advantage for the Turks of generating goodwill and catching the British off-balance, but it left them with little with which to barter: they ended up with a payment of a mere £500,000 for the province when they could have had £1,000,000 – the secret British fall-back position (Berridge 2009: 145–51).
- Third, if concessions are nevertheless extracted incrementally, the impression of weakness might be reduced by exploitation of various tactical expedients. Among these are making the concessions contingent on a final package deal, periodically suspending the talks in order to remind the other party that too much pressure might lead to their collapse, and raising the question of the formula again.
- Fourth, a tough attitude in negotiations is most appropriate to parties confident that they can walk away without major damage to their position, which helps to explain the attitude of the Begin government during the Camp David negotiations. It is equally appropriate to regimes based on religious fanaticism or police terror, because the governments of such states are relatively indifferent to the costs imposed by diplomatic failure on their own people.

Whichever strategy, or combination of them, is adopted for making and seeking concessions will depend on circumstances and the established style of the negotiators. When the negotiators come from different cultural traditions, there can be problems (Cohen 1997).

Summary

Negotiation is generally a lengthy and laborious process, proceeding through prenegotiations and a formula to the details phase. In each stage, there is a risk of breakdown, although this is probably most acute in the first and last stages – in the first, not least because the 'exit costs' (Stein: 482) are low, while, in the last, because this is the negotiators' moment of truth. The momentum of the negotiations might thus falter, even if both parties in a bilateral negotiation, or a majority of parties in a multilateral negotiation, are serious about making them a success. How diplomatic momentum might be sustained is a serious question, and it is to this that we must next turn.

Further reading

Berridge, G. R., 'Diplomacy and the Angola/Namibia accords, December 1988', *International Affairs*, 65(3), 1989.

Binnendijk, H. (ed.), *National Negotiating Styles* (Center for the Study of Foreign Affairs, Foreign Service Institute, US Department of State: Washington, 1987).

Cohen, R., *Negotiating across Cultures*, 2nd edn (US Institute of Peace Press: Washington, 1997).

Crocker, C. A., *High Noon in Southern Africa: Making peace in a rough neighbourhood* (Norton: New York/London, 1992).

Faure, G. O. and J. Z. Rubin (eds), *Culture and Negotiation: The resolution of water disputes* (Sage: Newbury Park, CA/London/New Delhi, 1993).

Golan, M., *The Secret Conversations of Henry Kissinger: Step-by-step diplomacy in the Middle East* (Quadrangle: New York, 1976).

Kazuo, Ogura, 'How the "inscrutables" negotiate with the "inscrutables": Chinese negotiating tactics vis-à-vis the Japanese', *China Quarterly*, 79, September 1979.

Kremenyuk, V. A. (ed.), *International Negotiation* (Jossey-Bass: San Francisco/Oxford, 1991).

Quandt, W. R, *Camp David: Peacemaking and politics* (Brookings: Washington, 1986): chs 8–12.

Ross, Dennis, *Statecraft: And how to restore America's standing in the world* (Farrar, Straus & Giroux: New York, 2007): chs 8 and 9.

Touval, S., 'Multilateral negotiation: An analytic approach', *Negotiation Journal*, 5(2), 1989.

Vance, C., *Hard Choices: Critical years in America's foreign policy* (Simon & Schuster: New York, 1983).

Webster, Sir C., *The Art and Practice of Diplomacy* (Chatto & Windus: London, 1961).

Zartman, I. W. (ed.), *International Multilateral Negotiation* (Jossey-Bass: San Francisco, 1997).

Zartman, I. W. and M. Berman, *The Practical Negotiator* (Yale University Press: New Haven/London, 1982): chs 4–6.

4
Diplomatic Momentum

The momentum of a negotiation might falter, even if the parties are serious about proceeding. This was a recurring problem with the Uruguay Round of the General Agreement on Tariffs and Trade (GATT) negotiations, which started in September 1986 and was not finally completed until April 1994. Why might momentum falter? Why is it serious? And what might be done to prevent it? The first two questions are not especially problematical and have, in any case, already been touched upon. As a result, the greater part of this chapter will discuss the practical stratagems falling under the heading of the third – other than inducements such as side payments and guarantees offered by a mediator, which will be dealt with in Chapter 15.

Some reasons why momentum might be lost, especially in the details stage of negotiations, have already been mentioned but will bear recapitulation here. First, there is the characteristic withdrawal of senior ministers or officials following conclusion of the formula stage of important negotiations, which might well lead to a slackening in pace because of the greater need for reference home for instructions when difficulties occur. Second, a party feeling that things are not going well might drag its feet in the hope that something to its advantage will turn up. Third, there is the effect of the sheer complexity of much contemporary international negotiation, especially multilateral negotiation. This much we already know.

Talks might, however, also be slowed down – or even temporarily interrupted – by a host of other factors. Key personnel might be withdrawn from any stage of negotiations by the need to attend to even more urgent matters. These include time-consuming commitments in annual national and international calendars such as party congresses, the opening of new parliamentary sessions, regular summit meetings, the start of the new session of the UN General Assembly in September, and so on. They might be delayed by disputes within delegations, which was notoriously the case with the European Community (EC) delegation in the GATT negotiations. They might be delayed by the serious possibility of a change in government of one or more of the parties. This is likely if it is feared that any agreement negotiated will be disavowed or, in practice, circumvented by the new government; or, alternatively, if the new government is expected to agree better terms. Final-term American presidents in their last years have notorious difficulty in being taken seriously as negotiators. (If one party expects worse terms from a new government, the talks might gain rather than lose momentum.) The talks might be delayed by the illness of a key player, or the incompetence or plain laziness of lesser officials. They might also be interrupted, as the Israel–PLO negotiations on the withdrawal of Israeli forces from Gaza and Jericho were interrupted for over a month, by an incident such as the Hebron mosque massacre on 25 February 1994. Such an occurrence makes it unseemly for one or other party to be seen pursuing negotiations for the time being.

If there is a lull in the talks, the great danger is that it will drag on and become permanent. This is because an absence of progress might demoralize the negotiators and, just as important, demoralize their supporters. Such a development will also provide the enemies of negotiations with fresh opportunities for sabotage, and provide them with further ammunition: 'we told you this approach would not work!'. Because, in a lull in negotiations, both parties are likely to remain on their best behaviour, one or other might be led to draw the conclusion that perhaps the *status quo* is not so bad after all, and the price of a deal is too high. Finally, and perhaps most fatally of all, a lull in the talks permits the attention of key personnel to be drawn to other items on the crowded international agenda. This, at one time, seemed to be the likely fate of the Uruguay Round in early 1991, when the Gulf War literally blew up at just the point when a pre-Christmas crisis left the talks drifting aimlessly and urgently in need of top-level attention. In such circumstances, what can be done to sustain momentum, and to regain it if lost?

One method is to employ the step-by-step approach discussed in the previous chapter. This minimizes the risk of stalemate by proceeding in piecemeal fashion, usually from the less to the more difficult issues; and, by building up a list of tangible achievements over a relatively long period, demonstrates the value of diplomacy. A good example is provided by the Cairo Accords on security, signed between the PLO and Israel in early February 1994, which broke months of deadlock in the details stage of this negotiation but left other issues for later. At the time of writing (June 2009), the Obama administration was contemplating a step-by-step approach to reviving the stalled nuclear negotiations with Iran.

If ratification of any initial achievements is contingent on a package deal, the step-by-step approach also gives the negotiators a vested interest in driving the talks towards a final conclusion. After all, they will not normally wish to see their achievements thrown away and have to admit that their time has been wasted. The step-by-step approach, however, is rarely able to maintain momentum unaided, not least because it has a downside: its unavoidable slowness, together with the impression that it generally gives of ducking the main issues, can generate exasperation. It is, then, perhaps the step-by-step approach that is the strategy of negotiation most in need of special assistance in the maintaining of momentum. How can this be provided?

Deadlines

A traditional device regularly employed by negotiators in order to keep up the momentum of their talks is to employ deadlines; that is, calendar dates by which either some partial, interim, or final agreement must be reached. Deadlines must allow sufficient time for the negotiations to be concluded. If they are too tight – especially when a multilateral convention is being negotiated under the lash of a coalition of NGOs and 'like-minded' states – the support of key parties might be lost. This is what has happened with the treaties banning anti-personnel landmines and establishing the International Criminal Court. But, as well as being realistic, deadlines must also be real: real penalties must be expected to flow from failure to reach agreement by the specified date, including the clear risk that one or more of the parties concerned will have to pay a higher price for a settlement, or that the opportunity for a settlement will slip away altogether.

Artificial deadlines

Deadlines that are determined by best estimates of the time required for a negotiation but are, in other respects, arbitrary do not usually carry penalties of the kind just mentioned, unless, that is, one of the parties feels that it has much the stronger hand (Box 4.1). Such 'artificial deadlines' (De Soto: 378) might have a positive impact on the momentum of talks, especially if they are publicly announced, because failure to meet them will be a minor blow to the professional reputations of

---

Box 4.1   The Chinese 'deadline' on Hong Kong

A party to a negotiation confident that it has much the stronger hand can announce a deadline without any discussion, and accompany it with the threat that it will take unilateral action on the issue if a settlement is not reached by this date. In effect, this is virtually an ultimatum, and the weaker party might well conclude that, if it wishes to retain some influence over events, it has no alternative but to adapt to this timetable. An example is provided by the Sino–British negotiations over the transfer of Hong Kong back to China. In September 1983, a few months after the start of the negotiations, the Chinese Communist government announced that if a settlement were not achieved within a year – that is, by September 1984 – it would simply make known its own decisions on the future of the island. The British fell in with this timetable, and the Joint Declaration on Hong Kong was initialled in this same month. A 'practical deadline' also stimulated progress in these talks: the expiry of the 99-year lease on the so-called 'New Territories' (which comprised 92 per cent of the territory of the colony of Hong Kong) on 30 June 1997 (Cradock: 162, 189–90, 196–7).

---

the negotiators. On the other hand, these individuals can usually gain more than compensating marks from their supporters by claiming that the terms on offer remained unsatisfactory, and that they would have been failing in their duty if they had settled by the agreed date. Missing the deadline would be considered evidence of a 'tough' stand rather than incompetence, sloth, or lack of seriousness of purpose. The best deadlines, thus, are either those that are deliberately pegged to some date that has significance more or less independent of the negotiations (symbolic deadlines), or those that are forced on the negotiators by circumstance (practical deadlines).

Symbolic deadlines

Symbolic deadlines are often dates that would have significance for the subject of the negotiations, whether the negotiations were taking place or not. Good examples in peace negotiations are the anniversaries of the outbreak of a war, a ceasefire resolution, or – especially suitable – some spectacular, grisly and altogether gratuitous massacre. The birthday or anniversary of the death of a great leader might serve equally well, as might the date of the founding of some major international organization. And such is the media-inspired fascination with multiples of ten that the most prized anniversaries are half-centenaries, centenaries, and bi-centenaries; even mere tenth anniversaries are eagerly commandeered. Dates in the calendars of the great religions are also useful – in the Christian tradition, especially Christmas itself.

The importance of symbolic deadlines is not difficult to understand. Dates of symbolic significance have long been exploited for propaganda purposes by lobbyists for whom they are important and, partly for this reason and partly because they are ideal pegs on which to hang articles and broadcasts, they have long been the stock in trade of the mass media. In the modern world, therefore, it is highly unlikely that any date of symbolic importance for some group or other will go unnoticed. In early 1994, the story of the Bosnian conflict was repeatedly pushed from the headlines in Britain by coverage of wrangles over the best way to commemorate the 50th anniversary of the Normandy landings of 6 June 1944, which presaged the defeat of Hitler in World War II.

The pressure exerted by a symbolic deadline is this: with unusual media attention focused on the negotiations in the weeks immediately preceding it, the negotiators can expect high marks for meeting the deadline and low ones for letting it slip by. Concluding by this time will show proper respect for the event that it commemorates, while failure to meet it will imply the opposite. The penalty is a propaganda penalty.

A good example of such a deadline was the proposal of the Cuban government in May 1988, endorsed by both Washington and Moscow, that the Angola/Namibia negotiations should be completed by 29 September (Crocker 1999: 229). The appeal of this was that it was the tenth anniversary of the passing of UN Security Council Resolution 435 on the arrangements for the independence of South African-controlled Namibia. Not taking this deadline seriously, therefore, would imply not taking seriously the question of Namibian independence – a 'motherhood' issue (Berridge 1989: 475–6). A more recent example is provided by the target date of midnight on Thursday 9 April 1998 deliberately chosen by George Mitchell, the American mediator, for a settlement of the internal conflict in Northern Ireland – in part because it was the start of the Easter holiday. 'As I studied the calendar,' he wrote later, 'Easter weekend leaped out at me. It had historical significance in Ireland. It was an important weekend in Northern Ireland, a religious society' (Mitchell: 143). In the event, his deadline slipped only by hours: agreement was finally reached at about 5.30 pm on 10 April, Good Friday. Not surprisingly, this settlement has been known ever since as the 'Good Friday Agreement'. British, Irish and American government spin doctors were in seventh heaven.

The usefulness of a symbolic date as a deadline will obviously vary with the importance attached to the event that it commemorates, and will be significantly reduced if it is forced by mediators on parties whose own estimation of the event varies. This was the case with the proposed deadline regarding the Angola/Namibia negotiations. This is because South Africa itself – a key player in these negotiations – could hardly have been expected to be unduly worried by the prospect of appearing indifferent to the celebration of the passage of what was a transparently anti-South African resolution. In the event, at South Africa's suggestion, the deadline for the Angola/Namibia negotiations was brought forward to 1 September. Nevertheless, the regularity with which symbolic deadlines are employed in negotiations is testimony to the value attached to them.

Practical deadlines

There is little doubt that – as the name for them that comes most readily to mind suggests – practical deadlines are usually the most valuable when it comes to sustaining momentum in negotiations. These are deadlines imposed by events that either are completely beyond the control of the negotiating parties or can only be cancelled at considerable cost. Into the last category fall deadlines imposed by summit meetings, discussed in Chapter 10. Into the former fall deadlines imposed by any number of events: scheduled elections, the opening of other conferences where the subject at issue might be high on the agenda, the expiry of the negotiating authority of a key party, the expiry of a ceasefire agreement or mandate of a peacekeeping force, and previously announced dates for the commencement and completion of military withdrawals where the details remain to be negotiated. It is true that practical deadlines might leave insufficient time to perfect an agreement, but an imperfect agreement is usually better than no agreement at all.

Significant practical deadlines are imposed by the US electoral cycle on American diplomacy, especially that in which the president plays a personal role. Only in the first year of the president's maximum of two four-year terms is he relatively free of the pressure of electoral deadlines and, in this first year, the emphasis is, in any case, usually on prenegotiations. In the second year, he begins to look for diplomatic breakthroughs in advance of the mid-term elections for Congress in November. In the third year, it is not long before he is worrying about the effects of his diplomacy on the notoriously protracted nominating process for presidential candidates. And, in the fourth year, unless it is his second term, he is obviously worrying about the general election in November (Quandt: ch. 2).

It is not altogether accidental that it was just two months before the mid-term elections in 1978 that President Carter devoted 13 days to summit diplomacy on the Middle East at Camp David. Nor is it accidental that his 'clear priority after Camp David was to conclude the [detailed] treaty negotiations as quickly as possible, literally within days' (Quandt: 260). It is, however, interesting that his sense of urgency was also heightened by an even tighter practical deadline: the ninth Arab League summit that was scheduled to meet in Baghdad in late October. For it was feared that the 'moderate' states of Jordan and Saudi Arabia would both come under intense pressure at this event from the 'radical' Arab states to denounce the Camp David Accords, and that this would cause Sadat to lose his nerve (Carter: 404–9; Vance: 229; Quandt: 260). By the beginning of 1979, at which point the details stage of the Egypt–Israel negotiations had still not been completed, Carter was in his third year. It is also worth adding here that the presidential election in November 1988, together with the imminent arrival of a new administration in the following January, encouraged all the parties to make tangible progress in the Angola/Namibia negotiations. It increased the pressure on the American mediator, Chester Crocker because, although Ronald Reagan was retiring, the Republican candidate, Vice-President George H. W. Bush, was anxious to highlight as many foreign policy achievements for the administration as possible in his own election campaign. As for Crocker, who had led the negotiations for such a long time, it was also natural that he would want a personal success before probably leaving office himself.

The prospect of a presidential election in the United States can also spur on America's negotiating partners towards a settlement. This will happen if they expect to get a worse deal from the rival presidential candidate than from the incumbent, and if there is a real possibility that the former might win. This was the calculation that was at work on the Iranians in the negotiations over the hostages held at the US embassy in Tehran at the beginning of 1981. Apprehensive of the attitude of the new conservative Republican administration of Ronald Reagan but, at the same time, determined to complete their humiliation of Jimmy Carter, they finally settled on the very day of the new president's inauguration, 20 January 1981.

Fear of the attitude of a rival presidential candidate also influenced the South Africans in the Angola/Namibia negotiations in 1988. They knew that they were unlikely ever to get a better deal from the Americans than under Ronald Reagan, and certainly not from the liberal Democrat, Michael Dukakis, who was running against Vice-President Bush. The prospect of a new administration in January – albeit still a Republican one, since Bush had won – also goaded *all* the parties to these negotiations to clear the final hurdles that appeared in early December. This was because the Americans advertised the fact that the new administration would 'likely mean a change of personnel and a basic policy review' (Crocker 1999: 229).

Another good example of a practical deadline working to keep a negotiation in motion was the Brussels ministerial meeting in GATT's Uruguay Round in the first week of December 1990. The deadline injected urgency into these talks because the US delegation's Congressional mandate was due to run out on 1 March 1991, and there was a real fear that, because of hostility in the United States to the direction of the negotiations, this would not be renewed. Since any package negotiated would have to be submitted to Congress by this date, Carla Hills, the US trade representative, insisted that she would need the time between December and the end of February in order to prepare the necessary legislation. Hence, the effective deadline on the negotiations was the December ministerial meeting.

Finally, the practical deadlines imposed on the details stage of the Israel–PLO negotiations by the dates agreed in the Declaration of Principles of September 1993 for the withdrawal of Israeli forces from Gaza and Jericho might be mentioned. On this occasion it was announced that the withdrawal would commence on 13 December 1993 and be completed by 13 April 1994. These dates were of particular importance to the PLO leader, Yasser Arafat, who was under intense pressure to deliver tangible progress from his own supporters, as well as from more radical Palestinian elements. It is true that the Israeli prime minister, Yitzak Rabin, subsequently declared that 'there are no sacred dates' (*Independent* 1994). Nevertheless, it was clear that failure by Israel to take the agreed withdrawal dates seriously would lead to intense international criticism – not least from the United States – and might destroy Arafat, who remained Israel's most promising negotiating partner. The Palestinian self-rule agreement was finally signed on 4 May under the equally intense pressure generated in the previous week by the public announcement on 28 April of a 'pre-signing summit' between Arafat and Rabin in Cairo. To this, more than 2500 guests and 40 foreign ministers were invited – another practical deadline.

The best deadlines of all are probably those that are both practical and symbolic. The symbolic significance of the start of the Easter weekend in April 1998 as a deadline in the Northern Ireland negotiations has already been noted. However, this was also a practical deadline because any agreement would need to be confirmed by referendums and then followed by the election of a new Northern

Ireland Assembly. This would take a minimum of two months, so, if a settlement were not reached by the middle of April, the whole process could easily fall foul of the North's 'marching season', when community tensions are always raised by numerous sectarian parades; these start every year at Easter and climax in early July (Mitchell: 143–4). In the event, with the deal concluded on 10 April it was possible to hold referendums in both the North and the South in May. The results of these referendums expressed overwhelming popular acceptance of the Good Friday agreement, and it was possible to elect the new assembly in late June.

It often happens that deadlines are passed by much larger margins than that of the negotiations producing the Good Friday agreement. The Angola/Namibia negotiations were not concluded for almost four months after 1 September 1988, the Egypt–Israel Peace Treaty was still unsigned at the time of the American mid-term elections and the Arab League Summit in early November 1978, and the Uruguay Round plodded on for over three years following December 1990. Nevertheless, it seems reasonable to suggest that, in light of the urgency these deadlines visibly injected into these negotiations, they would have taken even longer in their absence and might not have been concluded at all.

Metaphors of movement

Our conceptual system mediates the manner in which we both think and act, and it is now uncontroversial that this system is fundamentally a metaphorical one. Metaphors, which are representations of one thing in terms of another (for example, 'time is money'), have their effect by highlighting and organizing certain aspects of our experience while hiding those inconsistent with it (Lakoff and Johnson: 3, 10, 156–8). Moreover, although most of the metaphors that shape the lives of peoples and governments alike do so unconsciously, they can be deliberately chosen and manipulated. 'War' and 'battle' are common metaphors employed by governments to encourage their citizens to 'close ranks' and make exceptional 'sacrifices' in situations that bear no resemblance to real warfare. The 'war on poverty' and the 'battle against climate change' are familiar metaphors that come to mind here. It is hardly surprising, therefore, that metaphors should also be deliberately employed by those seeking to preserve the momentum of negotiations, and that these metaphors should chiefly be metaphors of *movement*.

A common instance of such a metaphor used in negotiations is that of the automobile. Negotiations are often said to be 'driven forward' and thus, by implication, be capable, like a car, of high speeds and versatility in manoeuvring around 'obstacles in the road'. If they come to a stop despite a 'green light', this is because they have 'stalled', a condition usually caused by the sort of embarrassing incompetence that is best corrected as soon as possible. In case the drivers of the talks are in any doubt about the direction in which they should be headed, a 'road map' of the sequence in which points should be agreed and implemented is routinely provided. The Americans did this in their negotiations over the normalization of relations with the Vietnamese in the early 1990s (Berridge 1994: 57–8), and in a fresh bid in 2003 to promote a two-state solution to the Israeli–Palestinian conflict. On the latter occasion, when the United States was associated with the European Union, Russia, and the United Nations ('the Quartet' – was this musical metaphor meant to encourage harmony?), a 'timeline' was also added. Ever since, with a shameless mixing of the car and train metaphors, there has been much talk of the need to keep the road map 'on track'.

Even more common in the language of negotiations than the automobile metaphor is the metaphor of the train, perhaps because trains have far fewer opportunities to make detours. If the negotiation is like a train, it will be perilous for all concerned if it does not stay 'on the track' – if, that is to say, it is 'derailed' – which is, in any case, a very rare occurrence. It will also be dangerous for anyone 'to get off' before it 'pulls into the station'; and general exasperation will ensue if the talks get 'shunted into a siding'. The train metaphor is particularly useful because it can cope with lulls in a negotiation: trains, after all, stop in stations – but only briefly. Trains also run to timetables, so the metaphor reinforces the use of deadlines. And only rare and terrible disasters prevent them from eventually arriving at their terminus. Complicated negotiations are also commonly described as 'dual track' or 'multi-track', and negotiations by unofficial bodies and individuals as 'track two' diplomacy (see Chapter 15). 'Back-tracking' is the worst of all sins in negotiations. The popularity of the train metaphor is not difficult to understand. In the Angola/Namibia negotiations, the Americans used it repeatedly (Berridge 1989: 477; see also the section on 'Publicity' below). And so they appear to have done again, in setting up the conference on the Middle East at Madrid in 1991, when James Baker, US secretary of state at the time, reports telling the Palestinians that 'the train was moving and they'd better not miss it' (Baker: 200).

Metaphors of movement of the kind just described help to prevent loss of momentum in negotiations by stimulating all of the participants, together with their supporters, to believe that they are on something fated to forward motion. In consequence, they are also encouraged to resign themselves to helping it reach its destination. At this point it will be clear, and needs to be emphasized, that implicit in the metaphor of movement is a further metaphor – the *metaphor of the journey* – and that both are, at the same time, *metaphors of collaboration*. A metaphor of movement sometimes used by negotiators that brings out the collaborative aspect particularly well is the 'race against time'. This is a race against one of the sorts of 'deadline' – themselves now revealed as an instance of this metaphor – that were discussed in the previous section. This kind of race is a race in which the parties collaborate against their common enemy, time, rather than one in which they compete against each other. In the negotiation that is like a race against time there are no prizes for 'not finishing' or 'dropping out early'. Obstacles that are met in the negotiation are 'hurdles', and it is the duty of everyone, including those for whom an early shower might, in reality, be the best option, to 'clear' them. Negotiators of countries on the verge of war, as in the case of the United States and Iraq in early 1991, are now generally expected to go 'the extra mile' for peace.

The importance of the metaphor of the *journey* – which has a point of departure and proceeds through stages to its destination – is stressed by Lakoff and Johnson (89–91). It is true that they use it as an example of a metaphor of argument rather than negotiation, but negotiation is no more than a special variant of this. The production by the US Department of State's metaphor machine of the 'road map' metaphor, an obvious instance of the metaphor of the journey, has already been noted. There is, however, another instance – one that is far more important – as demonstrated by the fact that it is the commanding concept of Part I of this book and, so far, has been taken for granted. This is the concept of 'stages of negotiation', and the related metaphor – also noted by Lakoff and Johnson (90) – of 'step-by-step' diplomacy.

In sum, metaphors of movement, especially those that imply the need for collaboration on a shared journey, are a common device employed by those anxious to preserve the momentum of a negotiation. The extent of their effectiveness in different situations must remain largely speculative, but the revelations of linguistic philosophy and the evidence of the repeated use of these metaphors in negotiations suggest that two conclusions are reasonable. The first is that the influence of these metaphors will often be considerable, and the second is that it will be most significant for the behaviour of those for whom continued negotiation is risky and for whom, therefore, metaphors of movement are a treacherous stimulus. The potency of such metaphors – especially if picked up, embellished and repeated by the mass media – must be difficult to resist. This brings us naturally to publicity.

Publicity

It is a cliché of studies of diplomacy that publicity is the enemy of negotiation, and this is often true. However, employed judiciously, publicity about a negotiation can also help to move it forward. In addition to implanting and constantly emphasizing appropriate metaphors, it can do this in at least three other ways: first, by flying kites to see how the other side will react; second, by mobilizing popular support for a negotiated solution; and third, by 'talking up the talks'. Propaganda and diplomacy are thus not necessarily antithetical; it all depends on the nature of the propaganda. This is one of the reasons why the press office is such an important department of heads of government and their foreign ministries.

Floating formulas or flying kites, both publicly and privately, is of special importance in prenegotiations, as already remarked, but it is not confined to this stage. For example, during the 14 weeks of substantive negotiations held on Rhodesia at Lancaster House in London in 1979, the head of the News Department at the Foreign Office, Sir Nicholas Fenn, often aired suggestions for the press to report (Dickie: 249). Flying kites openly can expedite negotiations by preparing the public for an eventual settlement. It can perhaps do this even more effectively by permitting negotiators to gain greater insight into the ambitions and anxieties of their interlocutors, by noting their reactions when the kites soar upwards. An idea *publicly* accepted – or, at least, not dismissed outright – will be regarded as a serious basis for negotiation, because this will be an indication that the party concerned believes it can sell this at home.

Even authoritarian regimes ignore their own popular opinion at their peril – as the Shah of Iran discovered in the late 1970s – and they are, in any case, almost always anxious to influence foreign opinion. As a result, mobilizing the public in support of important negotiations will be a priority for any government committed to them, especially if they appear to be flagging. This was why the Egyptian leader, Anwar Sadat, took the dramatic step of journeying to the disputed city of Jerusalem in November 1977 to address the Israeli people over the heads of its government. It was also why the Carter administration decided, shortly afterwards, to 'mount a public campaign' directed at both American and Israeli opinion to bring pressure to bear on the government of Menachem Begin (Quandt: 162).

Another important way of sustaining momentum in negotiations is to give the public the impression that they are nearer to success than is, in reality, the case. 'Talking up the talks' cannot be done repeatedly, or in circumstances when it is manifestly obvious that success is nowhere in sight. This will result in a loss of public credibility. It might also rebound by angering the delegation of the more recalcitrant party, which might find itself unfairly in hot water with its own supporters. Nevertheless, used sparingly and when clear progress in one or other stage of the negotiations has been made, talking up the talks can prove very useful indeed. It was employed by the British Foreign Secretary, Lord Carrington, at the Lancaster House talks on Rhodesia (Dickie: 250), by the UN mediator in the Afghanistan talks in the 1980s (Harrison: 35), and also by Chester Crocker in the Angola/Namibia negotiations. Crocker's tactic, as in the case of the other two negotiators, was to sound optimistic at press briefings once it was clear that there was a genuine chance of a breakthrough. Any party then deserting the talks or behaving in an obstructive manner would be the target of attack from the many influential quarters that, in the current atmosphere of superpower *rapprochement* and war-weariness in southern Africa, favoured a settlement. A report written a few days after the final breakthrough at Geneva, in November 1988, summed up this particular ploy very neatly, as well as highlighting the use of the train metaphor in these negotiations:

Once a little momentum was achieved, Mr Crocker would drive the talks train faster and faster, briefing journalists on how well negotiations were going and how close to agreement they were. If the participants tried to stop the train or get off they would be seen as wreckers. It failed a few times, but each time Mr Crocker put the train back on the tracks and started again. 'If anyone had got off the train when they arrived in Geneva they would have sprained a wrist,' one US official said after agreement was reached on Tuesday night. 'If anyone tries to get off now they will break both legs' (*Independent* 1988).

Raising the level of the talks

A negotiation might lose its momentum because those employed in it lack the authority to grant significant concessions. In this event, the obvious solution is to insert or reinsert more senior personnel. Raising the level of the talks has the added advantage of once more bringing these decision-makers face to face with the realities of the negotiation, and dilutes the influence on them of their home constituencies. It might also provide an opportunity to bring different people with fresh ideas into the process and, providing it is done publicly, it will be symbolically significant: raising the level of the talks will indicate that the parties to the negotiation continue to attach high priority to progress. This will generally raise public expectations of success and, thus, increase the pressure for a settlement.

There are various ways of raising the level of negotiations. It can be done in set-piece fashion. For example, following confirmation at the Leeds Castle conference in July 1978 that no further progress in the Egypt–Israel negotiations could be made at foreign minister-level, Jimmy Carter decided to propose a summit at Camp David. The same tactic was employed, as already noted, in the Israel–PLO negotiations in May 1994. A more common method is to inject senior personnel into a negotiation in a more *ad hoc* manner. Thus, in order 'to speed up the talks', Jimmy Carter briefly joined the foreign minister-level negotiations that were held at Blair House in Washington in October 1978, in order to flesh out the details of the Camp David Accords agreed the previous month (Quandt: 272). A further method is to create a second channel at a higher level, and often in a different place, while leaving the lower-level channel untouched. This has the advantage of achieving a division of labour on the agenda while retaining the lower-level channel as an all-purpose fall-back in the event of difficulties. For example, US–North Korea talks began to take place at ministerial level in New York following admission of Pyongyang to the UN in September 1991, but counsellor-level talks continued in Beijing.

Finally, it is important to stress a variation on the latter strategy: the creation of a higher-level channel that, on important issues, short-circuits the lower-level channel and concerning the activities of which the latter is kept in complete ignorance. This is what Henry Kissinger called a 'backchannel' (Kissinger 1979: 138–40, 722–3), and was illustrated notably by his Washington discussions on arms control with Soviet ambassador to the United States, Anatoly Dobrynin. This subject was under formal negotiation alternately in Helsinki and Vienna. The advantages of backchannels are secrecy, speed, and the avoidance of internal bureaucratic battles, and were also a tactic notoriously favoured by Yasser Arafat. The disadvantages of backchannels, however, are also numerous. They include the possibility of overlooking key points, damaging the morale of the 'front-channel' negotiators when they find out what is going on, and the related difficulty of getting those who have been excluded from the decision-making to support the implementation of any agreement that emerges.

Summary

The momentum of negotiations might falter for any number of reasons, even though the parties remain committed to progress. This is serious because a slow-down can turn into a lull, and a lull can become a full stop. In order to prevent this, negotiators characteristically resort to both artificial and symbolic deadlines, and lean on such practical ones as are to hand. They also employ publicity and metaphors of movement, and they raise the level of the talks as a last resort. None of these devices is the best for sustaining or regaining momentum in all circumstances: which is the most suitable turns on the nature of the negotiation concerned, the stage it has reached, the personalities involved, and the nature of the threat to its momentum. Many permutations of these points could be made but it would be an idle exercise: in the end, it is a matter of political judgement.

If an agreement is eventually reached, with or without the assistance of these devices (and it will be a rare agreement that needs none of them), it will still need to be packaged and followed up. It is to these questions that we must now turn.

Further reading

Berridge, G. R., 'Diplomacy and the Angola/Namibia Accords, December 1988', *International Affairs*, 65(3), 1989.

Carter, J., *Keeping Faith: Memoirs of a president* (Bantam Books: New York, 1982): 267–429, on the Egypt–Israel negotiations.

Cradock, P., *Experiences of China* (John Murray: London, 1994): chs 16–20, 23, on the negotiations in 1983–84 for the transfer of Hong Kong from British to Chinese sovereignty.

De Soto, A., 'Ending violent conflict in El Salvador', in C. A. Crocker, F. O. Hampson and P. R. Aall (eds), *Herding Cats: Multiparty mediation in a complex world* (United States Institute of Peace Press: Washington, DC, 1999).

Harrison, S., 'Inside the Afghan talks', *Foreign Policy*, Fall, 1988.

Lakoff, G. and M. Johnson, *Metaphors We Live By* (University of Chicago Press: Chicago/London, 1980): esp. chs 1–3, 11, 16 and 23.

Mitchell, George J., *Making Peace* (Heinemann: London, 1999): 126–83, on the Good Friday agreement on Northern Ireland.

Moore, Christopher, *The Mediation Process: Practical strategies for resolving conflict*, 2nd edn (Jossey-Bass: San Francisco, 1996): 291–300, on deadlines.

Quandt, W. B., *Camp David: Peacemaking and politics* (Brookings Institution: Washington, DC, 1986).

Ross, Dennis, *Statecraft: And how to restore America's standing in the world* (Farrar, Straus & Giroux: New York, 2007): 205–7, on deadlines.

Sullivan, J. G., 'How peace came to El Salvador', *Orbis*, Winter, 1994: 83–98.

5
Packaging Agreements

Diplomatic agreements vary in form to an almost bewildering degree. They vary in title or style, being given such descriptions as treaty, final act, protocol, exchange of notes, and even plain 'agreement'. They vary significantly in textual structure, language, whether they are written or oral, and whether or not they are accompanied by side letters. They also vary in whether they are publicized or kept secret. The purpose of this chapter is to explain this variation, and to indicate what form an agreement might take depending on its subject matter and the political needs of its authors.

There are a number of reasons – aside from accident and changing linguistic preferences – that help to explain the multiplicity of forms taken by international agreements. Some create international legal obligations, while others do not. Some forms of agreement are better at signalling the importance of the subject matter, while others are better at disguising its significance. Some are simply more convenient to use than others; they are easier to draw up and avoid the need for ratification. And some are better than others at saving the face of parties who have been obliged to make potentially embarrassing concessions in order to achieve a settlement. The form taken by any particular agreement will depend on what premium is attached to each of these considerations by the parties to the negotiation. It will also depend on the degree of harmony between them on these questions, and – in the absence of harmony – the degree to which concessions on form can be traded for concessions on substance.

International legal obligations at a premium

The parties to a negotiation might agree that the subject of their agreement is not appropriate to regulation by international law. This could be because, as with many commercial subjects, it is more suited to municipal law, but it might also be because the agreement merely amounts to a statement of commonly held principles or objectives. Such was the case with the Atlantic Charter of 1941 and the Helsinki Final Act of 1975, which was the product of the 35-nation Conference on Security and Cooperation in Europe (Gore-Booth 1979: 238–9; Shaw: 372–3, 1289). If, however, the parties to a negotiation concur that their agreement should create obligations enforceable in *international* law, then they must put it in the form of a treaty (Box 5.1).

In view of the widespread cynicism about the effectiveness of international law, why might the parties to a negotiation want to create an agreement entailing international legal obligations? They do this because they know that such obligations are, in fact, honoured far more often than not, even by states with unsavoury reputations (Henkin: 47). This is mainly because the obligations derive from consent; because natural inhibitions to law-breaking exist in the relations between states that do not obtain in the relations between individuals – notably the greater ability of states to defend their interests, and the far greater likelihood that the fact and the authorship of international law-breaking will be detected; and because a reputation for failing to keep agreements will make it extremely difficult to promote policy by means of negotiation in the future (Bull: ch. 6; Berridge 1997: 154–7).

Box 5.1   What is a 'treaty'?

The term 'treaty' derives from the French word *traiter*, to negotiate. It was defined by the Vienna Convention on the Law of Treaties (1969), which came into force in 1980. This stated that a treaty is 'an international agreement concluded between States in written form and governed by international law, whether embodied in a single instrument or in two or more related instruments and whatever its particular designation'. It is important to add to this that, in order to be 'governed by international law', an agreement must (under Article 102 of the UN Charter) 'as soon as possible be registered with the Secretariat and published by it'. This is because unregistered agreements cannot be invoked before 'any organ of the United Nations', which includes the International Court of Justice (Ware 1990: 1). In short, parties who want their agreement to create international legal obligations must write it out and give a copy to the UN; in so doing, they have created a 'treaty'. The Vienna Convention on the Law of Treaties between States and International Organizations or between International Organizations (1986) extended the definition of 'treaty' to include international agreements involving international organizations as parties – although, as yet, it has not entered into force.

Signalling importance at a premium

Creating a treaty is one thing; calling a treaty a 'treaty' is another. In fact, treaties are more often than not called something quite different. A few of these alternative titles were mentioned at the beginning of this chapter; others include act, charter, concordat, convention (now applied to a multilateral treaty with a large number of signatories), covenant, declaration, exchange of correspondence, general agreement, joint communiqué, memorandum of understanding, *modus vivendi*, pact, understanding, and even agreed minutes (Gore-Booth 1979: book IV). Some treaties are, nevertheless, still called treaties, usually when there is a desire to underline the importance of an agreement. This is because of the term's historical association with the international deliberations of rulers or their plenipotentiaries, and because the treaty so-called is presented in an imposing manner, complete with seals as well as signatures (Box 5.2). Agreements on matters of special international significance that have accordingly been styled treaties include the North Atlantic Treaty of 4 April 1949, which created the West's Cold War alliance; the Treaties of Rome of 25 March 1957, which created the European Communities; and the various Treaties of Accession of new members to the EU. Agreements ending wars are commonly called peace treaties, as

---

Box 5.2   The treaty so-called

The treaty so-called usually has the following characteristics:

- Descriptive title
- Preamble, including the names and titles of the High Contracting Parties (if in heads of state form), the general purpose of the agreement, the names and official designations of the plenipotentiaries, and an affirmation that the latter have produced their full powers, and so on
- Substantive articles, which are numbered I, II,..., commonly beginning with definitions, and usually leading from the general to the more specific
- Final clauses, which deal with matters such as the extent of application of the treaty, signature, ratification, accession by other parties, entry into force, duration, and provision for renewal
- Clause stating 'in witness whereof' the undersigned plenipotentiaries have signed this treaty
- Indication of the place where the treaty is signed, together with the authentic language or languages of the text, and date of signature
- Seals and signatures of the plenipotentiaries.

Sources: Gore-Booth 1979: 240–1; Grenville and Wasserstein: 13.

in the case of the Treaty of Peace between the Arab Republic of Egypt and the State of Israel of 26 March 1979. Agreements providing all-important guarantees of a territorial or constitutional settlement are invariably called treaties of guarantee. In this case, a good example is the Cyprus Guarantee Treaty of 16 August 1960. These, however, are not so common today (see Chapter 6).

It is important to note, however, that, as the Foreign Relations Committee of the US Senate has complained, trivial agreements are sometimes sent to the Senate as treaties, while much more important ones are classified as 'executive agreements' and, thus, withheld. A trivial agreement sent as a treaty was one to regulate shrimp-fishing off the coast of Brazil (Franck and Weisband: 145). The executive branch presumably deals with trivial agreements in this way to make the Senate feel that its constitutional prerogatives in foreign policy-making have not been entirely ignored (executive agreements are discussed later in this chapter).

If an agreement is believed by its authors to be of great political importance but is not of such a character as to warrant the creation of legal obligations, its importance cannot be signalled, neither can its binding character be reinforced by calling it a treaty: it is not a treaty. However, precisely because the parties have rejected the possibility of clothing their agreement in international law but remain politically bound by it, as well as deeply attached to the agreement's propaganda value, it is doubly important to dress it in fine attire of a different kind. Hence the use of imposing titles such as Atlantic Charter and Helsinki Final Act, as mentioned in the previous section.

Convenience at a premium

Since states today negotiate on so many matters, an international agreement does not have to be of merely routine character for convenience to be an important consideration in dictating its shape (Aurisch: 281). Convenience argues for informal agreements: treaties not styled as treaties, or agreements that, because they remain unpublished, are treaties in neither form nor substance. What inconveniences are avoided by packaging an agreement informally?

First, the complexities of formal treaty drafting and its attendant procedures, such as the production of documents certifying that the plenipotentiaries have full powers, are avoided. This is probably of special benefit to smaller and newer foreign ministries, but is also likely to be regarded as an advantage by the overburdened ministries of the bigger powers as well. Not surprisingly, therefore, exchanges of notes or exchanges of letters, which consist simply of a letter from one of the parties spelling out the terms of the agreement and a reply from the other indicating acceptance, are now the most common form of treaty. They require none of the elaborate construction of the treaty so-called; neither do they require the presentation of full powers (Gore-Booth 1979: 247–8).

The second inconvenience that can be avoided by informal packaging is ratification of the agreement, although it should first be stressed that ratification is still widely valued, and provision for it is a feature of almost all written constitutions. It is also a feature of the unwritten constitution of the United Kingdom (Ware: 1; Shaw: 152–3, 911–13).

Ratification means confirmation on the part of the negotiators' political masters that they will honour an agreement negotiated and signed on their behalf. It became normal practice when poor communications made it difficult, if not impossible, for there to be any certainty that negotiators had not exceeded their powers, or that their masters had not changed their minds altogether since dispatching them on their diplomatic errand. The revolution in communications has virtually removed this problem, although governments still sometimes favour a form of agreement that requires ratification. This might be because they have certain anxieties about the agreement: perhaps it had to be negotiated under the lash of an over-tight practical deadline (see Chapter 4), and so requires time for second thoughts. They might also insist on provision for ratification because they know that the significance of the agreement is such that it will be politically unsupportable at home and, thus, unimpressive to their foreign interlocutors in the absence of some expression of popular approval, typically by a special majority in a representative assembly. In a genuine democracy, the ultimate form of ratification is a referendum, such as that held by the Labour government in Britain in 1974 on the issue of whether or not the United Kingdom should remain a signatory of the Treaties of Rome.

There are, nevertheless, many occasions when governments do not feel the need either for an opportunity for second thoughts on an agreement or for its popular endorsement. In these circumstances, they are naturally keen to avoid the delay in the coming into force of an agreement caused by the need for its ratification; and they are especially anxious to avoid the risk of a demand for its renegotiation that this might entail. This was the notorious fate of the Treaty of Versailles, signed in June 1919 but, in the following November and again in March 1920, refused the two-thirds majority by the US Senate needed for American ratification. The strain of campaigning for ratification – coming, as it did, on top of the mental and physical exertions of the peace negotiations – had also caused the American president, Woodrow Wilson, to have a severe stroke, from which he very nearly died (Dimbleby and Reynolds: 70–3). Six decades later, President Jimmy Carter had an equally acute problem of ratification with the second Strategic Arms Limitation Treaty, although fortunately it did not have the same effect on his health.

An executive that feels no need for ratification is, then, unlikely to invite certain delay and possible trouble by casting its agreements in a form that requires endorsement by a popular assembly. Since the American view is that treaties, by definition, require ratification (Shaw: 912–13), it is obvious that the United States executive branch will avoid this form of agreement in these circumstances, and will probably have little difficulty in persuading its negotiating partners to concur. It is in order to avoid the possible embarrassments of the ratification process in the Senate that there has been massive resort to the executive agreement, in place of treaties so-called, by successive American administrations since Wilson's time. Technically, these are international agreements entered into by the president, either after Congress has, by law, given him a *general* authorization in the field concerned (Bradshaw and Pring: 407–8), or, in the case of 'pure' executive agreements, by virtue of certain unfettered plenary powers that the president possesses under the constitution – for example, as Commander-in-Chief. In practice, they are simply any international agreement entered into by the US executive branch that is not called a treaty and therefore does not require the 'advice and consent of the Senate' (Franck and Weisband: 141–9 *passim*). Since World War II, US presidents have entered into roughly seven times more executive agreements than treaties; of the 1271 international agreements entered into by the second Reagan administration, only 47 were treaties (Ragsdale: 76–7).

Another way of sidestepping the Senate is for the US executive branch and its foreign negotiating partner each to issue a 'unilateral non-binding declaration', which, in practice, nevertheless is expected to be politically effective. The classic example here is provided by the separate but virtually simultaneous declarations of the United States and the Soviet Union immediately prior to the date of expiration of the Interim Agreement on Strategic Offensive Arms on 3 October 1977. Each indicated in its separate statement that, provided the other showed similar restraint, it would continue to honour the provisions of the technically dead Agreement (Glennon: 267–9).

One of the titles common to a large proportion of the thousands of executive agreements to which the US government is a party, as well as to a large proportion of the international agreements entered into by other states, is, as already mentioned, the exchange of notes or exchange of letters. This does not normally require ratification, and so comes into force immediately upon signature. As a result, it is popular for this reason as well as because it avoids the formal complexities of the treaty so-called. Informal agreements with other titles might, however, also be so framed in order to avoid pressure for ratification.

The final inconvenience that can be avoided by packaging agreements informally is the inconvenience of unwanted publicity; that is, publicity that might stir up political opponents at home, or present intelligence gifts to unfriendly states. To avoid the former, agreements on sensitive matters might be published (and, thus, become binding) but in such informal style as to be unlikely to attract attention. Two examples might be cited here. The first is the so-called Simonstown Agreements between Britain and the Union of South Africa concluded in 1955. The British wanted to play these down because they entailed surrender of Royal Navy facilities (the Simonstown naval base) to Afrikaner nationalist control and, at the same time, close military cooperation with racist South Africa. The agreements took the form of an exchange of letters (Berridge 1992: ch. 5). The second good example is the Anglo–Argentine agreement on the Falkland Islands of 1971. The Argentineans were not anxious to advertise this because they had gained nothing on sovereignty. The British were not anxious to advertise it either because the practical schemes dealing with access and technical cooperation to which they had agreed could, nevertheless, have been interpreted as the thin end of the wedge of surrendering sovereignty. The agreement was in two parts. First, there was a joint statement initialled (rather than signed) by delegation heads on 1 July, thus indicating only that negotiations were closed (Wood and Serres: 221). Second, there was an exchange of notes on 5 August between the British *chargé d'affaires* in Buenos Aires and the Argentine minister of foreign affairs, which referred to and qualified the joint statement (Grenville and Wasserstein: 11, 433–6).

To avoid presenting intelligence gifts to unfriendly states, the parties to a successful negotiation may not only conclude an informal agreement, but withhold publication. This means that it is not a treaty. But there are circumstances in which international legal obligations are relatively unimportant; for example, in the case of certain kinds of defence agreements between close allies, bound to each other by urgent common interest and strong ties of sentiment. As Ware has noted, a good example of such an agreement is the UK–US Memorandum of Understanding on British participation in the Strategic Defence Initiative. This was signed in 1985 but, in Britain, revealed in its details only later, and in confidence, to the Defence Select Committee of the House of Commons (Ware: 3).

Saving face at a premium

In politically sensitive negotiations where publicity for any agreement achieved is unavoidable, and even desirable, what excites special interest in its packaging is the issue of 'face' – reputation for strength. This means the necessity to save from excessive embarrassment those parties whose concessions would otherwise make them vulnerable to the wrath of their supporters. Face is a particularly important consideration in shame cultures, such as those of the Arab Middle East (Cohen 1997: 183).

Where face is a vital issue, the composition and structure, as well as the title of any agreement, might not only be an important, but also a controversial element in a negotiation. It will be important because some kinds of packaging will be better than others at disguising the concessions that have had to be made. It is also likely to be controversial because what one side wants to disguise, the other will usually wish to highlight. Settlement of the Iranian hostages crisis was helped by using a form of agreement – a declaration by the Algerian mediators – that suggested Ayatollah Khomeini had made his own concessions to the third party rather than to 'the Great Satan' (see Chapter 15; Grenville and Wasserstein: 11). It is fortunate that this was of no great concern to the diabolical United States. In what other ways can agreements be packaged in order to save face and, thus, ease a settlement?

Both languages, or more

Language is fundamental to nationality, so diplomatic agreements must be acutely sensitive to it. This has not always been the case, in part because nationalism is a relatively modern ideology. Until the seventeenth century, most treaties were written in Latin, thereafter in French, and in the twentieth century chiefly in English (Grenville and Wasserstein: 10). However, since the end of World War II it has become much more common for copies of agreements made between parties speaking different languages to be translated into the language of each. Furthermore, as might be imagined – and as was confirmed by the

Vienna Convention on the Law of Treaties – each version is typically described as 'equally authentic' or 'equally authoritative'.

The diplomatic advantage of drafting agreements in the language of each party is that it fosters the impression – whether true or not – that negotiated agreements reflect relationships of equality and provide for an exchange of concessions on an equal basis. After 1945, to take some examples, agreements between the United States and the Soviet Union were written in English and Russian, and, between the United States and South American countries, in English and Spanish. The Paris Peace Accords of 1973, which ended the Vietnam War, were drawn up in English and Vietnamese. The agreement concluded between Cuba and Angola in 1988, which concerned the withdrawal of the forces of the former from the territory of the latter, was written in Spanish and Portuguese. In each of these cases, there were good political reasons for doing everything possible to suggest equality of status.

It should be added, though, that while there is a diplomatic advantage to having equally authoritative versions of agreements in different languages, there is also a disadvantage. This is because an agreement might be vague or loose at certain points and, in the course of its implementation, it might transpire that one interpretation of these points is favoured more by the language of one text than it is by the language of the other. Where there are only two languages, this is a recipe for trouble. It is for this reason that states sometimes wisely agree to have the text also drawn up in a third language – usually English – and agree that this shall prevail in the event of a divergence of interpretation between the other two, as in regard to the Hindi and Russian texts of the India–Russia Agreement on Illicit Trafficking in Narcotics and their Precursors signed in Moscow in November 2007 [www]. It is even more likely that this arrangement, provision for which was made in the Vienna Convention on the Law of Treaties, will be used in agreements where an English-speaking state has been employed as a mediator. Many agreements, however, have no master text, thereby underlining the greater importance that is generally attached to saving face compared with avoiding possible future misunderstandings. To take but one example, the first of the two Angola/ Namibia Accords, signed in December 1988 – to which South Africa, Cuba, and Angola were each a party – was signed in English, Spanish, and Portuguese versions, 'each language being equally authentic'. No text was nominated as the one that would prevail in the event of disagreement.

Small print

Sensitivity to language only addresses the question of face in the most general way, and negotiators must needs turn to other devices when they are confronted with the problem of disguising a sensitive concession in the text of an agreement. Perhaps the most common way of achieving this is to say very little about it, tuck it away in some obscure recess, and ensure that the rest of the agreement is padded out with relatively trivial detail. A good example of this strategy can be found in the UN-brokered agreements of 1988 between the Soviet-backed Afghan Communist government and the American-backed Pakistanis, one of the most important provisions of which concerned the withdrawal of Soviet troops from Afghanistan. The Soviet Union was extremely sensitive to any suggestion that it was abandoning its clients in Kabul to the ferocious, if disorganized, *mujahedin*. The trouble was that the Soviet concession – troop withdrawals – was the sort of event that was considerably more attractive to television news editors than the American *quid pro quo* that Moscow hoped would enable the Afghan Communist regime to survive; that is, the termination of material support to the *mujahedin*. As a result, in the three agreements and one declaration that made up what were popularly known as the Geneva Accords on Afghanistan, only two short sentences were devoted to the Soviet troop withdrawal. Furthermore, they were tacked onto the end of a paragraph (number 5) that gave no signpost at the beginning as to what was to come at the end. And the agreement of which these two sentences were the most pregnant part was padded out, rather in the manner of a 'final act', with a résumé of the history of the negotiations, the titles of the other agreements reached, and general principles of international law (Berridge 1991: 148–51).

Another 'small print' technique for saving face is to place embarrassing concessions in documentary appendages to the main text. These take many forms: side letters, interpretive notes, appendices, additional protocols, and so on. Whatever their title, the point remains to make the concessions binding by putting them in a written, public agreement, but to do so in such a way as to make them less likely to attract attention and be easier to play down for those obliged to grant them. Numerous side letters – exchanges of correspondence that are, figuratively speaking, placed at the side of the main documents – were published to accompany the two main agreements in the Camp David Accords of September 1978 and the Egypt–Israel Peace Treaty of the following March. While most of these served purposes other than face-saving, some existed for precisely this reason. These included the anodyne restatements of existing positions on the incendiary question of the status of Jerusalem. The Egyptians wanted the matter dealt with in side letters to obscure the fact that they had made no progress on the issue. As for the Israelis, they happily concurred in order to obscure the fact that they had been prepared to talk about it at all (Carter: 395, 397–9; Vance: 225–6). The Israelis even persuaded the Americans not to restate the substance of their own position on East Jerusalem, which was that it was occupied territory. Instead, they merely stated in their own letter that their position remained that outlined in statements by two former American ambassadors to the United Nations (Quandt: 252).

Tucking sensitive matters away in documentary appendages to the main agreement also has disadvantages. First, in a complex and tense negotiation under great pressure of time, there is more chance of a slip-up. For example, in September 1978 the Americans failed to secure unambiguous written Israeli agreement to a freeze on new settlements in the West Bank and Gaza until the autonomy negotiations had been concluded, which proved to be a serious oversight. It is inconceivable that this could have occurred had this issue been addressed in the general framework accord, rather than by means of a side letter which, in the event, the Israelis never signed (Vance: 228). Second, it can subsequently be claimed that ancillary documents do not have the same value as the main text of an agreement. This is what the Israeli premier, Menachem Begin, alleged of the side letter of 17 September 1978 from Sadat to Carter. This was the one in which the Egyptian president indicated his readiness to negotiate on the West Bank and Gaza on behalf of the Palestinians in the event of a refusal by Jordan to assume this responsibility. Begin hoped to persuade the Americans that there was no point in discussing the West Bank at all if the Jordanians refused to take part (Quandt: 299, 386–7). Naturally enough, Irish republicans also refused to admit that the side letter hurriedly written by the British prime minister, Tony Blair, to the Ulster Unionist leader, David Trimble (which contained assurances about the British attitude permitting the Unionists, at the last minute, to sign up to the Good Friday agreement (see p. 59)) was part of that agreement at all.

Euphemisms

It is notorious that politicians who live by the vote also live by the euphemism, and that the more difficult the positions in which they find themselves, the more creative they become in this regard. This is rarely an edifying spectacle. In diplomacy, however, the use of euphemisms is more defensible. Indeed, in the description of concessions, the use of words or expressions more palatable to the party that has made them is another face-saving feature of almost all politically sensitive international agreements, although at some price in terms of accuracy.

A good example of the use of euphemisms is to be found in the Geneva Accords on Afghanistan referred to earlier, in which Soviet sensitivities on the issue of the withdrawal of their troops were so solicitously handled by confining the relevant provisions to the small print. The risk of humiliating the Kremlin was reduced further by the complete absence of any reference whatever to the withdrawal of 'Soviet' troops. What were to be withdrawn instead were 'foreign' troops. It might be added, too, that the agreement containing the provisions on 'foreign' troop withdrawals had a title which was, itself, a masterpiece of euphemistic obscurantism: 'Agreement on the Interrelationships for the Settlement of the Situation relating to Afghanistan' (Berridge 1991: App. 5). Brilliant.

These examples illustrate the fact that euphemistic language can help states to sign agreements providing for the withdrawal of their military forces from situations where their prestige is at stake. Others can be found to demonstrate its usefulness where they are being bought off; that is, induced to surrender some principled position by a delivery of hard cash or payment in kind. Rich states negotiating with poorer ones often find it possible to smooth the road to an agreement by discreetly handing over extremely large amounts of money. Since, however, it would be humiliating to the poorer state if this were to be too obvious, and not present the richer one in an especially flattering light either, these large amounts of money are never called 'large amounts of money'. Instead, they are usually called 'reconstruction aid'. This is what the Americans called the large amounts of money repeatedly offered to the North Vietnamese, from as early as April 1965, to encourage them to negotiate an end to the Vietnam War. They were finally referred to – coyly and briefly – in Article 21 of the peace settlement of January 1973. The North Vietnamese wanted to call them 'reparations' (Kissinger 1982: 37–43).

'Separate but related' agreements

Where an agreement is based on linkage, it might be necessary to obscure this as much as possible, especially if one party has, for years prior to the settlement, insisted that it would have nothing to do with any such deal. This had been the position of the Angolans and their supporters (more so the latter) in regard to the proposal that South Africa would withdraw from Namibia if, in return, Cuba would withdraw from Angola. Linkage, as mentioned earlier, is deeply offensive to those who believe that issues should be resolved on their merits. It is, thus, significant that, when a settlement of the south-west African imbroglio was achieved at the end of 1988 (which was based on this linkage), it was embodied not in one agreement but two. One dealt exclusively with Namibian independence and the other only with the withdrawal of Cuban troops from Angola. Moreover, South Africa was not even presented as a party to the latter, and so did not sign it (Berridge 1989).

The same device had been employed in the Camp David Accords a decade earlier. The draft Egypt–Israel peace treaty was presented as one of two accords published simultaneously, while the other was a much more general 'Framework for Peace in the Middle East', the nub of which dealt with the West Bank and Gaza. Having the two related in this way satisfied the Egyptian president, who was anxious to preserve his position that progress on the Egypt–Israel front was linked to progress on the Palestinian question. Having them, nevertheless, separated in the text satisfied the Israeli prime minister, who was even more anxious to avoid the suggestion that progress in bilateral relations was conditional on any such thing (Quandt: 211, 230).

Summary

The form taken by diplomatic agreements, especially those giving expression to settlements of great political sensitivity, is often of considerable significance. When creating an international legal obligation is at a premium, the parties to an agreement will want to package it as a treaty; that is, write it out and give a copy to the UN. If they want to draw attention to it as well, they might go so far as to call it a 'treaty'. If the press of business is great and their agreement is not so important, they will readily settle for an informal agreement such as an exchange of notes – which might or might not be published and which, therefore, might or might not be a treaty. If saving face is at a premium, the parties to an agreement can resort to any number of expedients, the tactical purposes of which are to obscure and minimize the most sensitive concessions. This is not disreputable; it is a significant part of the art of negotiation.

Further reading

Cohen, R., *Negotiating across Cultures*, revised edn (US Institute of Peace Press: Washington, 1997): ch. 9.

Cradock, P., *Experiences of China* (John Murray: London, 1994): chs 19, 20, 23.

Franck, T. M. and E. Weisband, *Foreign Policy by Congress* (Oxford University Press: New York/Oxford, 1979).

Glennon, M. J., 'The Senate role in treaty ratification', *American Journal of International Law*, 77, 1983.

Grenville, J. A. S. and B. Wasserstein, *The Major International Treaties since 1945: A history and guide with texts* (Methuen: London/New York, 1987).

Johnson, L. K., *The Making of International Agreements: Congress confronts the executive* (New York University Press: New York/London, 1984).

Roberts, Sir Ivor (ed.), *Satow's Diplomatic Practice*, 6th edn (Oxford University Press: Oxford, 2009).

Shaw, M. N., *International Law*, 6th edn (Cambridge University Press: Cambridge/New York, 2008).

UN Treaty Collection: *Treaty Reference Guide* [www]. The notes and definitions provided here are extremely valuable.

6
Following Up

The great Florentine statesman and historian, Francesco Guicciardini, wrote:

> In matters of business take this as a maxim, that it is not enough to give things their beginning, direction, or impulse; we must also follow them up, and never slacken our efforts until they are brought to a conclusion. Whoso conducts business on this system contributes in no small measure to its settlement; while he who follows a different plan will often assume things to be ended which in truth are hardly begun (Guicciardini: 85).

Guicciardini's maxim on following up applies with as much force today as when it was written in the early sixteenth century, not least in the case of international treaties, despite the incentives that states have to honour them (see p. 71) and some evidence that they are now more willing to submit disputes over them to judicial procedures. For the jurisdiction in such disputes of bodies like the International Court of Justice continues to rest on the consent of states, which is invariably withheld where matters of vital interest are concerned; where consent is given, the means of enforcement are generally inadequate; and there is no settled, general principle that international law should prevail over domestic rules (Shaw: 177–8, 1057–117). Even when international agreements are self-executing or subsequently embodied in domestic legislation, states might fail to act or act properly on their terms through deliberate evasion, distraction, lack of capacity, inadvertent error, or administrative weakness. If, therefore, international agreements – however well constructed, appropriately packaged, and solemnly ratified – are to be properly implemented, it is, today, usually on *diplomacy* that the responsibility for ensuring this must fall.

In practice, diplomatic follow-up means careful monitoring of implementation so that sticks and carrots might be applied to those falling down on their obligations as and when necessary. This has always been an element in ensuring implementation but, in earlier times, it was by no means so easy, and other methods were usually more prominent. It will be interesting to note these briefly before concentrating on the varieties of the characteristic method of the present.

Early methods

Until about the seventeenth century, rulers sought to make their agreements more durable by inviting their gods to bear witness to them in an oath-swearing ceremony (Vattel: book 2, para. 225; Anderson: 47–8). Implementation was, thus, a divine responsibility presumed to take the form of smiting down with ferocious blows any backslider, however powerful in the world of ordinary mortals. At oath-swearing ceremonies in western Asia in the second millennium BCE, the nature of the divine punishment to be inflicted was symbolized by ritual gestures and sacrifices (Munn-Rankin: 84–92).

Wisely enough, where agreements of special importance were concerned, an additional precaution was usually provided in the form of a tangible surety for the performance of promises. One such surety that was popular was the surrender unilaterally or exchange of valuable hostages (typically nobles, and even the sons or daughters of ruling families), but this method expired in Europe with the Treaty of Aix-la-Chapelle in 1748 (Vattel: book 2, paras 245–61; Hall: 357, 439; Anderson: 48). Another form of surety was the pawning or mortgaging of towns or provinces, which would be lost for good in the first case, and liable to seizure in the second, if the promise were not kept (Vattel: book 2, paras 240–4). This method lasted longer but was problematical to execute, struggled (especially in the age of nationalism), and did not survive the first half of the twentieth century – except when employed by victors in war to ensure implementation by the vanquished of the terms of peace treaties (usually with the help of commissions of control) as, for example, in the Treaty of Versailles of 1919 (Avalon Project, articles 428–31).

Another device occasionally employed to ensure treaty observance was to entrust the task to men of standing from both signatory states. Appointed to a standing commission with certain powers of enforcement, these men were known as *conservatores pacis* – conservators of the peace. This device was certainly obsolete by the beginning of the twentieth century, and probably well before.

A final method was the treaty of guarantee, by which powerful states undertook to enforce, if necessary, an international agreement; such an agreement would invariably deal with a subject of great importance – such as the position of a dynasty, the possession of specified territory, security against aggression, the independence and territorial integrity of a state, or permanent neutrality (Hall: 351–6; McNair: 240). This method continued to be employed until 1960, when it underpinned the unusual treaty regime by which the Republic of Cyprus was established. But this – at least, in the grand style – appears to have been its last gasp. The treaty of guarantee had always been of limited use because of the onerous responsibility it placed on the guarantor. The result was that this responsibility was only likely to be shouldered by a state with an indirect interest in the observance of an agreement or a special friendship with one or more of the parties; and then to be so riddled with escape clauses that there was always serious doubt as to whether a guarantor would ever stand by its own promises. That it would do so became even less likely with the enhanced risks of warfare in the twentieth century (Vattel: book 2, paras 235–9; Morgenthau: 300–1; Dinstein: 267).

For one reason or another, then, virtually all of the diplomatic devices customarily employed to ensure that agreements were honoured had become obsolete by the middle of the twentieth century. Thus bereft, treaty implementation has, as a general rule, needed to rely more and more on expert and systematic monitoring. However, the form this takes varies with the subject of the agreements concerned, and whether they are multilateral or bilateral. What costs follow any defaulting depend on the reasons for non-compliance but, at a minimum, will usually mean bad publicity and consequent damage to reputations. In some cases, assistance in what is now generally known as 'capacity-building' is more appropriate than sanctions. Diplomats are not always to be found at the sharp end of following-up although, even when not prominent in the activity, they are invariably to be found in its wings. What are the chief methods by which international agreements are followed up today?

Monitoring by experts

Agreements that are complex, technical and sensitive always have to be followed up by experts, including scientists, engineers, and lawyers, and sometimes by national intelligence agencies. Arms control agreements and UN Security Council-imposed disarmament regimes, especially those limiting chemical, biological and nuclear weapons – weapons of mass destruction (WMD) – provide the best-known cases in point. Compliance with these has long been monitored by national intelligence agencies employing technical means, including the electronic interception of communications (signals intelligence or SIGINT) and observation via spy satellites. The US Department of State houses an inter-agency organization – the Bureau of Verification, Compliance, and Implementation – with intimate links to the intelligence community, which is dedicated to the analysis of compliance with arms control, non-proliferation, and disarmament agreements. But multilateral bodies also play a major part in this work, as was clearly seen in Iraq.

The International Atomic Energy Agency (IAEA) has a whole division – the Department of Safeguards – devoted to verifying compliance with the promise not to obtain nuclear weapons made by signatories of the Nuclear Non-Proliferation Treaty (NPT), of which Iraq was one. After the ejection of the forces of the Iraqi leader, Saddam Hussein, from Kuwait in 1991, the UN Security Council also established a special commission of weapons inspectors to oversee compliance with the disarmament obligations which were then imposed on his regime. The first commission, UNSCOM, was dominated by the United States and discredited by well-documented media allegations that it had allowed Western intelligence agencies to piggy-back on its activities in Iraq for purposes of military planning. As a result, it was replaced in 1999 by the UN Monitoring, Verification and Inspection Commission (UNMOVIC), the entire staff of which was on the payroll of the UN (Blix: 36–40).

Weapons inspectors from both the IAEA and the UN struggled for a long time to establish, in the face of immense difficulties, whether Saddam was concealing WMD. In 1998, he opened the highly sensitive 'Presidential sites' only after the United States threatened air strikes and the then UN Secretary-General, Kofi Annan, negotiated a short-lived agreement with his foreign minister on special arrangements for the inspections (see Box 6.1). The cat-and-mouse game played by Saddam with the weapons inspectors certainly contributed to the impression that he was concealing WMD. Nevertheless, the inspectors were highly professional and, having found nothing significant in 1998 or later, became highly sceptical about their existence. Prior to the attacks on the United States on 11 September 2001 ('9/11'), even the Bush administration was content that Saddam was being successfully contained by the 'regime of inspection, eradication and monitoring by the UN,

---

Box 6.1   Special Group on Visits to Presidential Sites: Iraq, 26 March–2 April 1998

The memorandum of understanding (MOU) establishing the Special Group provided, among other things, that the IAEA and UNSCOM weapons inspectors should be led by a Commissioner appointed by Kofi Annan and accompanied by foreign observers comprising 'senior diplomats', also to be appointed by the UN Secretary-General. In the event, the group was headed by the Sri Lankan diplomat, Jayathan Dhanapala, then UN Under Secretary-General for Disarmament Affairs. Following a canvass by Dhanapala for volunteers from senior diplomats already based in Baghdad or in the region, a group representing 20 different states was selected. This arrangement clearly helped to reconcile the Iraqis to the exercise. The diplomats also helped to smooth relations between the inspectors and lower-level Iraqi officials when misunderstandings occurred as a result of 'cultural differences and miscommunication'. However, as a model arrangement the need to organize a large and diverse body of diplomats had the drawback of making it more difficult for UNSCOM and the IAEA to make surprise inspections.

Sources: MOU between UN and Rep. of Iraq, 23 Feb. 1998, UN Doc. S/1998/166 27 March 1998; Report (1998); *USIS Washington File*.

---

supported by military pressure from the U.S. and the U.K.' (Blix: 259, 273). It is a great pity that UNMOVIC, which was wholly concerned with Iraq, was disbanded by the Security Council in 2007 and not given a wider brief. The IAEA remains very active, especially in connection with Iran and North Korea, but its remit does not include chemical and biological weapons.

There is also great need for monitoring by experts to try to ensure compliance with multilateral human rights agreements; for example, the Convention against Torture and Other Cruel, Inhuman or Degrading Treatment or Punishment (CAT), which entered into force in 1987. Torture is conducted in secret and might leave no obvious physical marks; furthermore, its victims – through fear for their families, as well as themselves – are understandably reluctant to testify against their tormentors even if they are eventually released. International NGOs such as Human Rights Watch and Amnesty International are particularly well-known for their work in monitoring torture and other abuses, publicising their findings, and reporting them in detail to governments and such bodies as the UN Human Rights Council. International NGOs have the advantage over states that share their repugnance for torture of not having to pull their punches for fear of harming other interests; they have the disadvantage that their staff do not enjoy diplomatic immunity and, so, are vulnerable to harassment or worse in the states where they are most needed. National NGOs are often enlisted by states and intergovernmental organizations as partners in monitoring compliance with human rights agreements, although they often work on a shoe-string and their position is usually even more exposed.

A body that has some of the advantages in the human rights field of both an NGO and an intergovernmental organization is the International Committee of the Red Cross (ICRC), which is a hybrid of the two. On the one hand, it is a private body, established under the Swiss Civil Code; on the other, 'its functions and activities – to provide protection and assistance to victims of conflict – are mandated by the international community of states and are founded on international law, specifically the Geneva Conventions' (Rona). As with an intergovernmental organization such as the UN, therefore, its staff enjoys special privileges and immunities that are widely recognized. These include the right to decline to testify before such bodies as the International Criminal Tribunal for the former Yugoslavia. The ICRC also provides its reports in confidence to the state whose activities are being monitored. It helps that Switzerland, where the ICRC is headquartered, has the firm legal status of permanent neutrality. These credentials make it effective to varying degrees in even the most viciously governed states, such as Zimbabwe, where other human rights bodies find it difficult, if not impossible, to operate. It carries out significant operations in nearly 80 countries (Rona; SIAC, Appeal No – SC/15/2005, para. 182).

Embassies

In a number of respects, embassies (see Chapter 7) are ideally placed to follow up agreements, whether bilateral, or multilateral ones in which the sending state has a close interest. As well as having the advantages of local knowledge and contacts that come from being on spot, the larger embassies, at least, are not without their own experts (traditionally known as 'attachés'); for example, in commerce, culture, defence, drugs, and immigration.

A good example of the role played by embassies in encouraging compliance with the terms of multilateral agreements is that of US embassies relative to the numerous conventions outlawing human trafficking. Under the national authority of the Trafficking Victims Protection Act (2000), the State Department's Office to Monitor and Combat Trafficking in Persons publishes an annual Trafficking in Persons Report. This places states at a point in a hierarchy of 'tiers' according to their degree of compliance with the Act's minimum standards for the elimination of trafficking. It is one of the responsibilities of US embassies, albeit in partnership with other agencies and NGOs, to supply the information on which this annual report is based. They are encouraged to be energetic in this and related activity by the annual award by the State Department of an honour named after a prominent Senate supporter of the Trafficking Victims Protection Act: the 'Paul Wellstone Anti-Slavery Ambassador of the Year'.

Embassy staff enjoy special privileges and immunities, and are therefore unlikely to fear the reprisals likely to be visited in authoritarian states on the representatives of campaigning NGOs, and especially on investigative journalists or opposition politicians whose questions prove too awkward. For example, apart from the ICRC, it was only the embassies in Harare that were able to provide any effective monitoring of the extreme and widespread flouting of international humanitarian law by the Zimbabwean authorities during their violent confrontation with the supporters of the opposition leader, Morgan Tsvangirai, in the election year of 2008. At one point, Tsvangirai actually had to take refuge in the Dutch embassy.

On the other hand, resident embassies have the general interests of their own state to protect, and this usually requires normal – if not good – relations with the government of the receiving state (it might even infect the embassies with a greater or lesser degree of 'localitis', see Chapter 7). Pushing too hard for compliance with the terms of an agreement on a sensitive subject such as human rights, therefore, might well completely compromise the rest of their work. This, as well as lack of expert knowledge, might render them ill-suited to take the lead in following up. It is clear, nevertheless, that they often play an unobtrusive but important supporting role where other bodies take the lead. In this context, it is instructive to look at the recent practice of the British government in attempting to secure compliance with bilateral MOUs on torture.

British embassies and 'No Torture' agreements

Since the July 2005 bomb attacks in central London, Britain has found itself detaining a growing number of foreign nationals suspected of engaging in or sponsoring terrorism but whom, for one reason or another, it has been unwilling either to subject to criminal trial or to release without charge. Anxious, therefore, on grounds of national security to despatch them to their countries of origin, which often wish to lay hands on these persons for reasons of their own, it has nevertheless been hindered by its status as a signatory of the European Convention on Human Rights (ECHR) and the CAT. For these instruments not only prohibit this kind of abuse, but also the deportation or extradition of persons to countries where there are substantial grounds for believing that they would be in danger of being subjected to such treatment. Unfortunately, many of the states to which Britain wishes to deport terrorism suspects – chiefly in the Middle East and North Africa – have precisely such reputations. As a result, it has been obliged to negotiate memoranda of understanding or other forms of agreement with them under which they give assurances that their nationals will not be subjected to unfair or inhumane treatment if returned to them by the United Kingdom. These are now usually known as 'diplomatic assurances'.

But what provision is made in these MOUs for ensuring that the receiving states live up to their assurances not to torture the returnees once they have got their hands on them? The UK–Jordan agreement, which became the prototype for those negotiated later (see Box 6.2), spelled out the arrangement as follows:

> If the returned person is arrested, detained or imprisoned within three years of the date of his return, he will be entitled to contact, and then have prompt and regular visits from the representative of an *independent body nominated jointly by the UK and Jordanian authorities*. Such visits will be permitted at least once a fortnight, and whether or not the returned person has been convicted, and will include the opportunity for private interviews with the returned person. The nominated body will give a report of its visits to the authorities of the sending state [emphasis added].

Insisting in a published agreement on the need for what has come to be known as an 'independent monitoring body' implies lack of trust in the willingness or ability of the receiving state to keep its promises; in a case such as this, it also amounts to interference in its domestic affairs, for the returnees are, after all, its own citizens; and accepting such a body might be construed as an admission that torture has previously taken place. These are among the reasons why the United States does not insist on publication of 'diplomatic assurances' (Deeks: 10).

Non-interference in internal affairs is a basic (if, now, somewhat embattled) norm of the society of states, and is a major theme of the Vienna Convention on Diplomatic Relations (1961) (on the VCDR, see Chapter 7). As a result, some states, such as Algeria, refused to sign MOUs

(SIAC, Appeal No: SC/02/05, para. 39), and those that did come to fruition provided for reciprocity: Britain agreed to identical procedures to guarantee its own good behaviour in the event that one of these countries should wish to deport British nationals back to Britain. More significantly, these MOUs gave the receiving state a veto in the choice of the so-called 'independent monitoring body'.

The British government describes the monitoring bodies that have emerged as a result of these agreements as 'local NGOS' (see Box 6.2) but, given the fact that they must be acceptable to the receiving government, it is clear that this is a typical official gloss. Some of these bodies are no doubt more independent than others and, in Jordan and Lebanon, the monitoring bodies both have links to the local Bar Associations. But independence and enthusiasm are not enough. The Adaleh Centre in Amman – which at the time of its selection was small, inexperienced and little known, even in Jordan – was not the British government's first choice (SIAC, Appeal No: SC/15/2005, paras 186–204). In Libya, the Qadhafi Development Foundation (QDF) is headed by Seif al-Islam, the second son of the Libyan dictator, Colonel Muammar al-Qadhafi; in Ethiopia, the monitoring body was established by the ruling party under the chairmanship of a former Ethiopian ambassador to Russia.

The nature of these monitoring bodies led organizations such as Human Rights Watch and Amnesty to charge that the MOUs were not worth the paper they were written on. They were not alone. In April 2007, the Special Immigration Appeals Commission (SIAC) in Britain declared unsafe the decision of the Home Office to deport two Libyan terrorism suspects to Libya; monitoring by the QDF, it declared, was unlikely to be effective. SIAC's judgement was subsequently supported by the Court of Appeal. It was against this background that it began to emerge that the British embassies in the countries concerned were also playing a role in monitoring compliance with the 'No Torture'

Box 6.2   States with which Britain has 'No Torture' agreements, and local NGOs appointed as monitoring bodies

Jordan	10 August 2005	Adaleh Centre for Human Rights Studies
Libya	18 October 2005	Qadhafi Development Foundation
Lebanon	29 December 2005	Institute of Human Rights
Ethiopia	12 December 2008	Ethiopian Human Rights Commission

There was also an exchange of rather vague letters on the subject with Algeria on 11 July 2006, which contained no mention of a monitoring body.

agreements. It also became clear that it was in the interests of the Foreign Office to let this be known, albeit discreetly, in order to try to meet the charge that Britain intended to wash its hands of these suspects once they had left the country.

Though the importance attached to these agreements had led to the direct involvement in their negotiation of senior officials and ministers in London, the British embassies in the receiving states had also been intimately concerned with them from the very beginning, having been asked by the Foreign Office, in 2003, to report on the prospects for negotiating a 'generic Mou' (SIAC, Appeal Nos: SC/42 and 50/2005, para. 209). Thereafter, they led in the search for suitable monitoring bodies and supported the negotiation of their terms of reference. This positioned them well to assume the role of local coordinator of the capacity-building assistance then provided by Britain to these bodies (for which there was great need), as also to prison officers, police officers, judges, and so on. Finally, the embassies not only monitored the monitors, but also *directly* monitored the treatment of returnees. If the experience of the embassy in Algeria is anything to go by (SIAC, Appeal Nos: SC/02/05, para. 39; and SC/32/2005, *passim*), this was especially true in those receiving countries with which there was no MOU and, therefore, no appointed monitoring body. However, it also appears to have been a normal expectation in those receiving countries, such as Jordan, where there was an MOU. As SIAC said, in dismissing the appeal of 'VV' against deportation to Jordan:

> Experience of deportations to Algeria has demonstrated that the British Government takes its obligations to see that diplomatic assurances in relation to deportees are fulfilled seriously. We have no reason whatever to doubt that the embassy in Amman would do the same (SIAC, Appeal No: SC/59/2006, para. 23).

In sum, while the British government maintained that diplomatic assurances of 'No Torture' were reliable chiefly because it was in the interests of the receiving countries to honour them, it also recognized the need to follow them up. In this, the role of its embassies was of the first importance.

Review meetings

The value of follow-up procedures is now so well-understood that formal 'compliance mechanisms', as they are sometimes known, are often created by, or pursuant to, the provisions of international agreements; these become permanently institutionalized. In multilateral diplomacy, the ultimate expression of this is an international organization (see Chapter 9), whether created at the time of the agreement or evolving into its final form only after some years. A good example of the latter is the Organization for Security and Co-operation in Europe (OSCE), which exists to consolidate and build on the Helsinki Final Act of 1975. A permanent structure had been proposed by the Soviet Union at the start but opposed by NATO countries, and it was another 20 years before *ad hoc* follow-up procedures evolved into the OSCE. But, as its history suggests, formal follow-up arrangements take different forms well short of a fully fledged international organization, and they are a common feature of bilateral as well as multilateral agreements.

The most common sort of formal follow-up procedure is a review meeting, sometimes also known as a 'conference of the parties', a 'joint commission' (in the case of bilateral agreements), or simply as a 'follow-up conference'. This is a gathering of representatives of the parties to the original agreement called for the express purposes of measuring progress on its implementation, and securing an understanding of what needs to be done to move matters forward. The original agreement usually stipulates that these meetings are to be held on a regular basis and at a venue rotating among the participant states. (If the venue is fixed, as at IAEA headquarters in the case of the review meetings of the Convention on Nuclear Safety, the president of the meeting might be rotated.) This puts all of the parties – especially the host – under pressure to make progress before the meeting so as to avoid the charge of backsliding, and possible public criticism.

Review meetings, although regular, often have large gaps between them, but it is unwise to jump to the conclusion that this means following-up is not being taken seriously. For example, the interval between review meetings of the Convention on Nuclear Safety, which entered into force in 1996, might be as long as three years, but an organizing committee must meet well before this. Moreover, six months prior to the review meeting the parties are required to submit a national report on the measures they have taken to implement their obligations under the convention. If they do not, they are named and shamed in the published summary report of the review meeting (Summary Report of the 4th Review Meeting, paras 5–6). Those of the NPT are held only every five years but meetings of a preparatory committee – which all states party to the treaty are entitled to attend, and which discuss substantive as well as procedural matters – are held in the intervening period; three

of these should have been held by the time of the next review conference in 2010. It is also not unusual for agreements to stipulate that
review meetings might be held at short notice in an emergency.

Since the flurry of global UN conferences in the economic and social
field in the 1990s, the idea has also been firmly planted that global
conferences should be followed up with regional ones. When 'implementation committees' – a feature of some multilateral environmental
regimes – come into being, progress has been made on the road to the
creation of an international organization.

In bilateral agreements, especially when there is no provision for review
meetings, follow-up may be facilitated by other means. For example, an
agreement might list (or require, by a deadline shortly after signature,
the identification of) the competent authorities in each state – and,
ideally, the named individuals in them – responsible for implementation. Such an agreement might also require the establishment of direct
channels of communication between these authorities or named persons. Provision for all of these procedures was made in the India–Russia
agreement on cooperation against illicit trafficking in narcotics signed
in Moscow on 12 November 2007 and published on the website of the
Indian embassy. But such, or similar, procedures need not be substi-
tutes for review meetings, as is clear from the US–Mexico agreement of
14 August 1983 on cooperation for the protection and improvement of
the environment in the border area. This provided for nomination by
each state of both a 'national coordinator' to be responsible for implementation and an annual review meeting to be held alternately in the
border area of the USA and Mexico.

In the case of fragile agreements painfully constructed, such compliance mechanisms might be a necessary condition of implementation,
but they are not a sufficient one. This is only too tragically revealed
by the 'road map' on the Middle East of 2003, which provides that
'The Quartet will meet regularly at senior levels to evaluate the parties'
performance on implementation of the plan'. This particular formulation has been criticized for its vagueness by the International Peace
Academy, but it is hardly that alone that has prevented the Israelis and
Palestinians from reaching the destination marked out on the map.

Summary

States often sign up to agreements that they have no intention of
observing, or of doing so only in limited and belated fashion. As a
result, however well-constructed, appropriately packaged, and solemnly

ratified these agreements might be, it is essential that steps be taken to follow them up. Agreements that are complex, technical and sensitive always have to be followed up by experts, whether employed by governments, international organizations, or NGOs. Embassies, too, are in some respects ideally placed to follow up agreements, as can be seen in their work in monitoring and encouraging compliance with 'No Torture' agreements. Review meetings are also valuable in following up bilateral as well as the better-known multilateral agreements. 'Naming and shaming' and assistance in capacity-building are the main levers in diplomatic follow-up but, if this is insufficient, the implementation of agreements might, in some circumstances, be sought through international courts and tribunals and – in extreme cases – by economic sanctions, blockade, or military intimidation.

Further reading

Adcock, Sir Frank and D. J. Mosley, *Diplomacy in Ancient Greece* (Thames & Hudson: London, 1975): 216–26.

Beyerlin, U., P.T. Stoll and R. Wolfrum (eds), *Ensuring Compliance with Multilateral Environmental Agreements: A dialogue between practitioners and academia* (Martinus Nijhoff: Leiden, 2006).

Blix, Hans, *Disarming Iraq* (Bloomsbury: London, 2004).

Carlson, John, 'NPT Safeguards Agreements – Defining Non-Compliance', 31 August 2008 [www].

Deeks, Ashley S., 'Avoiding transfers to torture', *Council on Foreign Relations Special Report*, 35, June 2008 [www].

Dinstein, Yoram, *War, Aggression and Self-Defence*, 4th edn (Cambridge University Press: Cambridge, 2005): 263–7, on treaties of guarantee.

Munn-Rankin, J. M., 'Diplomacy in Western Asia in the early second millennium B.C.', *Iraq*, 18, 1956, on oaths.

Reynolds, David, *Summits: Six meetings that shaped the twentieth century* (Allen Lane: London, 2007).

Roberts, Sir Ivor (ed.), *Satow's Diplomatic Practice*, 6th edn (Oxford University Press: Oxford, 2009): ch. 32, on NGOs.

Rona, Gabor, 'The ICRC's status: in a class of its own', 17 February 2004 [www].

SIPRI, 'Iraq: The UNSCOM Experience', October 1998 [www].

UK FCO, *Human Rights Annual Report 2007*, Cm 7340, March 2008. [This and other *Annual Reports* are available as pdf downloads from the Foreign Office website.]

UNEP, *Manual on Compliance with and Enforcement of Multilateral Environmental Agreements* [www].

UNMOVIC, *Compendium: Observations and lessons learned* (UNMOVIC: 27 June 2007) [www].

US Department of State, *Trafficking in Persons Report 2008* (Office to Monitor and Combat Trafficking in Persons: 4 June 2008) [www].

Vattel, Emmerich de, *Le droit des gens* [*The Law of Nations*] (first publ. Neuchâtel, 1758) [English trsl. www], book 2: chs 15 and 16, on hostages, oaths, and treaties of guarantee.

See also the websites of the following bodies:
Canadian Centre for Treaty Compliance
Human Rights Watch
IAEA (Department of Safeguards)
OSCE (*History of the OSCE*)
US Department of State (Bureau of Verification, Compliance, and Implementation).

Part II
Diplomatic Relations

Introduction to Part II

On 10 February 2004 the Republic of Ireland established diplomatic relations with the oppressive government of Myanmar (Burma). 'In view of Ireland's responsibilities during our EU Presidency,' said the Irish foreign minister, 'this decision ... will ensure that, during the Presidency, we can contribute more directly to promoting the process of democratisation and national reconciliation there.' This example illustrates the fact that when states are in diplomatic relations they can, in principle, communicate freely with each other and, so, in the most effective manner possible.

To be in diplomatic relations is the normal condition as between states enjoying mutual recognition; hence, diplomatic relations is often spoken of as 'normal relations'. This condition might have grown up naturally and be taken for granted, as in the case of states having dealings with each other over centuries. In other cases, the establishment of diplomatic relations – or the 'normalization' of relations – might be the result of a well-advertised written agreement to this effect, today typically taking the form of a joint communiqué signed by their permanent representatives to the United Nations in New York, as in the case of Sri Lanka and Paraguay in April 2009. Such communiqués commonly add that the step has been guided by the principles and purposes of the Charter of the UN and the VCDR (1961), and indicate both the date when and the manner in which normalization will commence.

The ways in which normal relations are conducted varies, and it by no means follows that they require an exchange of ambassadors. It is true that resident embassies are frequently established, but diplomatic relations – broadly understood – might also be conducted by means of consulates, summit meetings, conferences, and telecommunications.

It is the different channels, or modes, of diplomacy that are the subject of this Part of the book.

It has been argued in Part I that the most important function of diplomacy is the negotiation of agreements between states. It has also been noted, however, that this is not always the function to which those professionally involved in the conduct of diplomatic relations devote most of their time, and that diplomacy has other important functions. These include political and economic reporting, lobbying, supporting the activities of businesses from home, assisting distressed nationals, and propaganda. The opportunity will be taken in Part II to examine these functions also.

7
Embassies

Formally accredited resident embassies are the normal means of conducting bilateral diplomacy between any two states. The British scholar-diplomat Harold Nicolson called this the 'French system of diplomacy', because of the dominant influence of France on its evolution and the gradual replacement of Latin by French as its working language (Nicolson 1954). This chapter will commence with a discussion of this system as it evolved from the early modern period to the twentieth century. It will then proceed to an examination of the working of the resident embassy today, in the course of which it will be seen that this institution has proved remarkably resilient.

The French system of diplomacy

In the Middle Ages, responsibility for diplomacy was placed chiefly in the hands of a *nuncius* and a plenipotentiary. The former was no more than a 'living letter', whereas the latter had 'full powers' – *plena potestas*, hence the later 'plenipotentiary' – to negotiate on behalf of and bind his principal. Nevertheless, they were alike in that they were temporary envoys with narrowly focused tasks (Queller: chs 1 and 2). It was the mark of the system that began to emerge in the second half of the fifteenth century that these *ad hoc* envoys were replaced or, more accurately, supplemented by resident embassies with broad responsibilities. Why did this occur?

Temporary embassies were expensive to dispatch, vulnerable on the road, and always likely to cause trouble over precedence and ceremonial because of the high status required of their leaders. As a result, when diplomatic activity in Europe intensified in the late fifteenth century, 'it was discovered to be more practical and more economical to appoint an ambassador to remain at a much frequented court' (Queller: 82; also Satow: vol. I, 240–1). Continuous representation also led to greater familiarity with conditions and personalities in the country concerned, thereby producing better political reporting; facilitated the preparation of important negotiations (although it long remained customary to continue sending higher-ranking, special envoys to conduct them); and made it more likely that such negotiations could be launched without attracting the attention that would usually accompany the arrival of a special envoy (Queller: 83). The spread of resident missions was also facilitated by the growing strength of the doctrine of *raison d'état*; that is, the doctrine that standards of personal morality were irrelevant in statecraft, where the only test was what furthered the interest of the state. This sanctioned what, in the seventeenth century, Richelieu called 'continuous negotiation': permanent diplomacy 'in all places', irrespective of considerations of sentiment or religion (Berridge, Keens-Soper, and Otte: ch. 4). Anticipating this doctrine by a century, in 1535 His Most Christian Majesty, François I, King of France, established a resident embassy in Constantinople at the court of Suleiman the Magnificent, Sultan of the Ottoman Empire, Shadow of God on Earth – and spear of the Muslim holy war against Christendom.

The resident embassy, which initially meant the ambassador and his entourage but came to mean the building they occupied, was at first treated with suspicion in most quarters. Nevertheless, its value was such that it was steadily strengthened by the customary law of nations, which evolved quite rapidly in this area after the late sixteenth century. Reflecting the change in practice, the premises rented for long periods by the envoy – as well as his person, domestic family, and staff – were soon attracting special immunities from local criminal and civil jurisdiction (Adair; Young 1966). As might have been expected, the more powerful states, including France itself, were slower to dispatch than to receive resident embassies. The Ottoman Empire did not experiment with residents of its own until 1793. As for Manchu China, this first had to be encouraged to view foreign states as sovereign equals rather than as barbarous vassals whose representatives must acknowledge this status by the delivery of tribute and performance of the kow-tow at the feet of the Emperor (Peyrefitte). As a result, it did not entertain occidental-style embassies until 1861.

Continuity in diplomacy via the resident embassy (or 'legation', if the mission were headed by the lower-ranked minister rather than an ambassador) was not the only characteristic feature of the French system. Another was secrecy. In current usage, 'secret diplomacy' can mean keeping secret all or any of the following: the contents of a negotiation, knowledge that negotiations are going on, the content of any agreement issuing from negotiations, or the fact that any agreement at all has been reached. Nevertheless, in the French system secret diplomacy normally meant keeping either the fact or the content of negotiations secret. This was considered important chiefly because a successful negotiation means, by definition, that each side has to settle for less than its ideal requirements, which is another way of saying that certain parties – radical supporters of the governments concerned, some other domestic constituency, or a foreign friend – have, in some measure, to be sold out. If such parties are aware of what is afoot at the time, they might well be able, and would certainly try, to sabotage the talks.

Another important feature of the French system was close attention in protocol to elaborate ceremonial with religious overtones. This was used to enhance a ruler's prestige, flatter his allies, and solemnize agreements (Anderson: 15). Ratification of agreements concluded by plenipotentiaries, which was juridically unnecessary, was also often accompanied by high ceremony, in order to reinforce the compact (Queller: 219–20). Ambassadors, in contrast to mere 'publick ministers', were of special value in ceremonials because they were held to have the 'full representative character'; that is, to represent their sovereigns 'even in their dignity' (Vattel: 367); accordingly, they came to be reserved for relationships of special importance.

Protocol, although it now has a reputation for stuffiness and excessive formality, has always had an important task: that of making it unnecessary for diplomats to have to argue afresh about procedure each time they meet, thereby enabling them to concentrate on the substantive issues that divide their governments (Cohen 1987: 142). A vital point of protocol has always been the regulation of diplomatic precedence; that is, the order in which diplomats are acknowledged on official occasions – who comes first and who last. This is because of the sensitivities of sovereign bodies to their prestige, which is such a valuable currency in international relations. It was a major achievement of the French system to overturn, at the Congress of Vienna in 1815, the controversial scheme of precedence laid down by the Pope in 1504 (Box 7.1). Henceforward, diplomats would take rank according to the date of the official notification of their arrival in the capital concerned, the longest serving being accorded the highest seniority. It also became customary that plenipotentiaries at a conference would sign treaties in alphabetical order.

Box 7.1   The papal class list

'The Pope, not unnaturally, placed himself first among the monarchs of the earth. The Emperor came second and after him his heir-apparent, "The King of the Romans". Then followed the Kings of France, Spain, Aragon and Portugal. Great Britain came sixth on the list and the King of Denmark last. This papal class-list was not accepted without demur by the sovereigns concerned' (Nicolson 1963: 98–9).

According to Nicolson, however, what really distinguished the French system was its adoption of the critical principle that deceit had no place in diplomacy. He probably exaggerated the depravity of the diplomatic methods popularized by Machiavelli (Hale: 272–5; Mattingly: 109; Queller: 109) but as the resident ambassador won acceptance, acquired higher social standing, and gradually became part of a profession, more importance did come to be attached to honesty in diplomacy. François de Callières, the theorist of this system, emphasized that the purpose of negotiation was not to trick the other side but, rather, to reconcile states on the basis of a true estimate of their enduring interests. This was right; it was also prudent. For agreements are only likely to endure if made on this basis – and, if they are unlikely to endure, they are unlikely to be worth concluding in the first place. By contrast, if a state secures an agreement by deceit, or subsequently throws over an agreement immediately it becomes inconvenient, it is likely to breed a desire for revenge in the breast of its victim (Callières: 33, 83, 110). It is also likely to find other states disinclined to enter negotiations with it in the future. Greater honesty in diplomacy was a sign of the maturing of the diplomatic system.

An additional feature of the French system was the professionalization of diplomacy: controlled entry, some form of training, a code of conduct, clear ranks, payment that was at least nominally regular, and a pension on retirement. For Callières, diplomacy was too important and too much in need of extensive knowledge and technical expertise to be treated otherwise (Callières: 99–100). The transformation of diplomacy into a profession was a slow and fitful process, and was not seriously under way, even in France itself, until well into the nineteenth century. Nevertheless, movement in this direction had been signalled well before this by the emergence of the *corps diplomatique*, or diplomatic body.

The 'diplomatic corps', as it was corrupted in English, is the community of diplomats representing different states resident in the same capital. (It is not be confused with the diplomatic *service* of individual states, although it usually is – not least by diplomats.) The evolution of this institution, with its own rules of procedure – such as the rule that the longest-serving ambassador should be the spokesman or dean of the *corps* on matters of common interest – was clear evidence of an emerging sense of professional identity among diplomats (Berridge 2007: 15). In other words, diplomats under the French system had come to recognize that they had professional interests that united them as diplomats, as well as political and commercial interests that divided them as, say, Englishmen, Frenchmen, or Austrians. Foremost among these professional interests was defence of their immunities under the law of nations. The diplomatic corps perhaps reached its apogee – or, at any rate, its most glorious moment – in the successful defence of the Legation Quarter in Peking during the Boxer uprising in 1900.

In his elegant lectures, Harold Nicolson remarked that the French method was 'that best adapted to the conduct of relations between civilised States' (Nicolson 1954: 72). Nevertheless, he was aware of weaknesses and drawbacks, and others were much less charitable. Indeed, although Nicolson vigorously disputed this, some held the old diplomacy – as the French system came to be more usually called – to have been one of the causes of World War I. Prominent among the charges against it were its secrecy, leisurely pace, domination by the traditional aristocracy, and tendency of its representatives to 'go native'.

Going native, or succumbing to 'localitis', is an occupational hazard experienced by professional diplomats who have been posted for a long time in the same part of the world. It has been recognized since the birth of resident missions during the Italian Renaissance. At best, they lose touch with sentiments at home; at worst, they become mouthpieces for the governments to which they are accredited, rather than those they nominally represent. Localitis is not difficult to understand. In order to be effective in a foreign posting, a diplomat has to learn at least something of the local culture and, ideally, the language. This does not, in itself, lead to sympathy for the local point of view but it presents the opportunity to acquire it, which might be the more enthusiastically taken if the culture in question prizes values and personal attributes that are important to the diplomat's own nation and social class. This was certainly a part of the explanation of the admiration developed by British diplomats for the desert tribes of Arabia (Monroe: 116–17). Diplomats can also be won over by gifts and decorations. This was why Queen Elizabeth I of England is said to have remarked, with her ambassadors in mind: 'I would not have my sheep branded with any other mark than my own' (Satow: vol. I, 369). A more important cause of localitis, however, is the fact that – as we shall see – resident diplomats need constant access to local officials and other influential persons. It is a short step from regularly having to listen to their point of view to showing sympathy for it as a professionally expedient courtesy – and it is perhaps not a much longer step to sharing it.

It was, in part, because it was known that diplomats might go native that it became normal to rotate them between postings, typically after three or four years. This means some sacrifice of hard-won area expertise but this should not be exaggerated, because rotating does not mean that diplomats must never be allowed to return to a previous post. In fact, it is quite common in properly run diplomatic services for ambassadors to have served at the same post earlier in their careers. Country expertise is also conserved by rotating diplomats between posts and the desks of the foreign ministry at home dealing with the same countries.

What of the stranglehold on the profession of the traditional aristocracy? Although the earliest resident diplomats were not generally of the highest social standing, special envoys normally were. This was necessary to maintain the prestige of their ruler and flatter the parties with whom they were dealing, as well as to make it easy for them to move in circles of influence. However, as the French system matured, resident embassies – at least in the important capitals – attracted leading notables, and the emerging foreign services of the various European states became the province of the traditional aristocracy.

Aristocratic dominance of diplomacy was significant because of the considerable uniformity of outlook that it fostered across the diplomatic services of different states. As Anderson says, 'The aristocracies which ruled so much of Europe could still see themselves even in 1914 as in some sense parts of a social order which transcended national boundaries... A diplomat who spent most of his working life in foreign capitals could easily feel himself part of an aristocratic international to which national feeling was hardly more than a vulgar plebeian prejudice.' For one thing, they often had foreign wives (Anderson: 121; Nicolson 1954: 78–9). Similarly, it made them uncomfortable with the growing trend towards more democratic control of foreign policy in Europe in the early twentieth century, and attracted hostility – generally unwarranted – towards their methods, such as secret negotiation. Since the traditional aristocracy was also contemptuous of trade, its dominance of diplomacy made this a poor instrument for promoting the commercial and financial interests of the state abroad (Platt 1968). This, along with other menial tasks, was generally left to consuls (see Chapter 8).

Finally, as the number of states increased, the complexity of the problems confronting them multiplied, and the urgency attending them grew, the operating pace of the French system of bilateral diplomacy became simply too slow. This was realized during World War I and was demonstrated by the rash of conferences – many of them achieving permanent status – that were hurriedly organized to cope with the crisis. Afterwards, multilateral diplomacy was properly inaugurated with the creation of the League of Nations, and it was widely believed that the old diplomacy had been replaced by a 'new diplomacy'. This was an exaggeration but some things clearly had changed, and these changes will be discussed more fully later in this chapter, as well as in Chapter 9. Nevertheless, the French system remained at the core of the world diplomatic system after World War I – and remains, albeit sometimes disguised, at its core today. It is necessary, therefore, to turn to an examination of its modern manifestation, which is legally anchored in the VCDR.

The Vienna Convention on Diplomatic Relations, 1961

By the 1950s, it was broadly accepted by jurists that diplomats must have special privileges and immunities under local criminal and civil law for the reason given two centuries earlier by Emmerich de Vattel, a native of Neuchâtel who was, at the time, in the diplomatic service of the Elector of Saxony. 'It frequently happens', he wrote, 'that a minister [diplomat] is entrusted with commissions that are disagreeable to the sovereign to whom he is sent. If that prince has any power over him, and particularly if he has sovereign authority over him, how is it to be expected that the minister will carry out the orders of his master with the requisite fidelity, courage, and freedom?' (Vattel 1758: book 4, para. 92). In short, diplomats needed special treatment under the law because, without it, they would be unable to carry out their functions properly.

The 'functional theory', as it was called, had certainly given a more persuasive justification of diplomatic privileges and immunities than the previously popular theories. (The theory of embassy exterritoriality mistook a metaphor for a justification, while that resting on the ambassador's character, as full representative of a sovereign power, protected His Excellency but left the rest of his staff in the cold.) It was one thing to accept that diplomats needed special treatment, and to agree on why this should be so; it was quite another to be complacent about the condition of the existing rules, which were found chiefly in customary international law. Indeed, there was growing anxiety, especially in the West, that looseness in the diplomatic rules was permitting some embassies to be used for illegitimate purposes and others to be subjected to improper harassment; that the existing rules were inadequate to cope with the size of the diplomatic corps – by the 1950s, being swollen by diplomats arriving in the major capitals from the many ex-colonial states; and that traditional diplomatic institutions would be tarred with the brush of neo-colonialism if the new states of Asia and Africa were not allowed to give them official sanction. As a result, the VCDR, which was shaped by a draft produced by the UN's International Law Commission (ILC), codified and 'progressively developed' the customary law on diplomacy: clarified and tightened it, adjusted its content to modern conditions, and relaunched it in the more impressive form of a multilateral convention.

Consistent with the functional theory, early attention was given in the new Convention to listing the proper functions of diplomatic missions (Box 7.2). In addition, privileges important to their functioning were generally strengthened, while the categories of those by whom they could be invoked were tightened. On the all-important point of the inviolability of embassy premises, which it later made clear applied equally to the private residences of diplomatic agents, the Convention made strong statements. 'The premises of the mission shall be inviolable', it stated baldly in Article 22.1, adding by way of clarification that 'The agents of the receiving State may not enter them, except with the consent of the head of mission'. So, there was no provision – as some

---

Box 7.2   Article 3 of the Vienna Convention on Diplomatic Relations, 1961

1. The functions of a diplomatic mission consist *inter alia* in:
    (a) representing the sending State in the receiving State;
    (b) protecting in the receiving State the interests of the sending State and of its nationals, within the limits permitted by international law;
    (c) negotiating with the Government of the receiving State;
    (d) ascertaining by all lawful means conditions and developments in the receiving State, and reporting thereon to the Government of the sending State;
    (e) promoting friendly relations between the sending State and the receiving State, and developing their economic, cultural and scientific relations.

2. Nothing in the present Convention shall be construed as preventing the performance of consular functions by a diplomatic mission.

had wanted – for such consent to be assumed in a public emergency, which would have permitted an unscrupulous receiving state to contrive such an event itself; for example, by deliberately starting a fire at the embassy. ('Aha! You have a fire. We must rush in and put it out! And...ahem...inspect your documents to make sure they have not been burned.'). The VCDR also placed a special duty on the receiving state to protect the embassy premises.

The Convention stressed that the inviolability of the mission extended to its contents, bank accounts, and movable property, especially its means of transport and documents. The inviolability of the mission's communications was the subject of a long article, although the controversial qualification was added that 'the mission may install and use a wireless transmitter only with the consent of the receiving State'. This was a concession to the developing states, which were particularly afraid that unrestricted diplomatic wireless communication would permit intervention in their internal affairs (Kerley: 111–16; Denza: 175–9).

The VCDR also made a strong statement of the customary position on the inviolability of the person of the diplomat, while reiterating the right of receiving states to expel those whose actions were regarded as pernicious. Among other things, it underwrote the freedom of movement of the diplomatic agent, so vital to a number of functions, not least that of political reporting. Affirmation of this right had been made necessary by the Soviet bloc policy, introduced following World War II, of limiting the travel of foreign diplomats to 50 kilometres from the capital, unless they obtained special permission to make longer trips. This had provoked a number of Western states, notably the United States, to retaliate in kind. However, freedom of movement was also qualified by permitting receiving states to bar a diplomat from certain zones on grounds of national security, and the result was that state practice did not change a great deal (Denza: 168–72).

The Vienna Convention also detailed the obligations of missions to the receiving state. This was hardly surprising, since resident missions had always run the risk of being suspected of espionage and subversion, and this had been heightened by the Cold War activities of the superpowers in the non-aligned world (Berridge 1997: 157–61). Thus, the Convention stressed that diplomats must 'respect the laws and regulations of the receiving State' and repeatedly referred to the duty of non-interference in its domestic affairs, making a number of practical stipulations to reduce its risk: diplomatic missions were required to confine their conduct of official business to the receiving state's foreign ministry unless agreed otherwise; failing prior permission, embassy offices could not be established 'in localities other than those in which the mission itself is established'; *agrément* might be required for service attachés (always suspected of being spies) as well as new heads of mission; receiving states could insist on the slimming down of missions they believed to be too large; and finally, as noted earlier, radio facilities could only be installed in missions with the consent of the receiving state.

The VCDR was signed in Vienna on 18 April 1961 and came into force three years later when, on 24 April 1964, it had been ratified by 22 states. When the PRC acceded to it in November 1975, it enjoyed the support of the entire Permanent Five (P5) on the UN Security Council. At the time of writing (June 2009), 186 states are parties to this Convention – all but a very small handful of the total number of states in the world. Practice has revealed certain gaps and ambiguities in this seminal instrument, but it remains as true today as when remarked in 1988 that it is 'without doubt one of the surest and most widely based multilateral regimes in the field of international relations' (Brown: 54).

The VCDR dealt only with traditional bilateral diplomacy, and thus excluded both relations with international organizations and special missions (on the later attempts to codify and develop the law in these areas, see Chapter 14). This limited brief was one of the reasons for its success. Among the others was the fact that all states send as well as receive diplomats, and that, where there were serious disagreements at the Vienna conference (as, for example, over diplomatic wireless communication), the major powers – whether East or West – had tended to be on the same side (Kerley: 128).

The case for euthanasia

It is one of the ironies of the history of diplomacy that, not long after the VCDR had reinforced the resident embassy, voices began to be heard – at least, in the West – claiming that it had become an anachronism. Prominent among these were those of Zbigniew Brzezinski and Henry Kissinger:

• First, it was maintained, direct contact between political leaders and home-based officials had been made much easier by dramatic improvements in travel and communications, and the growth of international organizations, thereby enabling them to bypass their ambassadors.

- Second, functions such as representation and negotiation (especially where experts are needed to deal with technical business) were actually better executed via direct contact.
- Third, embassy political reporting had been overtaken by the huge growth in the international mass media, an argument reinforced by the dramatic broadcasting from Baghdad of Cable News Network (CNN) reports during the Gulf War at the beginning of the 1990s.
- Finally, it was suggested, serious ideological tensions and deepening cultural divisions across the world meant that the exchange of embassies by hostile states provided – quite literally – dangerous hostages to fortune.

The Iranian crisis at the end of the 1970s, during which the Shah's regime was replaced by a revolutionary theocratic government under Ayatollah Khomeini, seemed to provide spectacular confirmation that the resident embassy was both an anachronism and a liability. The US ambassador in Tehran, William Sullivan (at the time, the most senior member of the US Foreign Service on active duty), was repeatedly by-passed by direct communication between the White House and the Shah, and subsequently took early retirement (Sullivan: 199–287). As for the embassy that he had left on 6 April 1979, nine months later this was seized by militant supporters of the new Islamic government and its staff held hostage for 444 days. This humiliated the administration of Jimmy Carter, and provoked a crisis that dominated his last year in office.

Against such a background, it is hardly surprising that supporters of the resident embassy should have been on the defensive throughout most of the post-war period. In Britain, traditional diplomacy came under increasingly hostile official scrutiny after the mid-1960s and suffered remorseless attacks on its budget. The same trend was observable in the United States and other countries. Nevertheless, not only are resident embassies still to be found everywhere, but some of them are also larger than ever. For example, the staff of the British embassy in Turkey is four times the size that it was during the heyday of Lord Stratford de Redcliffe in the Crimean War, and twice the size it was in 1878 despite the fact that, in that year, it was temporarily inflated by the first cohort of student interpreters from the newly-created Levant Consular Service and a flood of military attachés caused by the outbreak of the Russo–Turkish war (Berridge 2009: 274). Why has the case for euthanasia failed to persuade? The best way to answer this question is to show how the functions of the resident embassy cannot be performed as well – if, in some cases, at all – in its absence.

Generalizing about the significance of the work done by resident missions is perilous, for it varies with the diplomatic services of which they are part and the countries in which they are located. Nevertheless, many important tasks are performed to some extent by almost all well-run embassies of at least medium size. It is to these that we must now turn.

Representation and friendly relations

Representation, that often overlooked or naively minimized function of diplomacy, is chiefly concerned with prestige and is, in certain instances, impossible to distinguish from propaganda. Principally involving the head of a mission, it embraces entertaining, giving public lectures, appearing on television and radio shows, and attendance at state ceremonial occasions. In principle, it can be conducted by government ministers and officials, but they cannot be everywhere and have important jobs at home. As a result, it devolves chiefly on ambassadors. On the occasions when it is, nevertheless, expedient for senior government figures to go abroad on representative duties – either to attend some special occasion, or simply on a goodwill visit – they are also highly dependent on the support of the local embassy: this applies as much to the forward planning and aftermath as to the period of the visit itself (Berridge 2009: 234–6).

The existence of a resident embassy also broadens a state's representative options and, thus, its repertoire of non-verbal signals. For example, at the funeral of Soviet leader Leonid Brezhnev in Moscow in 1982, most foreign delegations were headed by dignitaries flown in for the occasion. Nevertheless, a few countries found it expedient to be represented merely by their resident ambassadors; in their absence, it might have been difficult to avoid showing either too much or too little respect (Berridge 1994: 142). For representational purposes, resident missions are generally of special importance to new states and established ones in declining circumstances. What of their duty to promote friendly relations?

The first duty of an embassy is to advance its country's interests, and this might require a diplomat to behave in an unfriendly manner (James 1980: 937–8). Nevertheless, it remains an important task of the embassy to promote friendly relations with local elites *insofar as this is compatible with policy*. The report of the Central Policy Review Staff (CPRS) into British diplomacy called this the 'cultivation of contacts' and commended it (CPRS: 259). A well-networked embassy will obviously find it easier to gain influence and gather information; it will also be better placed to handle a crisis in relations should one subsequently develop. It is for this reason, as well as others, that a good embassy will honour local customs (provided they are not flagrantly objectionable), mark important local events, and make extensive social contacts.

It is also an important job of the embassy to ensure that gratuitous offence is not given to the host government in the event that some unpleasant message has to be delivered. Diplomats who are liked, familiar with the understatement of their profession, fluent in the local language, fully acquainted with protocol, and sensitive to local prejudice – in short, professionals – are more likely to achieve this than anyone else. Friendly relations can be cultivated by other means – for example, by summitry (see Chapter 10) – although this can have the opposite effect when there are personality clashes between leaders. For this task, then, the resident embassy has the greatest opportunities, and is likely to have the most appropriate knowledge and skills.

Negotiating and lobbying

In negotiation, the most important function of diplomacy broadly conceived, resident ambassadors and their staff also continue to have more than a walk-on part. Indeed, the settlement of some matters might still be left largely, or even entirely, to the embassy, acting under instructions that are now so easy to issue and update electronically. These include: subjects of relatively minor importance; amendments to existing agreements of greater significance, such as the rescheduling of the repayment of a loan; and important topics that require many months, perhaps years, to conclude and sometimes need great secrecy (CPRS: 117–18; Henderson: 335; Berridge 2009: 278–9; Jackson: 149–51). Among the latter in some parts of the world, and often with the assistance of secret service officers, are negotiations with kidnappers, which for good reasons Western governments regularly deny conducting but which, under intense and understandable pressure from the families and friends of victims, they are widely suspected of doing nevertheless.

When home-based experts or, more rarely, government ministers take the lead in a bilateral negotiation abroad, embassies still play an important role, although one that is less visible. The prenegotiations are often left entirely to them and these, as we know (see Chapter 2), can significantly influence the atmosphere in which the negotiation proper is conducted – and so shape its outcome. For example, in conducting the prenegotiations with Turkey for the International Road Transport

Agreement of September 1977, which had long been sought by Britain, the commercial counsellor of the British embassy in Ankara negotiated an important interim agreement in February 1976, an extension of this in March 1977, and several other points of substance shortly after that, quite apart from making all of the other preparations for the visit of the negotiating team from the British Department of Transport. As it was, the Department's specialists only needed to be in Turkey for a few days. During a negotiation led by home-based experts, it is also normal for the embassy to occupy seats at the table, as well as provide bed and breakfast for the visitors and briefs on key local personalities; and the vital task of following up any agreement reached usually falls chiefly to them as well, as already noted in the previous chapter in the case of bilateral MOUs on torture (Trevelyan 1973: 72; Henderson: 214–16, 225–6; Berridge 2009: *passim*).

Sometimes, too, ambassadors are brought back to reinforce a negotiation being conducted at home. The US ambassador to Egypt, Herman Eilts, and to Israel, Samuel Lewis, were so respected for their knowledge of their respective countries (see p. 118) that they were called home to be members of the 11-man US negotiating team at the Camp David summit in September 1978 (Carter: 327).

Closely related to negotiating is lobbying by the embassy: encouraging those with influence in the receiving state to take a favourable attitude to its country's interests. The targets of the embassy's attention, the extent to which lobbying is even prudent, and the style judged most efficacious vary with the receiving state's constitution and political culture. In general, however, personal contact is the most effective device of lobbying, and typical targets are government departments and opinion leaders in business and the media. Only where elected assemblies have real influence, as in the United States, do legislators (especially the chairmen of key committees) also attract an embassy's attention. All former ambassadors to the United States report their heavy involvement in lobbying during their periods in Washington. Allan Gotlieb, who was Canadian ambassador in the US capital from 1981 until 1989, gives the impression that the head of mission in Washington has time for little else (Gotlieb: 44, 56, 76). Increasingly, too, embassies in Washington are calling on the assistance of its numerous public relations and law firms, and many states now rely entirely on them for lobbying purposes. They do this for the same reason that European embassies employed dragomans to pursue their cases in Constantinople – the vast and baffling character, to outsiders, of its government and legislative institutions (Newhouse: 74).

Clarifying intentions

States always need to make sure that others know enough in order to behave conveniently. Depending on the situation, another government might need to be reassured ('relax – we're only invading your neighbour'), alarmed ('these sanctions are just the first step'), encouraged ('we like what you're doing'), or deterred ('do that and you'll regret it'). Once more, the resident embassy is not the only option. For example, if a message needs special emphasis or flattery is important, telephone diplomacy might be employed (see Chapter 12) or a special envoy might be sent (see Chapter 14). Nevertheless, there remain situations in which the resident embassy is either at least equally appropriate, or distinctly preferable, as the vehicle of clarification.

An ambassador can supplement a written message with an oral explanation and be more appropriate than a special envoy, if it is thought advisable to keep the exchange in a low key. The manner of the ambassador's presentation might also reinforce the message, as might the local reputation that the envoy has acquired. If reassurance is the import of a message, a statement by a trusted ambassador will be as good a medium as many, and better than most. In time of war, the ambassadors of allies play a particularly important role in this regard. The embassy might also be employed for the clarification of intentions in order to avoid erosion of its local standing, which needs preserving for other aspects of its work.

Political reporting

Gathering information on political – and, indeed, on military, economic and other developments – and reporting it home has long been recognized as one of the most important functions of the resident embassy. Immersed in the local scene and swapping information with other members of the diplomatic corps, embassy personnel are ideally situated to provide informative reports, and it is difficult to see this function ever being adequately performed in any other way. Only in unusual circumstances – such as those of Beijing during the Cultural Revolution in the late 1960s, when the diplomatic quarter was virtually besieged by Red Guards – is an embassy not peculiarly well-placed to know what is going on. It is true that service attachés (army, air force and navy), who are charged with obtaining military information, sometimes find this difficult even in friendly states, and next to impossible in hostile ones, but what they manage to discover continues to be valued by military intelligence.

A mission at the UN can obtain some information from another on conditions in its country of origin, but it would be sanitized and limited. Special envoys can also obtain information, but the brevity of their visits and their slender resources make it likely that their reports will be impressionistic. Spies – except for that rare specimen, the agent in place – do not enjoy regular, high-level access. Neither do journalists, who, in any case, do not always ask the questions in which governments are interested, or attach the same priority to the *accuracy* of their information. And, while a journalist's dispatch might be censored, a diplomat's might not. In closed societies, the information provided by a diplomatic mission is especially important.

What is particularly impressive is the extent of reliance on embassies for knowledge of the mind of the local leadership. For example, during the American-mediated negotiations between Israel and Egypt in the 1977–79 period – in which accurately sensing the mood of the Egyptian president, Anwar Sadat, was of vital importance to the Carter administration – great reliance was placed on the reports of the US ambassador in Cairo, Herman Eilts, who, by 28 November 1978, had had more than 250 meetings with the Egyptian leader (Carter: 320–1; Quandt: 166, 284). Carter also paid close attention to the on-the-spot reports of the US ambassador in Tel Aviv, Samuel Lewis (Carter: 321).

It is true that during the last days of the Shah, President Carter ultimately lost faith in the reports of his ambassador in Tehran, William Sullivan, despite his regular meetings with the Iranian leader. However, Carter continued to rely on some of Sullivan's reports for a while after the two men found themselves at odds over policy. Moreover, when the president lost faith in him, he did not dispense with a resident envoy but sent another (Carter: 443–9). This case shows, too, that intelligence on a foreign government can also be sought by gentle interrogation of its own ambassadors abroad. Both Carter and Brzezinski testify to the usefulness in this regard of the Iranian ambassador in Washington, Ardeshir Zahedi, who was known to be close to the Shah (Carter: 441; Brzezinski: 359–60).

It follows naturally, from the respect still generally accorded to the local knowledge of the competent embassy, that its advice on policy is usually welcomed as well. The Duncan Report in Britain picked this out for special emphasis in 1969 (HCPP 1969: 18, 91), as did the Murphy Commission Report in the United States six years later. Advice on policy is particularly valued when ambassadors have acquired a high professional reputation. Moreover, advances in telecommunications, widely believed to have weakened their office, also enable heads of mission to communicate their views to their own governments with great rapidity. The advice of an ambassador can be obtained by recalling him for consultation, as well as by direct telecommunication. In some countries, there is also a tradition of discussing policy at periodic or *ad hoc* conferences where chiefs of diplomatic and consular missions from a particular region meet senior foreign ministry officials for brain-storming sessions.

Commercial diplomacy

Until well into the twentieth century, the diplomatic services of most states regarded commercial work either as the responsibility of the socially inferior consul or of an autonomous or semi-autonomous foreign trade service. However, a major change was foreshadowed in the 1960s when trading states such as Britain began to grow increasingly concerned at their diminishing share of total world exports, and took off against the background of the global economic turbulence of the 1970s. Since that time, commercial diplomacy has generally been regarded as a first order activity (Rana 2000: 96–7). This is true even in Germany, where the powerful chambers of commerce were formerly left to deal with matters themselves. In Britain, the first major postwar push to commercial diplomacy came from the Duncan Report in 1969, which concluded that export promotion 'should absorb more of the [Diplomatic] Service's resources than any other function' (HCPP 1969: 68).

Commercial diplomacy includes use of the embassy's resources to promote both exports and inward investment; and, in the case of poor countries, the cultivation of aid donors. Important features of the work of the embassy's commercial section are the supplying of market intelligence, opening doors for trade missions and companies from home (especially small and medium-sized businesses that cannot afford their own agents), and contributing to the negotiation of bilateral commercial agreements; for example, on landing rights for a national airline. If the sending state is an arms exporter, service attachés are expected to exploit their contacts with the local defence establishment to assist in promoting weapons sales. When the foreign government is itself the customer, or when businessmen are trying to create new markets in 'closed, remote, or unfamiliar places', the embassy's political expertise is especially valuable to them (Rana 2000: 111).

Versatility and adaptability

Embassies can fulfil any number of subsidiary functions, symbolic as well as practical. In recent years, they have also shown themselves able to cope with changing circumstances abroad and a difficult climate at home. Their versatility and adaptability are further explanations of their survival in the world of advanced transport and communications.

The opening or maintaining of an embassy highlights the recognition of the receiving state by the sending state, but the simple presence of an embassy can be used to good symbolic effect in other ways. For example, the opening of embassies by Canada in francophone Africa in the 1960s was designed, in part, to establish Canada's own credentials as a francophone state (Wolfe: 34). Similarly, the decision by the Soviet Union in the mid-1920s to be one of the first states to shift its embassy in Turkey from Istanbul to Ankara – the new capital so cherished by the Turkish leader, Mustapha Kemal – was not just a sensible practical move, but also a gesture designed to consolidate a new relationship. And when, in 2006, Costa Rica and El Salvador, the only states with embassies in the disputed Israeli capital of Jerusalem, removed them to join the rest of the diplomatic corps in Tel Aviv, it was a sign that they wished to come in from the cold.

Embassies are also valuable in the administration of foreign aid by donor states in the developing world. One reason for this is that the bigger powers commonly have a variety of agencies involved in aid work and the embassy is the natural vehicle for the coordination, as well as the protection, of their efforts. Another is that the political relationship between givers and receivers is notoriously fragile and, thus, needs delicate handling (Trevelyan 1973: 106).

Embassies are also expected to provide cover for the activities of intelligence officers. This is a function that has always made ambassadors uneasy, and there is sometimes an agreement between the foreign ministry and the 'intelligence community' stipulating the maximum proportion of embassy staff that can serve as agents. Similarly requiring diplomatic cover in embassies because of the sensitivity and dangers of their work are drugs liaison officers (DLOs) and immigration liaison officers (ILOs). These agents are now quite strongly represented in European and American embassies in countries along the transit routes of illegal narcotics and people trafficking. Their work consists chiefly, but by no means exclusively, of intelligence gathering (Berridge 2009: 255–61). All sorts of different officers working for the Department of Homeland Security are now making some US embassies bulge at the seams (OIG 2006; see also Box 7.3).

A further non-core function of the embassy, and one in which intelligence officers are sometimes involved, is intervention in the political affairs of the receiving state. The major powers – during the Cold War,

---

Box 7.3   US Embassy Singapore: sections and attached agencies

Department of State

- Consular Section
- Economic/Political Section
- Public Affairs Section
- Management Office
- Regional Security Office

Department of Homeland Security

- Immigration and Customs Enforcement Attaché Office (ICE) (including Customs and Border Protection)
- Transportation Security Administration (TSA)
- US Coast Guard Marine Inspection Detachment Singapore

Other Agencies and Sections

- US Commercial Service
- Defense Attaché Office
- Drug Enforcement Administration
- Federal Aviation Administration
- Office of Agriculture Affairs
- Office of Defense Cooperation

Source: Embassy of the United States Singapore [www].

---

notably the Soviet Union and the United States – have found their embassies to be excellent forward bases from which to conduct political operations. Such operations might be aimed at propping up a friendly regime or undermining a hostile one, and involve anything from the secret channelling to the friendly faction of funds, arms and medical supplies, to organizing a military coup against the opposition. Zbigniew Brzezinski, who saw no use for embassies before he joined Jimmy Carter's administration, wanted the US ambassador in Tehran to persuade the Iranian military to seize power. The ambassador had no objection to this in principle, opposing it only on the grounds that it would not work.

Resident missions have also proved useful to some states in providing cover for the prosecution of their wars. These include wars against exiled opposition movements, and even other states. It is notorious that North African and Middle Eastern embassies have been involved in this sort of activity. As for US embassies, since 9/11 many of them have become 'command posts in the war on terror' and witnessed a major influx of military personnel – including members of special forces, as well as military propagandists. Better resourced than the civilians, as well as increasingly numerous, these personnel have quite changed the character of many missions and, with the tacit encouragement of the Pentagon and the Bush White House, presented a serious challenge to the traditional idea that a US embassy consists of a 'country team' of which the ambassador is in charge (*Foreign Service Journal*, 2007a: 55–6; 2007b). British embassies in countries, such as Turkey, that were neutral in World War II served exactly the same military purposes – and had exactly the same problems, especially with the hell-raisers of the Special Operations Executive (SOE) (Berridge 2009: ch. 8).

Finally, embassies might well be useful in conducting relations between hostile states on the territory of a third. If the United States and the PRC had not both had resident missions in such places as Geneva, Warsaw, and Paris, a channel of communication that played an important role in limiting their conflict and ultimately in facilitating their *rapprochement*, would have been unavailable (Berridge 1994: ch. 5). Similarly, communication between the United States and the Socialist Republic of Vietnam was facilitated by their missions in Bangkok, and between the United States and North Korea by their missions in Beijing. Following a breach in relations, disguised embassies might serve the same purpose (see Chapter 13).

The embassy has also proved remarkably adaptable to changed circumstances, including increased violence against its buildings and staff, and budget cuts imposed or threatened by legislators at home. To improve security, the design, building standards, and location of new embassies – especially those of the United States – have, where possible, been changed to make them less vulnerable to car and truck bombs (Berridge and James: 134–5; *Inman Report*). To achieve economies, as well as increase local knowledge and institutional memory, many more locally engaged staff ('Foreign Service Nationals', in US embassies) are being employed; they raise security concerns, but are much cheaper to hire than staff sent from home. This trend can even be seen in the PRC, which abandoned a long-established prohibition on the employment of locally engaged staff in the mid-1990s (Xiaohong Liu: 165). The missions of some closely aligned states, particularly the Nordic countries and those within the EU, have also begun to share premises. This 'co-location' of posts obviously facilitates coordination of local tactics and information pooling, as well as saving money. And a recent trend in American practice is to concentrate certain embassy functions in major embassies or consular posts, such as the US embassy in Singapore, which is a major 'regional platform' for south-east Asia. Perhaps the most extra-ordinary evidence of the adaptability of the embassy, however, is the appearance of the 'flat-pack' or 'rapid reaction' embassy. This is a basic facility which, flat-packed and containerized – along with equipment and essential supplies – can be swiftly assembled in a city where peace has only recently been restored and where any former building might still be unsafe to occupy. A British embassy of this sort was established in Baghdad in early May 2003.

Summary

The resident embassy, concerning which obituaries were so confidently drafted in the 1970s and early 1980s, is still alive. It has survived the communications and transport revolutions, chiefly because it remains an excellent means by which to support, if not lead in, the execution of key diplomatic functions. However, it is also versatile and adaptable, and enjoys a strong legal regime in the Vienna Convention on Diplomatic Relations. Furthermore, the communications revolution has made it both more responsive and more able to make inputs into policy-making at home. It is not surprising that the death of the resident ambassador has been indefinitely postponed.

Further reading

Berridge, G. R. and Alan James, *A Dictionary of Diplomacy*, 2nd edn (Palgrave Macmillan: Basingstoke/New York, 2003). Includes the full text of the VCDR and 'A Guide to the Key Articles' by Lorna Lloyd.

Berridge, G. R. (ed.), *Diplomatic Classics: Selected texts from Commynes to Vattel* (Palgrave Macmillan: Basingstoke/New York, 2004).

Berridge, G. R., 'The counter-revolution in diplomatic practice', *Quaderni di Scienza Politica*, 1 April 2005.

Berridge, G. R., *British Diplomacy in Turkey, 1583 to the Present: A study in the evolution of the resident embassy* (Martinus Nijhoff: Leiden, 2009).

Cleverley, J. Michael, 'How to measure an ambassador', *Foreign Service Journal*, March 2007 [www].

Cradock, P., *Experiences of China* (Murray: London, 1994).

Denza, E., *Diplomatic Law: A commentary on the Vienna Convention on Diplomatic Relations*, 3rd edn (Oxford University Press: Oxford, 2009).

Edwards, R. D., *True Brits: Inside the Foreign Office* (BBC Books: London, 1994).

Faber, R., *A Chain of Cities: Diplomacy at the end of empire* (Radcliffe Press: London/New York, 2000): esp. ch. 10.

Foreign Service Journal, 'Focus on Iraq and the FS', March 2006 [www].

Foreign Service Journal, 'Embassies as command posts in the war on terror', March 2007a [www].

Foreign Service Journal, 'Focus on country team management', December 2007b [www].

Gotlieb, A., *I'll be with you in a minute, Mr. Ambassador: The education of a Canadian diplomat in Washington* (University of Toronto Press: Toronto, 1991).

Henderson, N., *Mandarin: The diaries of an ambassador, 1969–1982* (Weidenfeld & Nicolson: London, 1994).

Inman Report, Report of the Secretary of State's Advisory Panel on Overseas Security (1985) [www].

Kaiser, P. M., *Journeying Far and Wide: A political and diplomatic memoir* (Scribner's: New York, 1992): esp. 262–99.

Kerley, E. L., 'Some aspects of the Vienna Conference on Diplomatic Intercourse and Immunities', *American Journal of International Law*, 56, 1962.

Lloyd, Lorna, *Diplomacy with a Difference: The Commonwealth office of high commissioner, 1880–2006* (Martinus Nijhoff: Leiden/Boston, 2007).

Loeffler, Jane, C., *The Architecture of Diplomacy: Building America's embassies* (Princeton Architectural Press: New York, 1998).

Loeffler, Jane, C., 'Fortress America', *Foreign Policy*, September/October 2007.

Melissen, Jan (ed.), *Innovation in Diplomatic Practice* (Macmillan – now Palgrave: Basingstoke, 1999): ch. 12.

Meyer, Christopher, *DC Confidential* (Weidenfeld & Nicolson: London, 2005).

Mustard, Allan, 'Recalling all-purpose duty in Russia', *Foreign Service Journal*, May 2007 [www].

Newhouse, John, 'Diplomacy, Inc.: The influence of lobbies on US foreign policy', *Foreign Affairs*, May/June 2009.

Office of Inspector General [US Dept of State], *Semiannual Reports to the Congress* [www].

Parsons, A., *The Pride and the Fall: Iran 1974–1979* (Cape: London, 1984).

Rana, K. S., *Inside Diplomacy* (Manas: New Delhi, 2000).

Shaw, M. N., *International Law*, 6th edn (Cambridge University Press: Cambridge, 2008): 750–72.

Stearns, M., *Talking to Strangers: Improving American diplomacy at home and abroad* (Princeton University Press: Princeton, NJ, 1996): esp. chs 5, 7 and 8.

Sullivan, W. H., *Mission to Iran* (Norton: New York, 1981).

Wolfe, R., 'Still lying abroad? On the institution of the resident ambassador', *Diplomacy and Statecraft*, 9(2), July 1998.

Wolfe, R. (ed.), *Diplomatic Missions: The ambassador in Canadian foreign policy* (School of Policy Studies, Canadian Centre for Foreign Policy Development: Queen's University, Kingston, Ontario, 1998).

Xiaohong Liu, *Chinese Ambassadors: The rise of diplomatic professionalism since 1945* (University of Washington Press: Seattle/London, 2001): chs 7, 8 and conclusion.

Young, John W., *Twentieth Century Diplomacy: A case study of British practice, 1963–1976* (Cambridge University Press: Cambridge, 2008): ch. 4.

8
Consulates

'Welcome to the Consulate in Lille', says the website of the British embassy at Paris beneath the heading 'Consulate-General in Lille', thereby neatly making the point that although, technically, a consulate is only one kind of consular post, in common usage it is the term used to describe them all. Only pedants, protocol departments and lexicologists wince at this and hasten to point out that consulates are distinct because there are vice-consulates on which they might look *down*, as well as consulates-*general* to which they must look *up*. This chapter therefore discusses all of them – as, indeed, also the consular sections of embassies, even though international law is unclear as to whether the latter should be treated as consulates.

Consulates today are attracting unprecedented attention. What are their origins? Why do they no longer inhabit what D. C. M. Platt, the historian of British consuls, called a 'Cinderella Service'? Why are they now so important? How is their work organized?

Merchants' representatives to public servants

The consulates of European states, which were first established chiefly around the Mediterranean and its adjacent seas, had their origins in international trade. When cargo vessels from distant lands arrived in a port, the scope for misunderstanding and trouble was obvious. Sailors speaking strange tongues, displaying unusual habits, and – having been cooped up at sea, sometimes for months – soon drunk, were rarely impressive advertisements for their homelands. Attitudes to commercial dealings and the civil and criminal law generally were also often at serious odds, especially when religions were different. To make matters worse, there was usually intense competition between ship-owners from different states; and, where foreign merchants settled and formed a community at an important port, they needed to be internally regulated, as well as defended against rivals and rapacious local officials. If trade between distant lands was to flourish, therefore, there had to be some representative of the merchants in the ports who had the authority and ability to sort out these problems. Enter the consul: spokesman for the merchants and, where this suited the local authorities – as in the Ottoman Empire – magistrate over them. Consuls appointed by Italian merchant colonies in the Levant pre-dated the emergence of the resident embassy in the late 1400s by at least three centuries, and probably encouraged it (Mattingly: 63).

The first consuls, then, were part-timers: merchants chosen from the ranks of a local trading settlement by the merchants themselves. They were supported financially by the small tax they were permitted to charge on the goods moving through their settlements ('consulage'), as well as by what they earned from their private trading; their duties concerned exclusively the affairs of their fellow merchants. In short, although home government authorization might sometimes be given to them and minor political duties performed in return (Mattingly: 63–4; Busk: 125), the first consuls were, in general, neither appointed nor paid by the state, and had nothing to do with advancing its interests, except indirectly.

In Britain, it was only in the middle of the seventeenth century that the state began to assert its control over the consuls and require them both to take on additional responsibilities (notably the organization of naval supplies) and place the national interest first: at this point only did private sector spokesmen become public servants (Platt 1971: ch. 1). But even after a partial reorganization in the early nineteenth century, many consuls – especially at minor posts – still survived for years on the basis of fees and private trading. These 'trading consuls', as they were known, were unpopular at home but they were cheap (Berridge 2009: ch. 4). It was to be the beginning of the twentieth century before the general consular service in Britain was put on a modern footing, although the French service had long been much better organized, as had certain specialized services in Britain itself, among them the Levant Service.

Amalgamation with the diplomatic service

Until well into the twentieth century, there was an entrenched view among diplomats not only that consular work and diplomacy were quite different, but also that a person suited to the one was not suited to the other. Diplomats busied themselves at royal courts and foreign ministries, where refined manners and the self-assurance that came from an aristocratic lineage were essential. By contrast, consuls, who were of middle-class origin, grubbed around in seaports and needed limited ambitions and the rough and ready ways of the tough ships' captains and corrupt provincial officials with whom they had to deal. Clearly, so the argument went, they had neither the money to live in the style of a diplomat nor the personal qualities necessary to deal with foreign leaders as equals.

From this perspective, therefore, it was entirely appropriate that there should be completely separate diplomatic and consular services. This also had the effect of making it still more unlikely that even the most outstanding consul-general would be able to obtain promotion to a diplomatic post, although in some states – such as Austria-Hungary – this was easier than in others. This state of affairs was deeply resented by the consuls.

By the late nineteenth century, consuls were engaged in a much broader range of duties – in the Ottoman Empire there were even many 'political consuls' – and they were shaking off their seaport image. Conversely, diplomats were being forced more and more to support the commerce of their nationals. In other words, the differences between diplomatic and consular work were eroding. The result was that a consul or consul-general at an important post was usually doing more or less the same kind of work in relation to a regional authority that a diplomat was doing in relation to the central government. In the embassy itself (which by then might also have a consular section), and especially in the European embassy in the east (where members of specialized consular services had usually come to take the senior positions in the 'oriental secretariat' or 'dragomanate'), the consuls might even find themselves doing most of the work of the diplomats, while the latter spent much of their time riding, picnicking, or bathing in local waters. For their troubles, the consuls were paid far less and often treated with breathtaking condescension. An easing of transfers between the services was not the solution to this situation: such concessions were seen by the consuls as acts of grace by the high and mighty aristocratic establishment that monopolized the diplomatic career. What the consuls began to push for instead was *amalgamation*: the creation of a unified foreign service in which, at least in principle, there was no such thing as 'a consul for life'.

Fortunately, in the late nineteenth century, political and social attitudes were slowly changing. It was beginning to be felt, even by some diplomats, that it was not only unfair, but also imprudent to deny diplomatic appointments to persons who were perfectly qualified for them in every way except for the fact that they had previously been a consul and came from the wrong social class. In a situation where the best person could not be placed in a vacant diplomatic post, and where there was contempt on the one hand and envy on the other, the first casualty was efficiency. Eventually, therefore, the consuls got their way. In the United States, the separate diplomatic and consular services were amalgamated by the Rogers Act of 1924, although it was not until 1943, as part of the general reform of the 'foreign service', that the same step was taken in Britain. The white paper announcing the change in Britain said:

> What is aimed at it is wider training and equality of opportunity for all. Every officer of the combined Service will be called upon to serve in consular and commercial diplomatic as well as in diplomatic posts and in the Foreign Office and will have the opportunity of rising to the highest posts. Interchange between the different branches, and between posts at home and those abroad, will be facilitated with the object of giving every man as wide an experience as possible and of enabling the best man to be sent to any vacant post (HCPP 1943, para. 6).

In the course of the twentieth century, the diplomatic and consular services of most other states were also amalgamated; for example, Germany in 1918, Norway in 1922, Spain in 1928, Belgium in 1946, and Italy in 1952.

A separate activity, if not a separate service

A strong trend towards the administrative fusion of their previously separate services, and a growing overlap between what consuls and diplomats actually did, there might have been. Nevertheless, it is still true, as the quotation from the British white paper of 1943 unmistakeably implied, that there remained – and remains – a great deal of difference between *typical* consular work and *typical* diplomatic work. (This is why the currently fashionable term 'consular diplomacy' is unhelpful.) The former deals chiefly with the problems of individuals and corporate bodies; the latter is concerned mainly with issues of general policy in intergovernmental relations, especially those of a political nature. Besides, a sending state can only establish one embassy in a receiving state; if it needs representation in provincial ports and inland cities, it must have posts of a different kind where the mission premises and staff, lacking the full representative character of the embassy and usually handling matters of less political sensitivity, will not be justified in claiming quite the same privileges and immunities. Traditionally, such posts have been called consulates and, until very recently, no one appears to have seen any reason to change the designation. So, while separate consular *services* might have been abandoned, consuls and consulates remain.

Reflecting this understanding that consular work remains a distinct activity, separate consular corps in major cities, as well as in major provincial centres, remain alive and well; for example, the Washington consular corps as well as the North Carolina consular corps. Analogous to the diplomatic corps (see Chapter 7), the consular corps is often better organized and more collegial; this is probably because of its relatively non-political interests and its strong leaven of honorary consuls who are either nationals or permanent residents of the same country – the receiving state (see p. 136). The consular corps of New York City, organized in 1925 into the Society of Foreign Consuls, claims to be the largest in the world. In the United States, where consuls are numerous and particularly well-organized, there is even a National Association of Foreign Consuls with its own 'Consular Corps College'. In Britain, the Manchester Consular Association, founded in 1882, claims to be one of the oldest in the world.

Recognition that consular work was a separate activity was acknowledged when the customary and treaty law on consuls was codified and amended in a separate multilateral convention in 1963: the Vienna Convention on Consular Relations (VCCR). This convention neither overrode existing bilateral consular treaties nor precluded the negotiation of new ones. Nevertheless, it became 'an accepted guide to international practice' (Gore-Booth 1979: 212) and, in so doing, brought the privileges and immunities of consuls closer to those of diplomats, although differences remain (see Box 8.1). In insisting on these differences, the conference held at Vienna in 1963 that produced the final convention played a more significant role than the ILC, the final draft of which had gone much further to assimilate consular into diplomatic law, notably by assigning complete inviolability to consular premises (ILC, 'Consular Intercourse and Immunities'). What is the burden of consular work today?

Box 8.1   **The main differences between diplomatic and consular privileges and immunities**

Immunity from jurisdiction

Consular officers and employees are immune from the jurisdiction of the receiving state's courts and administrative authorities only in respect of their official acts. By contrast, diplomats generally enjoy this immunity in respect of their private acts as well; as, indeed, where criminal jurisdiction is concerned, do members of the administrative and technical staff of embassies.

Liability to give evidence

Consular officers might be called upon to give evidence at judicial or administrative proceedings (except in matters connected with the exercise of their functions), although not under threat of coercive measure or penalty. By contrast, diplomatic agents are under no such obligation.

Personal inviolability

In the case of a grave crime, a consular officer might be liable to arrest or detention pending trial; required to appear in court in person, if facing a criminal charge; and be imprisoned in execution of a final judgement. By contrast, the personal inviolability of a diplomatic agent is unqualified.

Inviolability of premises

Consular premises may be entered by the authorities of the receiving state without the express consent of the head of the post 'in case of fire or other disaster requiring prompt protective action', and may also be expropriated with compensation. By contrast, inviolability in the case of embassies is unqualified.

The private residence of a career consular officer (including the head of a consular post) is not part of 'consular premises', and so does not enjoy its inviolability or protection. By contrast, the private residence of a diplomatic agent shares these rights in equal measure with the premises of the diplomatic mission.

Freedom of communication: the consular bag

A suspect consular bag may – if a request to open it is refused – be sent back. By contrast, no diplomatic bag may be detained, let alone opened.

Consular functions

The work of consuls is famously rich in variety and is easily appreciated by looking at the list of consular functions in Article 5 of the VCCR, or at the consular services page of the website of any large embassy or consulate-general. A more detailed list of consular functions can be seen in the European Convention on Consular Functions (1967), the handiwork of a committee of experts appointed by the Council of Europe in 1960. This has not entered into force, most European states seeming to prefer the greater flexibility afforded by the VCCR's more summary treatment of consular functions; its list is also not exhaustive, although certainly exhausting. Nevertheless, the European Convention's influence should not be discounted because of the great political and economic weight of Europe, and the continuing use of west European consular practice as a model in the world beyond (Lee and Quigley: 113).

Reflecting their origins, many consuls are still greatly preoccupied with encouraging the exports of their countries in the receiving state, promoting inward investment, and – depending on their location – supervising and assisting, as need arises, the progress of any national flag shipping and aircraft. However, commercial work is less characteristic today of the consular sections of embassies (see p. 119), since the large embassies, at least, now tend to have separate commercial sections. More characteristic of their daily diet, as also a high priority of the consular posts in the provinces, is providing help to any nationals in need. This is to be expected because the modern media coverage of this aspect of consular work makes it probably the most important activity by which the diplomatic service, as a whole, is judged.

As foreign travel has become easier and cheaper, so population movements across national frontiers have increased enormously, whether for purposes of holiday, education, business, political asylum, or better paid employment. For example, in recent years hundreds of thousands of skilled and semi-skilled workers have flooded out of India to the oil-rich states of the Gulf and north Africa (Rana 2000: 198), while the number of overseas trips from the United Kingdom has tripled in the last 20 years (FCO 2007: 27). Many states now have large communities of their nationals living permanently abroad; in 2005, Britain had over 13 million (National Audit Office: 8).

Whatever their reasons for being abroad, individuals might find they need the services of one of their consuls. It might be for a relatively routine matter, such as the issue or renewal of a passport, the registration of a birth or death, or the issue or witnessing of a certificate of life – a document verifying that a retired person living abroad is still alive and entitled to continue receiving a pension from home. However, individuals might also need a consul when they are in difficulty or acute distress, whether because they have lost a passport, had an accident, fallen ill, been a victim of crime, arrested on a charge of committing a crime, been caught up in a natural disaster such as the Asian tsunami that devastated holiday resorts around the Indian Ocean in December 2004, or found themselves in the middle of a civil emergency such as the fighting in Lebanon in the summer of 2006. In situations such as these, consuls are required to do anything from providing new travel documents, advising on local lawyers, visiting in prisons, trying to trace the missing, arranging evacuation – and, all the while, keeping family at home in the picture. In the worst cases, consuls help to identify the dead, look after such of their relatives and friends as might fly out, and make arrangements for funerals or (if necessary) the transport home of bodies or ashes. In *True Brits*, there is a grim photograph of a British vice-consul in Bangkok overseeing the cremation of a British national who died in the city, one of an average of six a month with whose deaths he was dealing; he was known as the 'Death Man' (Edwards: 172). The stresses of this kind of consular work are not made easier by the public's unreasonably high expectations of what consuls can do for them. They might not be expected to revive the dead, but many of those thrown into foreign prisons assume that their consul will be able to secure their immediate release. Others behave so badly abroad that the odd consul, weary of having to clear up after them and ashamed of their behaviour, resigns in disgust (see Box 8.2).

Another consular responsibility that is related to the last function – now, more so than ever – is that of information gathering. As with embassies, consulates have always been required to report on conditions and likely developments in their regions, although it has traditionally been commercial and, to a lesser degree, political intelligence that they were expected to supply. But, a priority now is reporting on

---

Box 8.2   Disgusted in Ibiza

In August 1998, after only 18 months at his post, the locally engaged British Vice-Consul on the Spanish holiday island of Ibiza, Michael Birkett, resigned in disgust at the way too many young Brits behaved when they turned up in their hundreds of thousands for sun, sex, booze, and drugs. 'I have always been proud to be British', he told *The Mail on Sunday*, 'but these degenerates are dragging us through the mud.' The officer who stepped into this particular breach, Helen Watson, was subsequently honoured with the MBE and given a pro-consul. (This is a British term for a senior administrator of a consular post – at a small one, typically a locally engaged individual serving as personal assistant to the head of post.) In 2008, the consulate was renovated and expanded, and opened in the presence of the Under-Secretary of State for Consular Affairs at the Foreign Office, the British Ambassador to Spain, and the President of the Island Council. Not a bad repair job.

conditions that might affect travellers, on the sensible argument that prevention is better than cure. 'Know Before You Go' campaigns and 'Travel Advice', which are prominent features of foreign ministry websites, depend heavily on information supplied by their consular networks. The State Department, for example, has a 'Consular Information Programme' consisting of country specific information, travel warnings, and travel alerts.

A third task that falls to the lot of some consuls, especially those of the richer states in the West, is that of entry clearance: deciding to whom, among the many applicants for travel to their countries, they should issue visas. In light of the spread of poverty, insecurity and disease in many areas of the world, the numbers of those seeking visas for travel to the safer and more prosperous countries has grown enormously; and people-smuggling by organized crime gangs has increased with them. This has produced a mounting concern in the West about a floodtide of immigrants and asylum-seekers. The outbreak of the so-called 'War on Terror' has also produced a much greater anxiety about the sort of people who are trying to cross borders, as well as about their numbers.

There is great variation in the emphasis given to the work of sifting travellers not only between consulates of the same diplomatic service located in different countries (not all are in 'migration hotspots'), but also between diplomatic services themselves. In Britain, for example, a great deal of the burden of processing potential immigrants is placed on consular posts, whereas in others, such as France, most of this is done at home. The British view, which is similar to that of America, is that, although expensive, offshore migration control reduces delays at ports of entry, facilitates investigation of the applicants' circumstances, and minimizes their inconvenience – especially if they are refused. Another probable reason is the avoidance of heartrending scenes at ports and airports, and fear of what the media would do with them. In migration hotspots in Africa and the Asian sub-continent, consular posts are increasingly outsourcing the more routine aspects of visa work to private sector companies, thereby allowing more time for consular visa staff to concentrate on difficult cases.

Where there are normal relations but there is no diplomatic mission, a consular post might also be employed – subject to the approval of the receiving state – to perform *diplomatic* functions. On grounds of economy, this idea was strongly canvassed by the smaller states at the Vienna Conference in 1963, although it is impossible to tell the extent to which it has been put into practice. It appears not to be popular, and why should it be? A poor state wishing to put some flesh on its diplomatic relations with another state can always concurrently appoint to it an ambassador based in a neighbouring country. And if it wants, instead, a permanent representation by career officers, it might as well designate it an embassy rather than a consulate, which will be more flattering to everyone concerned and give its staff more privileges and immunities. On the other hand, sometimes an existing embassy has to be closed for reasons of economy, and it might prove useful to be able to transfer its functions to an existing consulate. Furthermore, use of an *honorary* consulate for diplomatic purposes saves money and might play some such role, provided the consul is not a national of the receiving state.

The least advertised role of consular posts, as with embassies, is providing cover for spies and serving as instruments of political warfare. In World War II, Britain's consulates in neutral Turkey were even used by SOE agents as dumps for explosives, in case the country should seem in danger of falling to Nazi Germany and it would be necessary to blow up key installations (Berridge 2009: ch. 8). It is not just the consulates of major powers that might be used for political purposes, as was vividly demonstrated by the activities in 2001 of the consulate of the Afghan Taliban regime in the Pakistani port city of Karachi. The head of this mission had supported Islamic movements in the country and addressed rallies in protest at Pakistan's pro-NATO policy. This, however, was obviously going too far, and the consulate was subsequently closed down by order of the government in Islamabad.

Career consuls

Career consular officers are so called in order to distinguish them from honorary consular officers, not to suggest that they are consuls for life, as would have been the case prior to the early twentieth century. They are members of a foreign service who happen to have a consular posting at the time but might have come from – and, in future, be destined for – a diplomatic posting. They are found in the consular sections of embassies (discussed separately later in the chapter), but chiefly at posts in the provinces of the receiving state, typically in major ports and inland cities. In descending rank order, these posts can be consulates-general, consulates, or vice-consulates, depending on the size of their staff or district, their importance, or the personal status of their head of post. Vice-consuls might be found in consulates (strictly defined), and both vice-consuls and consuls might be found in consulates-general, although the last is always headed by a consul-general.

In theory, this traditional hierarchy suggests a pyramidal structure, with a broad base of numerous vice-consulates tapering upwards to just a few consulates-general at the top. However, in practice, this was only ever seen, as a rule, with the consular networks of major or medium powers in receiving states of particular importance to them – as when, in 1879, Britain had 30 vice-consulates, 9 consulates, and only 4 consulates-general in the Ottoman Empire. Today, a pyramidal structure of career consular posts is difficult to discern, even in similar situations to this. In fact, the picture is often turned upside down: vice-consulates (as opposed to vice-consuls) have virtually disappeared, while consulates, and especially consulates-general, have multiplied. The Dutch and the British still use vice-consulates occasionally, especially on islands such as Ibiza; and the American 'presence post' – with its single foreign service officer – looks very much like a vice-consulate by another name. But most states appear to have consigned them, along with the diplomatic legation, to the past, and chiefly for the same reason – their lowly status makes them unflattering to both the receiving local authorities and to those who have to run them. France, for example, has a total of only 4 vice-consulates against 97 consulates-general and consulates. Nevertheless, it must not be concluded that the disappearance of the pyramidal structure of career consular posts means the disappearance altogether of the pyramidal structure of consular representation as a whole, as we shall see in a moment.

Many states have a number of consular posts in countries where they have important interests, and where many of their citizens are regular visitors and permanent residents. In France, for example, Britain has a consulate-general at Lille and consulates at Bordeaux, Marseilles, and Lyons. These are supplemented by numerous honorary consulates and consular correspondents (explained later in the chapter). Each post has its own consular 'district' (see Box 8.3).

All consular posts are formally subordinate to their 'sovereign' embassy in the state in which they are established. This no longer extends to hiring and firing consular staff, as it often did in earlier centuries, but it still gives an ambassador a considerable degree of authority over the general lines of their conduct. As subordinate posts, therefore, and except in emergencies, consulates usually take their orders from the embassy and report to it. (By the same token, those vice-consulates that remain are superintended by consulates.) Nevertheless, a consul-general in a major provincial city might accept this subordination only with reluctance and, in practice, act in some respects as if it did not exist. It can well be imagined that this is particularly likely to be so if the post is

---

Box 8.3   Consular districts

When a state has more than one consulate in a particular receiving state, each is given a 'district' in which to exercise its functions. If the receiving state is large and the number of consulates is relatively small, the districts will inevitably extend far beyond the urban area in which they are located. The district covered by the British Consulate-General in Lille, for example, includes all five of the northernmost *départements* of France: Nord, Pas-de-Calais, Somme, Aisne and Ardennes. But this is nothing compared to the jurisdiction of the Indian Consulate-General at San Francisco, where Kishan Rana, the author of *Inside Diplomacy* (see 'Further reading'), was once head of post. This embraces Alaska, Arizona, California, Colorado, Hawaii, Idaho, Montana, Nebraska, New Mexico, Nevada, Oregon, Utah, Washington, and Wyoming.

---

physically remote from the capital, as is, say, Perth in Western Australia or any of the major cities on the west coast of the United States; it is likely to be even more so if the consul-general had previously been an ambassador. It is not necessary to look far to find such cases (Berridge 2009: ch. 10).

Consulates have always placed great reliance on locally engaged staff, and this has increased even more in recent years: some posts are run entirely by nationals of the receiving state or permanent residents who are nationals of the sending state. Another trend – prompted by concerns over security, as well as economy, especially on the part of the United States – has been the creation of 'virtual consulates'. These are websites that are locally branded and customized, although they are ideally supplemented by periodic visits to the region in question by staff from the nearest 'real' consular post or embassy, and also by cultural and commercial initiatives, telephone links, and video-conferencing facilities.

Honorary consuls

At this point, it is appropriate to consider those consular officers who have, to some extent, rescued the pyramidal structure of consular representation as a whole; namely, honorary consuls and their close cousins – consular agents and consular correspondents. These represent the second category of consular officers.

At the ILC in 1960, honorary consuls were reckoned to be in charge of half of all of the consulates in the world (ILC 1960: vol. 1, 171). But they were thought by some of the jurists – and hoped by others, as earlier by the League of Nations Committee of Experts for the Progressive Codification of International Law – to be on the way out (Lee and Quigley: 515–16). The Soviet Union and its client states, together with the PRC, regarded them as nothing more than bourgeois spies and, with little tourism in either direction, had little use for them in any case; accordingly, they refused either to appoint or accept them. Other states were less squeamish and more in need of their services.

Honorary consuls are usually nationals of the receiving state with close connections to the sending state, or nationals of the sending state permanently resident in the receiving state; in either case, they know their way around. Honorary consuls are frequently self-employed businessmen, shipping agents, or professionals of one sort or another who have control over their own time. They undertake the role on a part-time basis; and they are paid (at most) a small salary (usually none at all), fees for certain services, and their expenses. Under the VCCR, they enjoy more limited privileges and immunities than career consular officers, largely because of their more limited functions and the suspicion of not being entirely respectable that they have tended to attract. The sad, whisky-drenched character of Charley Fortnum in Graham Greene's novel *The Honorary Consul* has probably done nothing for the reputation of the institution either. Fortnum supplemented his income by importing, duty free, and then selling a new Cadillac every two years, although he had redeeming features.

While some honorary consuls simply like helping people in difficulties, it is usually assumed that most of them undertake the responsibility chiefly for the social, commercial, and other advantages generated by its prestige. Honorary consuls can at least fly the national flag, display the national coat-of-arms, and have freedom of official communication; they have the same immunity from jurisdiction in respect of their official acts as career consular officers; and, among other things, they are entitled to especially respectful treatment in the event that criminal proceedings are instigated against them.

Despite the arrival of virtual consulates, honorary consulates, at least, are not in retreat; on the contrary, since the 1960s resort to them has been steadily growing. They found vigorous – even outspoken – support in the ILC and at the Vienna Conference in 1963 – especially from the Scandinavian countries, and the separate chapter on them in the VCCR both stabilized and legitimized their role. The United States, it is true, still does not appoint honorary consuls, and – although it has accepted them since 1895 – as with some European countries, it no longer admits those appointed for purely political or honorific reasons

(Dunham; Rana 2004: 239, n. 35); the PRC still holds out against them altogether. But China is now alone among major states in this regard. The Soviet Bloc began to relent on its hard line in the 1970s, and the later collapse of the Soviet Union itself merely accelerated the process. The Russian Federation now embraces honorary consuls, as do the numerous states formerly in the Soviet orbit (Lee and Quigley: vii, 518).

States that have traditionally had large merchant fleets, as well as the many poor countries in the modern world, depend heavily on honorary consuls, despite the fact that they are usually unable to offer the full range of consular services. In 2008, the representation in the United States of Iceland – then still rich, as well as small – consisted of an embassy in Washington, a consulate-general in New York, and 20 honorary consulates in major cities across the country. In 2009, 400 of Sweden's 413 consular posts were honorary ones. But even larger states also find them immensely useful. For example, in 2009 Germany had 35 honorary consuls in the United States, in addition to its 8 consulates-general and its embassy; it had 350 honorary consuls worldwide.

The base of the pyramid of consular representation is broadened further by consular agencies, although this venerable institution is more problematic. The VCCR identifies consular agents as a class of the category of *career* consular officer – the lowliest, ranking below vice-consuls – but not all states accept this or even recognize the term, and practice varies among those that do.

In Britain, 'consular agent' (or 'commercial agent') was actually the title first given to those now more often called 'honorary consuls', the preference for the latter title gradually gaining ground in the twentieth century because it sounded better to the ears of 'merchants of standing' and gave them an edge in the tussle over precedence in the consular corps of provincial ports and cities – although the need for grander titles for these purposes had been recognized in parliament much earlier (HCPP 1858: *passim*; HCPP, 1872: paras 2313–36). 'Honorary Consul-General' sounded even better. Similarly, in the French service, the terms 'honorary consul' and 'consular agent' are virtually synonymous. The United States employs consular agents and pays them according to how much work they do, but this is exceptional: generally, there is little doubt that they are 'more akin to honorary consuls than career consuls' (Lee and Quigley: 35). In other words, consular agents are either a component of, or identical to, the *category* of honorary consuls, rather than being a fourth *class* of the category of career consuls. The functions of consular agencies also vary: some, such as the 'Honorary British Consular Agent' at Nis in Serbia, have responsibility only for the protection and relief of distressed nationals; others have more extensive duties. In 2009, the United States operated 14 consular agencies in Mexico, all of which were explicitly described as 'extensions' of their superintending consular posts in the country, including the embassy in Mexico City.

The final addition to the pyramidal base to be noted is the consular correspondent, an individual employed by states such as Italy, the Netherlands and Britain. Such persons are voluntary representatives who serve as contact points between a consular post and a particular section of the community of their nationals resident in the receiving state. Their liaison role is particularly useful when such a group finds itself in a hostile environment, as is the case with the British community in Zimbabwe. It is a moot point whether consular correspondents are 'consular officers' in the meaning of the VCCR.

Consular sections

Last, but by no means least, it is necessary to say a few words about the consular sections of embassies, which are staffed chiefly by career consular officers. Most embassies had been concerned with consular affairs in their immediate vicinity long before the twentieth century, especially when the capital city in which they were located was also a major port, as in the case of Constantinople. In these circumstances, consular matters might be dealt with in a separate building, closer to the dockside – but still close enough to the embassy to be regarded as, more or less, a part of it. Sometimes, the head of a diplomatic mission, whether the capital was a port or not, even doubled as consul-general, as at the British missions in Tokyo, Tehran, Cairo, and elsewhere. Nevertheless, encouraged by the merging of the two services and the need to reduce expenses, following World War I a trend developed physically to re-house consular staff within the embassy proper (Strang: 124; ILC 1961: vol. 1, 271). But numerous anomalies remain. For example, the consular 'section' of the British embassy in Paris, at 35 rue du Faubourg St Honoré, is still located some distance away in the rue d'Anjou; it is also described officially as the 'British Consulate-General'.

Only larger embassies tend to have whole sections devoted to consular affairs. At the other extreme, some embassies are so small that one officer has to combine functions of both a consular and diplomatic character. But, whether in a full section or not, the discharge of consular functions by the embassy has another great advantage to the sending state: the consular staff has full diplomatic privileges and immunities, awkward though this is for the functional theory of these immunities. This was useful to the representation of Western states in Moscow during the Cold War (ILC 1961: vol. 1, 7), and it remains useful to many states today. In this connection, it is a striking fact that, in 2009, over half of the states with embassies in London had no consular representation – honorary or career – outside the capital but all handled consular affairs themselves. Whether this is to the advantage of their own citizens is another matter.

Summary

Consulates have a longer history than the resident embassy. In the twentieth century, consular services merged with diplomatic services, and the differences between their respective privileges and immunities narrowed. But typical consular work remains, in many respects, different from typical diplomatic work, and is often more stressful; this is why it tends to be less popular. This is a pity because consulates are the foreign service's shop window to both foreigners and its own nationals abroad. To the latter, this should represent protection; to the former, a warm welcome if entry can be permitted, and a polite and regretful farewell if it cannot. As international trade has expanded (at least, until recently) and population movements have increased dramatically, the demand for consular services has grown commensurately. This is why the consular representation of larger states still tends to have a pyramidal structure, even though, for reasons of economy, honorary consuls now play an even more important role in supporting the broad base. Nevertheless, many smaller states rely entirely on the consular sections of their embassies. In Chapter 13, we shall see how consular posts also play an important role when diplomatic relations are severed.

Further reading

Berridge, G. R., *British Diplomacy in Turkey, 1583 to the Present: A study in the evolution of the resident embassy* (Martinus Nijhoff: Leiden, 2009): ch. 4.

Coates, P. D., *The China Consuls: British consular officers, 1843–1943* (Oxford University Press: Oxford, 1988).

Dickie, John, *The British Consul: Heir to a great tradition* (Hurst: London, 2007).

Edwards, R. D., *True Brits: Inside the Foreign Office* (BBC Books: London, 1994): ch. 11.

European Convention on Consular Relations (1967) [www].

FCO, *Delivering Change Together: The consular strategy, 2007–2010*, 2007 [www].

Godsey, William D., Jr, *Aristocratic Redoubt: The Austro-Hungarian Foreign Office on the eve of the First World War* (Purdue University Press: West Lafayette, IN, 1999): 76–81.

Hertz, Martin F. (ed.), *The Consular Dimension of Diplomacy* (University Press of America: Lanham, MD, 1983).

ILC, 'Consular Intercourse and Immunities' [ch. 2], in *Report...to the General Assembly on its work, 1 May–7 July 1961* [www].

Lee, Luke T. and John Quigley, *Consular Law and Practice*, 3rd edn (Oxford University Press: Oxford, 2008).

Mattingly, Garrett, *Renaissance Diplomacy* (Penguin Books: Harmondsworth, 1965): 63–4.

National Audit Office, *Consular services to British Nationals: the Foreign and Commonwealth Office* (TSO: London, 2005).

Office of the Historian, Bureau of Public Affairs, *History of the Department of State during the Clinton Presidency (1993–2001)*: ch. 09 ('The Consular Function') [www].

Platt, D. C. M., *The Cinderella Service: British consuls since 1825* (Longman: London, 1971).

Rana, Kishan, *Inside Diplomacy* (Manas Publications: New Delhi, 2000): ch. 8.

Rana, Kishan, *The 21st Century Ambassador* (DiploFoundation: Malta/Geneva, 2004): 154–6.

Rand Europe, *International Review of Consular Services*, Vol. II, 23 June 2005 [www].

Roberts, Sir Ivor (ed.), *Satow's Diplomatic Practice*, 6th edn (Oxford University Press: Oxford, 2009): book V.

Shaw, L. M. E., *The Anglo-Portuguese Alliance and the English Merchants in Portugal, 1654–1810* (Ashgate: Aldershot, 1998): chs 4 and 5.

UN Conference on Consular Relations, Vienna, 4 March–22 April 1963, *Official Records. Vols. I and 2* [www].

Vienna Convention on Consular Relations, 1963 [www].

9
Conferences

If the role of the resident ambassador was modified in the course of the twentieth century, this is, in part, because of the explosion in the number of conferences attended by three or more states – multilateral diplomacy. These conferences vary hugely in subject, scope, size, level of attendance, longevity, and extent of bureaucratization. At one extreme is an *ad hoc* conference on a mundane topic lasting perhaps for a week, and attended at the level of officials and experts; in between will be found an 'informal forum' such as the Group of 20 (see Box 9.1); and, at the other extreme, a major permanent conference, or international organization, such as the United Nations, grappling with many topics of major importance. In 1909, there were already 37 international organizations and, by 1962, the number had risen to 163. In 1985, a peak was reached when the existence of 378 was recorded (IO: 2357). This chapter will consider why this enormous expansion has occurred, and look at the characteristic procedures associated with what, in the earlier decades of the twentieth century, was inevitably called the 'new diplomacy'.

Origins

It is common to assume that multilateral diplomacy is essentially a twentieth-century phenomenon, but its origins lie much earlier. It was important in diplomacy between allies in ancient India, and even in diplomacy beyond alliances in the Greco-Persian world of the fourth century BC (Watson: 91, 85–8). Within the European system of states, somewhat chaotic multilateral conferences devoted to peace settlements (referred to as 'congresses', when of special importance) were a feature of the seventeenth century. Multilateral diplomacy began to take on

---

Box 9.1 The Group of 20 (G20)

This multilateral body received unprecedented attention in late 2008 and early 2009, when the world plunged into deep financial crisis. Comprising finance ministers and central bank governors, it is an informal forum launched in 1999 in order to bring important emerging-market countries into the discussion of key issues of the global economy, hitherto reserved to the G8. Its members are: Argentina, Australia, Brazil, *Canada*, China, EU, *France*, *Germany*, India, Indonesia, *Italy*, *Japan*, Mexico, *Russia*, Saudi Arabia, South Africa, South Korea, Turkey, *UK*, *USA* (G8 members are italicized). The IMF and the World Bank are also strongly represented. The G20 has no permanent staff, continuity being preserved instead by a chair that rotates between member states and is part of a troika of past, present, and future chairs. The state occupying the responsible chair at any one time establishes a temporary secretariat for the duration of its term; this coordinates the group's work and organizes its meetings. In normal times, these meetings occur only once a year, but are usually preceded by two deputies' meetings and much technical work. Because of the seriousness of the financial crisis, the G20 met at summit level in Washington in November 2008 and in London in April 2009.

---

modern form in the early nineteenth century, following the end of the Napoleonic Wars. Since the global states-system of today emerged most directly from the European states-system, the immediate origins of modern multilateral diplomacy are to be found here.

Multilateral conferences emerged most emphatically in the nineteenth century, and blossomed in the twentieth because they were essential to the conduct of negotiations when states became more numerous, the number of international issues multiplied, and more urgency attached to their resolution. A conference is subject-focused and concentrates minds on one issue or series of related issues, brings together all the parties whose agreement is necessary, and encourages informality; its members might even develop a certain *esprit de corps*. It has a president with a vested interest in its success, and – at least if it is an *ad hoc* conference – will provide a deadline to concentrate minds because it cannot go on forever (see Chapter 4). Sir Maurice Hankey, who played such an important role in the development of multilateral diplomacy, laid great stress on the impetus given to this device by 'the perils and the overwhelming press of war business' during the great conflict of 1914–18 (Hankey: 14).

Multilateral diplomacy also owed its growing popularity to the fact that conferences in the European states-system were essentially conferences of the great powers. (Small states were allowed to attend if their vital interests were touched, but were usually condemned to the margins.) They were, therefore, a device for identifying and advertising membership of the great power club. For the state able to play host to such a conference – and thus, by custom, secure the presidency – so much the better; this counted not only in terms of prestige, but also in influence over the conduct of conference business. Because it raised the question of the authority under which the great powers presumed to dispose of the fate of the world, the great power conference was also an unrivalled opportunity to affirm and justify their special rights. Finally, such a conference was a subtle device whereby a great power could express respect for, and a bond of solidarity with, its most dangerous rivals (Webster: 59–6, ch. 9; Bull: ch. 9). With such a calculus of great power interest behind it, it is hardly surprising that multilateral diplomacy should have gathered such momentum once the idea got off the ground. It reached its twentieth-century apogee in the Security Council of the United Nations.

The great power conferences of the nineteenth century that gave birth to the multilateralism of the twentieth might have been important because they advertised the great powers. However, they were also important because they advertised national priorities, and the vastly improved opportunities for propaganda provided by the revolution in mass communications in the twentieth century made the advertising potential of such conferences even more attractive as time passed – for NGOs, as well as states. It is much easier to demonstrate a commitment to the resolution of an urgent international problem by staging a conference on it than it is by discussing the issue through normal diplomatic channels. Even if an invitee thinks that a conference on a subject is untimely, it might find it difficult to resist participation. Apart from the possibility that it might wish to avoid giving offence to the conference sponsors and the fear that any decisions taken in its absence might threaten its interests, it might not wish to risk being thought hostile to its aims. It is in this light that the conference attendance of some states should be seen – not least that of the United States under the presidency of George W. Bush at the rolling conferences of the parties to the UN Framework Convention on Climate Change, which started with the Earth Summit at Rio de Janeiro in 1992.

Conference diplomacy has also prospered because of the impetus that it can give to bilateral diplomacy. This point has two aspects. First, a multilateral conference can provide opportunities for participants to discuss matters outside the formal agenda. This is particularly true of major standing conferences such as the United Nations, and is of special value to states not enjoying diplomatic relations. Second, powerful mediators can hold a multilateral conference in order to kick-start, and then discreetly shroud, a series of essentially bilateral negotiations taking place elsewhere. This was the function performed for the Arab–Israeli bilateral by the Geneva Conference of December 1973 (Kissinger 1982: ch. 17) and then by the Madrid Conference in October 1991, and for direct US–North Korea negotiations on the latter's nuclear programme by the Six-Party Talks in Beijing after March 2007.

Multilateral diplomacy was also encouraged in the early years of the twentieth century by that strain in liberal thought that emphasizes the importance of popular consent in sustaining political authority. If governments were to be democratically accountable in the domestic sphere, it followed that they should be similarly accountable in the international sphere. An important means for achieving this was 'open diplomacy': the conduct of negotiations under the glare of a public scrutiny that (this was axiomatic) was 'creative and pacific' (Keens-Soper: 76–7). In an extension of the same thinking, the procedures of open diplomacy also permitted some formal influence, however limited, to the smaller states. In practice, conference diplomacy was not necessarily open diplomacy. This was certainly not what Hankey, for example, had in mind when he sang its praises in his lecture to the Royal Institute of International Affairs in 1920. Nevertheless, conference diplomacy was a necessary – if not a sufficient – condition for open diplomacy; hence, the one tended to encourage the other. The League of Nations Assembly was the first great example of open diplomacy, and was followed after World War II by the United Nations.

Finally, multilateral conferences hold out the prospect of making agreements stick. They do this partly by solemnizing them through signing ceremonies that display the consensus achieved in the most visible manner conceivable; and partly by their reflexive disposition to provide monitoring or follow-up machinery of one sort or another (see Chapter 6).

International organizations

The advantages of multilateral diplomacy noted so far do not altogether explain why some conferences have become permanent: standing diplomatic conferences or, as they are more commonly known, international organizations. No doubt they have achieved this status partly because, in the case of those that are politically important – such as the

United Nations or the International Monetary Fund (IMF) – it suits the powers with the greatest influence in them to have the world permanently reminded of their claims to high status. After all, the alternative – the periodic calling of *ad hoc* conferences – would cause much justified anxiety to those whose real international weight had been called into question in the interval between one meeting and the next. Indeed, had a series of *ad hoc* great power conferences been employed for the purposes of preserving 'international peace and security' instead of the UN, Britain and France would probably have lost their seats at the top table many years ago. Some multilateral conferences have also become permanent under the impact of the enduring functionalist notion that it is out of such structures that regional – and perhaps even, ultimately, global integration – will grow. Nevertheless, it seems clear that the multilateral conferences that achieve permanent status do so principally because the problem with which they were established to grapple is itself seen as a permanent problem. The paradigm case is the unceasing problem for the UN of preserving international peace without jeopardizing the immediate security of its member states.

An international organization has a constitution or charter in which its aims, structure, and rules of procedure are laid out. Most important is provision for a governing body and a permanent secretariat housed in permanent headquarters. In important cases such as the UN, the governing body – in this instance, the Security Council – is in virtually continuous session. The international organization will also have periodic meetings of the full membership. In normal circumstances, these meetings do not have much influence, but this might be greater in emergencies, when special meetings can be held. It is also important that substantial contributions to the budget of the international organization should come from at least three countries (IO: 2404). A good example of an international organization, and one of great significance, is the International Atomic Energy Agency (Box 9.2).

Apart from their permanent secretariats, none of the assemblies, councils, committees, or working groups of international organizations would find it possible to operate in the absence of temporary delegations and diplomatic missions permanently accredited to them by the member states. As a result, in 1975 an effort was made to extend to them the same sort of privileges and immunities in which permanent missions accredited to states had been confirmed by the Vienna Convention on Diplomatic Relations, 1961 (see Chapter 7). This attempt foundered because most international organizations are hosted by a small number of wealthy Western states. Evidently appalled at the extent to which the

---

Box 9.2   The International Atomic Energy Agency

The IAEA, which was established in 1957, is an autonomous organ linked to the UN General Assembly. In 2009, the Agency had 146 states members and 64 international organizations and NGOs formally linked to it. Its chief aims are to promote the peaceful uses of atomic energy, and ensure that any assistance given to its development is not diverted to military ends. Thus, its 'safeguards system' is of great importance and, in 2009, it had 237 safeguards agreements for inspections in force with 163 states. It is this activity that brought it into conflict with Saddam Hussein's Iraq and continues to cause tension in its relations with North Korea and Iran. The IAEA has a General Conference that meets annually; a 35-strong Board of Governors that meets five times a year and, in early 2009, was chaired by the Algerian ambassador in Vienna, Mrs Taous Feroukhi; a Secretariat with 2200 professional and support staff from 90 countries; and a plethora of scientific committees, advisory groups, and working groups. In addition to its headquarters in Vienna, it has offices in New York, Geneva, Toronto, and Tokyo.

Source: IO: 1231–2; and IAEA official website.

---

armies of specially privileged diplomats in their capitals would be swollen were this proposal to go through, in effect, they killed it (Fennessy). Nevertheless, the representatives of states at the headquarters of international organizations were not left without protection, their positions having been already regulated by specific agreements between individual host states and the organization concerned.

A multilateral conference that settles down to permanent status has obvious advantages. It permits the initial breakthrough to be consolidated, keeps the problem under constant surveillance (see 'Review meetings' in Chapter 6), encourages the accumulation of specialized knowledge, signals serious commitment, creates a lobby for the cause in question, often provides technical assistance to states requiring it, and does all this without raising the excessive expectations often generated by *ad hoc* conferences. There is a price to be paid for this, it is true: permanently constituted conferences tend to freeze the power structure in existence at the time of their creation, together with the culture convenient to it. In this connection, it is perhaps significant that the real negotiations seeking to restrain the nuclear ambitions of North Korea in the late 1980s and early 1990s did not take place within the ambit of the IAEA, from which it resigned in June 1994. Neither did they take place within the UN, of which it had never been a member. Instead, they took place in an altogether bilateral context with the United States (Berridge and Gallo).

Procedure

Whether multilateral conferences are *ad hoc* or permanent, they tend to share similar procedural problems, although the solutions with which they come up are by no means identical. Among others, these problems include questions of venue, participation, agenda, style of proceedings, and decision-making.

Venue

This question of sometimes symbolic, and always practical, signifi-cance in prenegotiations has already been discussed at some length in Chapter 2. Nevertheless, it must also be mentioned here, since venue is of special importance when the creation of an international organ-ization is contemplated; and the more important the organization, the greater the excitement that this issue tends to generate.

A case in point is the controversy surrounding the site for a per-manent home for the United Nations, a question that fell into the lap of the UN's Preparatory Commission in late 1945. Although many different sites were suggested, the argument – inspired in the main by concerns over prestige, but rationalized in a different language – resolved into one over whether it should be located in Europe or America. The argument for Europe was that this had always been the major cockpit of international conflict and, hence, where the UN was likely to have most of its work to do. Besides, the pro-Europe camp maintained, the old buildings of the League of Nations remained available in Geneva, itself in a neutral country and within easy reach of the Middle East and the east coast of the Americas, as well as from Europe. As for the case for the United States, this rested on the view that a US headquarters was essential to sustain American interest and prevent a return to isolationism, while many Latin Americans pre-ferred this solution for practical and political reasons of their own. In the end, a decision was made for the United States – but where in that country exactly? New York was finally chosen over the oppos-ition of the Arabs, who disliked its strongly Jewish character and favoured San Francisco instead (Gore-Booth 1974: 151–2; Nicholas: 44). For sound political reasons, the UN's other major agencies were distributed among important cities elsewhere – notably Paris, Vienna, Geneva, Washington, and Rome.

Venue might be of special importance for permanent conferences, but it is also significant for those of an *ad hoc* nature. Today, this is princi-pally because only a limited number of cities have the communications systems, hotel space, and pools of qualified interpreters to cope with the huge size of many of these conferences. Venues are also sometimes chosen, however, because it is believed that they will assist the publicity of the conference, which is no doubt why Botswana was chosen as the site for the 1983 meeting of the signatories of the Convention on Endangered Species (Aurisch: 283–4). Finally, an old and enduring reason why the venue of *ad hoc* conferences is important is that it is customary for the presidents of such conferences to be the foreign minister or principal delegate of the host country. Conference presidents have important duties: stating the background and purposes of the conference, and setting its tone in an opening speech; directing administrative arrangements; orchestrating any 'diversions' (which might include showing off local achievements); and, above all, chairing plenary sessions and perhaps drawing up any final report. It is true that the host country will generally have a special interest in the success of the conference, and that this might put it under pressure to make concessions of its own to ensure that this is achieved (Putnam: 61). But its possession of the conference presidency is a position of influence, as it was in the Concert of Europe in the nineteenth century. 'The question of president never raised any difficulty,' noted Sir Charles Webster. 'It belonged to the state in whose territory the meeting took place, an advantage', he added, 'of which both Palmerston and Metternich were very conscious' (Webster: 63).

For largely political reasons, the presidents of plenary sessions of permanent conferences tend to be less influential than those of *ad hoc* conferences. They are commonly chosen from smaller states, and also lack the ability to determine the ambience of a conference that is available to a senior politician operating on home territory. Furthermore, UN Security Council presidents, for example, rotate every month in the English alphabetical order of the names of the Council's members.

Participation

The sponsors of conferences dealing with matters of peace and security are traditionally great powers or regional great powers. In other matters, they are those – great powers, or not – who have a major interest in the subject and are anxious to get something done about it, willing to shoulder the administrative and financial burden, and prepared to risk the possible political complications of staging the conference.

Who should be invited? This is a sensitive question, since an invitation acknowledges the importance of the invitee to the outcome of the conference, and might even amount to *de facto* recognition of a government or state. An invitation also acknowledges legitimacy of interest, which might have far-reaching consequences.

Before the twentieth century, the rule of thumb was that invitees should be limited to important states with a direct interest in the subject matter of the conference. Those with an important indirect interest, or whom it was hoped might be encouraged to take a future interest, could be accorded observer status. This remained substantially the case in the twentieth century with the great majority of *ad hoc* conferences, other than those of the 'open-to-all' type spawned by the UN system. For example, the Geneva Conference on Indo-China in 1954 was limited to the United States, the Soviet Union, France, Britain, the PRC, Vietnam, Cambodia, Laos, and the Vietminh. To cite another case, the Arab–Israeli multilaterals, inaugurated in January 1992, were limited to the main regional parties, together with those external parties who had, in effect, assumed a mediating role of some kind (Peters: 6).

Employment of the criterion of interest in determining the membership of a conference is often insufficient to remove all problems. For one thing, the concept of interest is so slippery that there is ample room for disagreement on whether or not a state or other agency has a legitimate interest in a subject. The twentieth century witnessed a more liberal attitude to the inclusion of small states in *ad hoc* multilateral diplomacy – liberal to the point of universality in the case of UN conferences. Nevertheless, there was resistance to including representatives of bodies other than states. This was particularly noticeable in conferences dealing with the termination of military hostilities and territorial settlements. For example, the Vietminh were not admitted to the Indo-Chinese phase of the Geneva Conference in 1954 until the last minute (Randle: 159–60); the Afghan *mujahedin* were not present at any stage of the Geneva talks on Afghanistan in the 1980s; and none of southern Africa's large and well-known guerrilla movements was a participant in any round of the decisive Angola/Namibia talks in 1988. In each of these cases, there is little doubt that the excluded, or nearly excluded, parties had an extremely strong interest in the outcome, and not a little power to shape future developments.

Conference participation is also problematical since, in practice, the sponsors are often influenced by considerations of political rivalry in deciding whom to invite, sometimes finding themselves in a classic dilemma: excluding interested rivals dents their prestige and makes the deliberations of the conference easier, but including them provides an opportunity to carry them along and forestall the subsequent sabotage of any agreement reached. This was the uncomfortable position occupied by US Secretary of State John Foster Dulles apropos the British agitation to invite the Chinese Communists to the Geneva Conference on Indo-China in 1954. It was also in a similarly uncomfortable position that US President Jimmy Carter found himself in 1977 in considering whether or not to keep the Soviet Union involved in the multilateral diplomacy over the Arab–Israeli conflict. In view of their quite different reputations, it is ironic that it was Dulles who agreed to open the door to his rival and Carter who decided to keep it closed.

A special case of problematical conference participation that, in some measure, reflects the dilemma described in the previous paragraph is the question of membership of the UN Security Council. Presently consisting of five permanent, veto-wielding members (the United States, Russia, France, Britain, and the PRC – the 'P5'), plus ten members appointed for non-renewable two-year terms, there has for many years been a growing belief that this membership is no longer appropriate. The General Assembly has had an Open-ended Working Group considering this and related questions since January 1994 and, in February 2009, an 'intergovernmental' negotiation on the subject finally commenced at the UN.

Supporters of reform claim that the Security Council comes nowhere near to reflecting the distribution of either power or diversity among the world's regions and, therefore, lacks authority. Britain and France, it is pointed out, are no longer great powers, while Russia is but a pale reflection of the former Soviet Union (in 2008, Russia contributed only US$20m to the UN's regular budget, a little over a half of that paid by Mexico); besides, the less-developed countries have no permanent representation at all. Features common to most of the more radical reform proposals are a net increase in the size of the Security Council from 15 to 24 or 25; election on a regional basis; no granting of the veto to any new permanent members for a long probationary period, if ever (an African proposal in 2005 dissented on this); and more restricted use of the veto by existing members. There is less agreement on the character of the additional members: whether they should be a mixture of permanent and non-permanent members; include non-permanent members of a different kind (for example, 4-years renewable – hence, in effect, semi-permanent); or just non-permanent members, however constituted. According to one view with strong support, the Security Council would carry more authority if permanent membership were to be given to the G4: Japan and Germany (the second- and third-largest contributors to the UN's regular budget after the United States), plus India and Brazil.

Against the reformers, it is argued that it is a mistake to tamper with the Security Council when, since the end of the Cold War, it has at long last started to work – 'if it ain't broke, don't fix it' sums up their position. In any case, it is stressed, steps have been taken to ensure greater transparency. It is also said that powerful members such as Japan are virtually permanent members anyway – since they are re-elected so often to a non-permanent seat, and are carefully consulted by the P5 even when they are not sitting. Defenders of the *status quo*, traditionally led by the United States, add that reform entailing enlargement would make the Security Council unwieldy; they conclude their case by underlining the undeniable fact that there is no consensus, either on how the membership should be restructured or on which states should be given the great prizes – permanent seats.

The defence of the *status quo* on the Security Council glosses over the issue of prestige. It also fudges the question as to whether the Council is working because of, or in spite of, its present composition – if it is, in fact, working that well anyway. And it wobbles, even if it does not fall, on a tension between the claims that consulting powerful outsiders informally enables the Security Council to function smoothly, while bringing them formally into the decision-making by enlargement would paralyze it. Nevertheless, the conservative rearguard is a sophisticated one and, although there were strong signs in late 2008 and early 2009 that the reformers were getting the upper hand, it will still be a miracle if a consensus on reform can be found in the current negotiations at the UN. Reform is urgently needed, but it generally takes a cataclysmic upheaval to alter the composition of the councils of the major powers.

Finally, it is important to note that states or other agencies that are widely acknowledged to have a legitimate interest in a particular subject, and that might be prepared to engage in confidential bilateral discussions, might be reluctant to be observed on the same conference platform. This was a constant problem for the multilateral diplomacy in Africa sponsored by the South African government in the 1950s, and – until the early 1990s – for all attempts to involve the Israeli government in multilateral talks in which the PLO was a participant.

In many international organizations, the problem of participation is in principle solved, as already noted, by admitting all states. These are the so-called universal membership organizations, which have the added advantage of permitting discreet contact between states lacking diplomatic relations, as in recent years between the United States and North Korea at the UN in New York – the 'New York channel'. However, the United Nations itself was not a universal organization at the start of its life or for many years after, during which period participation was confined to the founding members and 'all other peace-loving states which accept the obligations' of the Charter and 'are able and willing to carry out these obligations'. This permitted the blackballing of many important states for long periods (Nicholas: 86–7), most signally in the case of the PRC, which was not admitted to membership until October 1971. Unpopular countries such as South Africa were also forced out of some international organizations, despite being founder members.

However, universal or near-universal membership brings problems of its own. The most important of these returns us to the concept of interest. This is because throwing the doors of a conference wide open permits, and might even encourage, each participant to have a say in the affairs of all of the others, whether they have a direct interest or not. Such problems will be exacerbated if discussion is conducted in public and decision-making proceeds, as it did for some considerable time in the UN General Assembly, by means of majority voting (discussed later in this chapter). In short, universal membership might well be anti-diplomatic, gratuitously worsening relations between states that, in an earlier era, would either have had little contact at all or would have had contact only on issues where both had a direct interest. It is, for example, unlikely that relations between Britain and Ireland (so important to resolving the problems in Ulster) would have suffered as a result of the Falklands crisis in 1982 had they not both been members (the one permanent, and the other temporary) of the Security Council of the United Nations.

Agenda

Problems concerning the agenda of a multilateral conference vary in some degree between *ad hoc* and permanent conferences. If a party is invited to an *ad hoc* conference, whether it will attend or not is likely to depend on the draft agenda. This might contain items that are embarrassing or, in themselves, innocuous, although prejudgement is obvious from the manner in which they are worded: for example, 'Chinese aggression against Vietnam', rather than 'the situation concerning China and Vietnam' (Nicol: 41; Bailey and Daws: 83–4). As in any kind of negotiation, the draft agenda might even be so framed as to amount to a proposed deal (see Chapter 2).

One agenda problem is peculiar to permanent multilateral conferences. Such conferences are provided with a general agenda by their founding charters or statutes, usually under the heading of 'functions' or 'purposes'. This is translated into a working agenda by the most influential members before each session (Peterson: ch. 2), and those who dislike it can only refuse to attend with difficulty, since they have already accepted permanent membership. Even one of the P5 on the Security Council cannot veto the inscription of an item on the agenda or veto its inclusion at a particular point on the agenda. This is because the customary law of the Security Council states that these are procedural, rather than substantive, matters (Bailey and Daws: 84–5).

On the other hand, devices exist to ensure that the sessional agendas of permanent multilateral conferences are broadly acceptable, typically the requirement that they should be approved by two thirds of the members present and voting; in any case, broad consultation usually ensures that a vote on the agenda does not need to be taken. If some states remain hostile to the inclusion of a particular item, they might be mollified by a vague, general, or altogether obscure formulation of it. This is the practice the UN Security Council has increasingly adopted (Bailey and Daws: 83–4). If all else fails, they can temporarily absent themselves from meetings or maintain only a token presence, as South Africa did at the General Assembly for several years after November 1956 in protest at the Assembly's insistence on discussing the policy of apartheid. States in a minority tend to stay for the discussion of items on which they would prefer silence to prevail. This is partly because they want their answer to any charges to be heard, and partly because they have other reasons for wishing to remain a part of the organization.

Public debate and private discussion

It is the character of public debate in the plenary sessions of international conferences that has caused multilateral diplomacy to gain a poor name. When discussion takes place between numerous delegations in a public setting, the political necessity of playing to the audience outside is inescapable, and the give and take of genuine negotiation goes out of the window. The style of proceedings is self-consciously point-scoring or 'parliamentary', and the result is that propaganda is substituted for diplomacy. Until recent decades, this was typically the case with both the UN General Assembly and the formal meetings of the UN Security Council. Even closed plenary sessions of conferences are hardly likely to encourage real negotiation when, as is often the case, well over 150 states are represented and the corridors outside are crawling with journalists and lobbyists from NGOs.

Widespread recognition of the drawbacks of over-reliance on public debate in multilateral diplomacy has led to increased employment of subcommittees, private sessions, and informal consultations. Since the 1970s, the UN Security Council itself has regularly met informally in private, and the P5 have caucused in secret since the mid-1980s (Berridge 1991: 3–6, ch. 5). Conferences within the broader UN system are now preceded by preparatory committees and, once launched, now employ an elaborate mix of different kinds of session – private and public, plenary and small group. In the Arab-Israeli multilaterals, overseen by a largely ceremonial steering group, the real business was conducted in five functionally defined and informally conducted working groups, and in their 'inter-sessional activities' (Peters: ch. 3). Where there is a constitutional tradition of public meetings, however, these are generally retained. In any case, while public sessions of conferences that effectively rubber-stamp agreements thrashed out in private might induce cynicism, they are valuable in demonstrating unity on important international problems.

The number of participants and the technicality of the issues in most multilateral conferences held today make them extremely complex. Despite the procedural advances just noted, therefore, it might be imagined that this alone would vitiate the advantages of conducting diplomacy by this method. Complexity is, indeed, a problem – but it is not normally fatal. This is because, in most large conferences, the order of battle is simplified by the formation of coalitions. In the UN Conference on the Law of the Sea, for instance, 150 states participated but, in reality, this boiled down to the West Europeans, the East Europeans, and the Group of 77 (Touval 1989: 164). Furthermore, there is invariably a small number of states both willing and able to make the running, while their need to carry the rest usually inclines them to make their own demands with moderation. In his memoir, Michael Alexander praised in this connection the 'informal directorate' in the NATO Council, consisting of the United States, Britain, Germany, and France (Alexander: 199–200). The opportunities for package deals are also far more numerous than in bilateral diplomacy.

Decision-making

The method by which decisions are finalized in bilateral talks has never been an issue: when there are only two parties, there can be no agreement unless both concur. By contrast, multilateral conferences provide the opportunity to make decisions by majority voting. As a result, the strength of the democratic idea, together with the fear that a rule of unanimity might induce paralysis when large numbers of states are involved, has produced widespread support for voting. Indeed, despite important exceptions such as the North Atlantic Council and the Council of the

Organization for Economic Co-operation and Development (OECD), this has been a formal feature of decision-making in all major international organizations, notably the United Nations, since 1945.

Where majority voting is employed there are, typically, differences in the treatment of procedural and substantive issues. Furthermore, some international organizations employ weighted voting while others do not, and some require special majorities while others require only simple majorities (over 50 per cent). In the UN Security Council, for example, an affirmative vote of only 9 of the 15 members is required for a decision on a procedural question. Decisions on 'all other matters', says Article 27 of the Charter, require 'an affirmative vote of nine members *including the concurring votes of the permanent members*' (emphasis added) – the great power veto. (It was subsequently accepted that an abstention did not amount to a veto.) For its part, the UN General Assembly was authorized to pass resolutions on a simple majority of members present and voting – except in the case of 'important questions', which require a two-thirds majority.

In practice, however, decision-making by voting has not been as significant across the whole spectrum of multilateral diplomacy as this picture might suggest. *Ad hoc* conferences, especially those with few participants and not constituted under UN auspices, have rarely employed voting, while those that have, including the permanent, large membership ones within the UN system, have generally found it necessary to qualify their voting arrangements. This has been observed since at least the mid-1960s.

The problem for the UN system is that its 'one state, one vote' rhetoric has collided head-on with political reality as a result of the admission (especially since the late 1950s) of a huge number of small, weak states. In these circumstances, even the requirement for a two-thirds majority can fail to block the 'wrong' decision. This has rendered 'majority voting increasingly useless for lawmaking decisions because of the danger of powerful alienated minorities' (Buzan: 326). Having lost its own majority following in the United Nations in the 1960s, the United States emerged as the most powerful member of just such a minority. Increasingly being expected to provide the lion's share of the money for programmes that it found objectionable, it drastically scaled back its funding of the organization in the 1980s. The result was that the UN, together with particularly anathematized satellites such as UNESCO, was threatened with collapse.

Could this dangerous position not have been prevented by giving more votes to the bigger battalions by using a system of weighted voting?

Although perhaps attractive in principle, this idea has three main problems: it is politically sensitive, because it draws attention to real differences between states when all are supposed to be equal; it might avoid the risk of alienating powerful minorities, but only at the price of running the opposite one – namely, alienating weak majorities; and it raises complex practical issues concerning the criteria to be employed in computing the differences between states. As a result, weighted voting has only proved acceptable in specialized economic organizations such as the IMF and the World Bank, where the size of financial contributions provides a ready claim on the size of votes.

Rather than weighted voting being generally adopted, then, what has happened is that multilateral diplomacy has witnessed a growing acceptance of decision-making by *consensus*, especially following its successful employment at the Third UN Conference on the Law of the Sea in the period from 1973 until 1982 (Buzan: 325–7; Peters: 7–8). In practice, most decisions are taken by consensus, even in the IMF and the World Bank. It is also this procedure that has saved the United Nations: the General Assembly itself has, for many years, been passing its own resolutions and decisions largely on the basis of consensus.

Consensus decision-making is the attempt to achieve the agreement of all the participants in a multilateral conference without the need for a vote and its inevitable divisiveness. A consensus exists when all parties are in agreement – which, on the face of it, is another way of saying that they are unanimous. However, a consensus might include some members whose support has been given only grudgingly and who have simply registered no *formal* objection, whereas unanimity implies broader enthusiasm – hence the view that, in fact, they are not the same. It might be more accurate to say that a weak consensus is not the same as unanimity, but that a strong one is.

But is consensus decision-making – that is to say, the method by which consensus is obtained – simply negotiation by another name? After all, if the reluctant agreement of all participants is to be obtained, those most in favour of a proposal must either water it down, make concessions to the unenthusiastic in some other area, or alarm them with the prospect of isolation. In short, they must negotiate with them. Nevertheless, it is now common to find even a strong consensus fostered by special procedural devices.

One of these methods is to give a secretary-general or chairperson the right to conduct straw votes – that is, count opinions by means of informal, confidential consultations with permanent missions or delegations; among other things, this provides the opportunity to hint at the way the wind is blowing to those being polled. Another device, which builds on this one, is 'silence procedure': the rule that a proposal with strong support is deemed to have been agreed unless any member raises an objection to it before a precise deadline: silence signifies assent – or, at least, acquiescence. This procedure relies on a member in a minority fearing that raising an objection will expose it to the charge of obstructiveness and, thereby, the perils of isolation. Silence procedure is employed by NATO, the OSCE, in the framework of the Common Foreign and Security Policy of the European Union (EU) and, no doubt, in numerous other international bodies. Finally, voting itself might still be employed, although its function is the limited one of ratifying a consensus already negotiated.

It seems reasonable to conclude, therefore, that consensus decision-making is something more than ordinary negotiation: it is the unanimity system adjusted to the prejudices of the twentieth and twenty-first centuries. More in tune with these prejudices although it might be, consensus decision-making is no guarantee that a decision can be reached, or reached in time, or that (if one is reached in time) it will be a good one. The notorious vagueness of UN Security Council Resolution 1441 of November 2002 on Iraq, notably in its reference to the 'serious consequences' that would follow non-compliance, is a case in point.

The return of a system of decision-making in which the more powerful states were able to exert the influence to which they thought they were entitled also marked a 'crisis of multilateralism' (Aurisch: 288). At least, it marked a crisis of the kind of multilateral diplomacy by means of which, in the 1970s, the weaker states had hoped to create a New International Economic Order. It is perhaps, therefore, not surprising that the number of international organizations should have gone into sharp decline after the mid-1980s, dropping by over one third by the turn of the millennium, although the level of universal membership international organizations remained steady. The total number of NGOs, by contrast, rose by roughly the same proportion.

Summary

Multilateral diplomacy took firm root in the early twentieth century under the impact of world war and the strength of the democratic idea. It blossomed after World War II with the great expansion in the number of states and the belief of the new ones that conference diplomacy within the UN system – based on majority voting – was their best chance of securing influence. Ultimately, they were disappointed.

The major Western powers became tired of paying for programmes to which they took strong political objection and, gradually, under the name of consensus decision-making, began to make their weight felt. In the 1980s, with the UN system reeling under the impact of American budgetary withholdings and the poorer states increasingly disillusioned with the meagre results obtained by their large voting majorities, a crisis of multilateralism set in. However, multilateralism is here to stay: it has weathered its crisis, and it has emerged a little leaner. It has also emerged a little more diplomatic.

Further reading

Alexander, Michael (ed.) with an introduction by Keith Hamilton, *Managing the Cold War: A view from the front line* (RUSI: London, 2005).

Armstrong, D., *The Rise of the International Organisation: A short history* (Macmillan – now Palgrave: Basingstoke, 1982).

Armstrong, D., L. Lloyd, and J. Redmond, *International Organisation in World Politics*, 3rd edn (Palgrave Macmillan: Basingstoke/New York, 2004).

Bailey, S. D. and S. Daws, *The Procedure of the UN Security Council*, 3rd edn (Clarendon Press: Oxford, 1998).

Bourantonis, D. and M. Evriviades (eds), *A United Nations for the Twenty-First Century* (Kluwer: The Hague, 1996): ch. 3, by Henrikson.

Bourantonis, D., *The History and Politics of UN Security Council Reform* (Routledge: London/New York, 2005).

Boutros-Ghali, B., *Unvanquished: A U.S.–U.N. saga* (I. B. Tauris: London/New York, 1999).

Buzan, B., 'Negotiating by consensus: developments in technique at the United Nations Conference on the Law of the Sea', *American Journal of International Law*, 72(2), 1981.

Caron, D. D., 'The legitimacy of the collective authority of the Security Council', *American Journal of International Law*, 87, 1993: 552–88.

'Congress', in *Encyclopedia Britannica* (1911 edn), written by Walter Allison Phillips [www].

Fennessy, J. G., 'The 1975 Convention on the Representation of States in their Relations with International Organizations of a Universal Character', *American Journal of International Law*, 70, 1976.

Global Policy Forum, Security Council Reform: Crucial documents [www].

Hampson, Fen Osler, with Michael Hart, *Multilateral Negotiations: Lessons from arms control, trade and the environment* (Johns Hopkins University Press: Baltimore, 1995).

Hankey, Lord, *Diplomacy by Conference: Studies in public affairs 1920–1946* (Benn: London, 1946).

Heikal, Mohamed, *Secret Channels: The inside story of Arab–Israeli peace negotiations* (HarperCollins: London, 1996): ch. 11, on the Madrid Conference, 1991.

Jenks, C. W., 'Unanimity, the veto, weighted voting, special and simple majorities and consensus as modes of decision in international organisations',

Cambridge Essays in International Law: Essays in honour of Lord McNair (Stevens: London; Oceana: Dobbs Ferry, NY, 1965).

Kahler, M., 'Multilateralism with small and large numbers', *International Organization*, 46(3), 1992.

Kahler, M., *Leadership Selection in the Major Multilaterals* (Institute for International Economics: Washington, November 2001): esp. 23–4, 62–75, 80, 85.

Kissinger, H. A., *Years of Upheaval* (Weidenfeld & Nicolson/Michael Joseph: London, 1982): ch. 17.

Langhorne, R., 'The development of international conferences, 1648–1830', in *Studies in History and Politics*, 11, pt 2, 1981.

Luard, E., *The United Nations: How it works and what it does*, 2nd edn, rev. by D. Heater (Macmillan – now Palgrave: Basingstoke, 1994).

Luck, E. C., *Mixed Messages: American politics and international organization, 1919–1999* (Brookings: Washington, DC, 1999).

MacMillan, Margaret, *Peacemakers: The Paris Conference of 1919 and its attempt to end war* (John Murray: London, 2001).

Parsons, A., 'The United Nations in the Post-Cold War era', *International Relations*, 11(3), December 1992: 189–200.

Peters, J., *Building Bridges: The Arab–Israeli multilateral talks* (RIIA: London, 1994).

Randle, R. F., *Geneva 1954: The settlement of the Indochinese War* (Princeton University Press: Princeton, NJ, 1969).

Steinberg, Richard H., 'In the shadow of law or power? Consensus-based bargaining and outcomes in the GATT/WTO', *International Organization*, 56(2), Spring, 2002: 339–74.

Thompson, K. W., 'The new diplomacy and the quest for peace', *International Organization*, 19, 1965.

UN Chronicle, 'The process of informals in the Fifth Committee', March–May, 2002. 'A More Secure World – Our Shared Responsibility: Report of the Secretary-General's high-level panel on threats, challenges and change' (United Nations: 2004): ch. 14 [www].

Walker, Ronald A., *Multilateral Conferences: Purposeful international negotiation* (Palgrave Macmillan: Basingstoke/New York, 2004).

Webster, Sir C., *The Art and Practice of Diplomacy* (Chatto & Windus: London, 1961): ch. 4.

Weiss, Thomas G., 'The illusion of UN Security Council reform', *Washington Quarterly*, Autumn, 2003 [www].

Zamora, S., 'Voting in international economic organizations', *American Journal of International Law*, 74, 1980.

10
Summits

Today an astonishing degree of multilateral diplomacy takes place at the highest level of political authority: heads of state and government, and heads of international organization, not forgetting the leaders of factions in civil wars (Young 2008: 118). But this is multilateral diplomacy of a special kind; besides, the bilateral diplomacy that also takes place at the summit is also special. For these reasons, it is necessary to treat summitry separately. This chapter considers the origins of summitry, its advantages and disadvantages, and the bearing on its contribution to diplomacy – as opposed to propaganda – of the different patterns it assumes.

Origins

Summits were not so-called until the 1950s, when the term was taken up in the press following its use by the British prime minister, Winston Churchill, during a speech in Edinburgh at the beginning of the decade. However, similar meetings occurred sporadically between the Bronze Age and the late Middle Ages, when they reached their pre-modern high-point. Thereafter, at least in Europe, they fizzled out. This was not only because resident missions had by this time become widely established. It was also because rulers had usually been poor diplomats; because they were more attractive than their envoys as targets for embarrassment, capture for ransom, or murder; and, above all, because the old idea that diplomacy was the prerogative of rulers because their territories were their private estates was being steadily undermined by the new notion of the modern state – among other things, a juristic person separate from and, in some sense, above its temporary custodians (Frey and Frey: 83–4, 130–1; Reynolds: 17–18).

In the nineteenth century, the Concert of Europe saw summit diplomacy flicker sporadically into life, but it did not become a significant technique again until the first half of the twentieth century. Growing out of the pall that had spread over professional diplomacy during World War I, the return of summitry was announced by the Paris Peace Conference in 1919. Here, Lloyd George, Georges Clemenceau, and Woodrow Wilson held centre stage. Its return was consolidated by the meetings in 1938 between Hitler and the British prime minister, Neville Chamberlain. These were prompted by the latter's belief that avoiding the terrible prospect of the aerial bombing of cities warranted the risks of personal diplomacy with the Nazi leader, and that coverage by the new cinema and arrival by plane would add drama to the proceedings (Reynolds: 6, 33–6, 47–9). In mid-century, the wartime conferences of the Big Three – Roosevelt, Churchill, and Stalin – confirmed that summits were unlikely to go away.

Encouraged at great power level especially by Churchill, summitry had really begun to take off within about a decade after World War II. In addition to be being stimulated by the same political and technological trends promoting multilateral diplomacy (see Chapter 9), summitry increased owing to the risk that the Cold War could lead to hot war between the superpowers: even more than in 1938, diplomacy in the nuclear age was believed to be 'too important to be left to the diplomatists' (Dunn: 5). Decolonization in Africa and Asia, where few of the new states possessed impressive diplomatic services, was another propellant; and the regional organizations that were becoming fashionable gave summitry a natural focus. The growing vulnerability to arrest on criminal charges of serving – as opposed to retired or deposed – heads of state, demonstrated most vividly by the case of President Bashir of Sudan (see Box 10.1), might in future dampen the enthusiasm for summit travel. However, the evidence for this is as yet slender.

Professional anathemas

The massive, twentieth-century return to summitry produced deep unease among professional diplomats, causing many to recall the objections to it of Philippe de Commynes (Box 10.2). Since summitry was an insult to their competence and, at least, a limited threat to their careers, this might be put down to special pleading. Nevertheless, their arguments are persuasive and find loud echoes outside their ranks. Most eloquent among their number was George Ball, US under-secretary of state during the Democratic administrations of the 1960s and author

---

Box 10.1   ICC arrest warrant for Sudan's president, March 2009: a dampener for summitry?

On 4 March 2009, the International Criminal Court (ICC) in The Hague issued a warrant for the arrest of the Sudanese President, Omar al-Bashir, on charges of war crimes and crimes against humanity committed during the conflict in Darfur. This required all 108 parties to the Rome Statute of the ICC of 17 July 1998 to arrest him if he entered their territory, including their airspace. (Note: The USA is not a party to the ICC.) However, while some Arab states, including Sudan itself, had signed the ICC's Statute, only Jordan among them had ratified it. The Arab League, together with the AU – where many leaders are afraid that one day they could end up in the same boat as President Bashir – condemned the ICC judgement, and the Sudanese leader was emboldened to visit the heads of state of three neighbouring countries in the following weeks: Eritrea, Egypt and Libya. He even attended the annual Arab League summit in Qatar at the end of March, and stopped off in Saudi Arabia on the way back, although this required him – unlike his visits a few days earlier – to fly through international airspace. Nevertheless, the Sudanese government had obviously been nervous about the visit to the summit in Qatar and the *ulema*, the state's highest religious body, had issued a *fatwa* advising that it was too risky. Special security precautions had to be taken for it, and the foreign ministry hinted that, in future, the President's summitry would have to be more selective and furtive. A visit to Ethiopia scheduled for 10 March was postponed until late April.

Sources: *UN Treaty Collection* (Status of Treaties); *Welt Online*; *Guardian Online*; *Sudan Tribune*.

Box 10.2   Philippe de Commynes

Commynes (c. 1447–1511) was a French diplomat and historian, and wrote the best-known political and diplomatic memoirs of the late fifteenth century. Great princes, he believed, were in general spoiled, vain, and badly educated. Unusually suspicious because of the many false stories and groundless reports brought to them by court intriguers, they were also too ready to believe the worst of any prince with whom they happened to be negotiating. Most seriously of all, summitry could place them in physical danger. Therefore, he famously concluded, 'two great princes who wish to establish good personal relations should never meet each other face to face but ought to communicate through good and wise ambassadors'. Commynes' attitude to summitry might not have been entirely unconnected to the role that he was required to play when his master, Louis XI, met Edward IV on a bridge over the Somme at Picquigny, in order to discuss the peaceful retreat of the English invasion force of 1475. Louis instructed Commynes to wear identical clothes to his own as a precaution against assassination.

of the account in *Diplomacy for a Crowded World* on which this section draws heavily.

The case against summitry turns chiefly on certain assumptions about heads of state and government as a class. They are held to be poor negotiators because they are vain, ignorant of details, pressed for time, addicted to publicity, over-tired if not actually suffering from insomnia or more serious form of ill-health, prone to cultural misunderstandings, and too readily swayed by personal likes and dislikes towards fellow leaders. Furthermore, in the event of a deadlock in a negotiation they are leading, there is, as a rule, no one at home to whom they can claim the need to refer in order to secure a postponement; after all, they are themselves the ultimate authority. (In states such as Britain and Israel, with a firm tradition of cabinet government, a prime minister can, however, claim to be only *primus inter pares* – first among equals – and therefore need to seek the approval of colleagues.) This means that, in these circumstances, they are always likely to make one or other of two mistakes: either they break off the negotiations prematurely, if faced by the prospect of failure; or they make unwise concessions in order to achieve a 'success', and one that is the more difficult to retrieve because it has been made on their personal promise rather than on that of a disavowable official. In short, diplomacy conducted at the summit is not only likely to lead to more mistakes, but also to mistakes that are irrevocable.

The scope for exacerbating relations between states by summitry is greater still, since key points in any agreement reached by this means might have been vaguely formulated in the absence of aides and, even, of any written record. In any case, agreements or understandings achieved by summitry, and thereby in some measure personalized, tend to be weakened by the fall from office of one or other of the leaders concerned. In short, summitry 'obscures the concept of relations between governments as a continuing process' (Ball: 40). Summing up the argument, David Watt wrote: 'Heads of government, with their massive egos, their ignorance of the essential details and their ingrained belief in the value of back-slapping ambiguity, simply mess everything up' (*Times* 1981).

The examples of summit failures are legion – quoted by the professionals sometimes with sadness, sometimes with anger. The mistakes made in the Treaty of Versailles were, in part, ascribed by Harold Nicolson to the decision of the American president, Woodrow Wilson, to attend in person – a 'historical disaster of the first magnitude' (Nicolson 1937: 71). In order to underline his own hostility to summitry, Dean Acheson chooses the example of President Truman. '[I]n the privacy of his study', he remarks, the president unwittingly altered American policy in a most sensitive area by informing the British prime minister, Clement Attlee, that the United States would not use nuclear weapons without first consulting the British (Acheson 1969: 484). William Sullivan's story is how the Shah of Iran, on a visit to the United States, told President Carter of his belief that the Organization of African Unity was an 'impotent' [powerless] body; the president – with the ear for words of a Southerner – agreed that it was indeed 'impohtant' [important] (Sullivan: 129). For his part, George Ball gives us a whole list of summits that have been a 'source of grief', among them the conference held by Chamberlain with Hitler at Munich in 1938, from which he returned with the conviction that he had secured 'peace for our time'; the East–West summits of the 1950s and 1960s that did nothing but raise false expectations; the meeting in 1962 at which US president, John F. Kennedy, gave Polaris missiles to British prime minister, Harold Macmillan, because he had a soft spot for the avuncular older man, though this fitted ill with American policy on nuclear proliferation and gave de Gaulle an excuse to veto Britain's application to the EEC; the personal encounters between another American president, Lyndon Johnson, and another British prime minister, Harold Wilson, in the 1960s that impaired Anglo–American relations because the two men simply did not like each other; the discussions, dogged with misunderstandings, between President Nixon and Prime Minister Sato of Japan that blighted US–Japanese relations in the early 1970s; and so on. Among recent summit failures, David Reynolds singles out the Blair–Bush meetings between 2001 and 2003 prior to the attack on Iraq, during the course of which Tony Blair – ignoring Foreign Office warnings – sold British military support to the United States too cheaply. The slide to this disastrous war, he argues persuasively, was 'lubricated by Blair's summitry' (Reynolds: 389).

But this is not the end of the case against summits. Their financial cost is also now enormous. Summits were always expensive, but their cost has risen exponentially over recent years as they have become a perfect target for anti-globalization protesters and opposition groups, as well as terrorists. In July 2001, the Italian government had to spend £100 million on the G8 summit in Genoa, which included the cost of installing a missile defence system at the airport. Even the slimmed down G8 summit in June 2002, hidden away from anti-globalization protesters at Kananaskis, a resort village in the Rocky mountains, cost the Canadian government at least £140 million. The cost to the Japanese government of the G8 summit at remote Toyako on Hokkaido Island in 2008 was reputed to be a staggering £238 million (*Guardian* 2008).

A leader who proposes to visit only one of two others locked in a traditional rivalry is stoking up trouble of a different kind, or makes the visit in the expectation of having to make a side payment to head it off. When President Obama announced that he would be visiting Turkey on his way home from the G20 summit in April 2009, he immediately provoked an outcry in Athens. Had he been proposing to go to Greece rather than Turkey the uproar would have emanated from Ankara. This is a well-established ritual that the British have found particularly trying ever since Cyprus – then its colony – poisoned Greece–Turkey relations in the mid-1950s; but it is no less consequential for that. A related problem is the need to return a visit paid by the leader of another state of roughly equal standing, even though this may be inconvenient.

Heads of state and government who over-indulge the summit habit, or just find themselves doomed to it, might also find themselves giving insufficient time to domestic affairs and might, in consequence, even lose their jobs. This was the fate of General Smuts in the election of 1948 that gave South Africa the hateful racist doctrine of apartheid. In June 1977, James Mancham, president of only recently independent Seychelles, was overthrown by an armed coup while attending a Commonwealth summit in London. While the cat is away, the mice will play.

Case for the defence

Summitry has been so roundly anathematized that it is, at first glance, not easy to understand why it remains so common – but only at first glance. It is valued chiefly for its enormous symbolic or propaganda potential, and it is no accident that it became an art form during the middle and later phases of the Cold War, itself essentially a conflict fought by means of propaganda. Summits between Soviet and American leaders symbolized the attachment of their governments to peace, while intra-alliance summits symbolized each side's internal solidarity; President Nixon's one-hour conversation with the legendary leader of Chinese Communism, Mao Zedong, in Beijing in February 1972, was 'an earthquake' in the conflict and symbolized the fact that 'the Eastern Bloc no longer stood firm against the West' (Macmillan 2006: 1); and the end of the Cold War was also symbolized by a summit, held in Paris in November 1990.

In democracies, summits are of special value to political leaders because they demonstrate to their voters that they are personally doing something about a current problem, and are important actors on the world stage. For this reason, bigger states might issue a summit invitation to the valued but insecure leader of a lesser one in order to boost his position at home (Young 2008: 120–1). Add to the pot of democracy the power of television, and sprinkle its contents with exotic locations of symbolic significance, and it is clear why summit diplomacy is an irresistible dish to those with an eye on a leader's poll ratings. Nixon simply could not pass over the opportunity virtually to kow-tow before Mao in 1972 – an election year – and pose for the television cameras at every opportunity, even though Washington still did not recognize the People's Republic of China.

Fortunately, while summitry might well be irrelevant and even highly damaging to diplomacy, and often serve principally foreign and domestic propaganda purposes, it can also have diplomatic value – provided it is employed judiciously. To help explain this, it is useful to distinguish between three main kinds of summit: serial summits, which are part of a regular series; *ad hoc* summits, which are generally narrowly focused, one-off meetings, although they might turn out to be the first of a series; and the less ambitious, high-level exchange of views, which might be part of a series but is more likely to be *ad hoc*. What are the diplomatic purposes served by all these summits, those served more by some than others, and those served by some but by others not at all?

Bearing in mind the functions of traditional diplomacy conducted via embassies discussed in Chapter 7, there are five functions that might usefully be advanced by summitry. These are: promoting friendly relations, clarifying intentions, information gathering, consular work (principally export promotion and interceding on behalf of detained nationals in high profile cases), and negotiation. Let us consider the degree to which the different types of summit are suited to carrying out these functions, broad though these categories are and treacherous though this makes the task of generalizing about them.

Serial summits

Important examples of the serial summit can be seen in Box 10.3. Of all types of summit, this is probably the best suited to serious negotiation, although the extent to which this is true turns, to some extent, on its length and frequency. Longer meetings allow subjects to be treated in greater depth and allow time for a return to the table following a deadlock. The Commonwealth Heads of Government Meeting (CHOGM),

---

Box 10.3   Serial summits: some important examples

- *US-EU summit.* Inaugurated in 1990. Now meets annually in June. An 'informal summit' was held with President Obama in Prague in April 2009.
- *US-Russia summit.* US-Soviet summits were occurring once a year by the second half of the 1980s. Following the breakup of the Soviet Union in 1991, US-Russian summits became more frequent but latterly less so.
- *EU-Russia summit.* Meets twice yearly under each 6-month EU presidency.
- *Franco-German summit.* Started in January 1963. Normally meets at least twice a year.
- *ASEAN summit.* Members of the Association of South-East Asian Nations, established in 1967. Over recent years has met on average roughly every 18 months. An experiment with holding 'informal summits' between three-yearly formal ones, which was launched following a decision in 1995, was short-lived.
- *SAARC summit.* Members of the South Asian Association for Regional Cooperation, established in 1985. Meets once in most years.
- *G8 summit.* The Group of 8 countries (Britain, Canada, France, Germany, Italy, Japan, Russia, USA) plus the EU. Meets annually.
- *CHOGM.* Meets every two years.
- *AU summit.* Formally known as the 'Assembly of the African Union', this meets at least once a year in ordinary session. First met in Durban in 2003.
- *Arab League summit.* Held annually since 2001.
- *Summit of the Americas.* Members of the Organization of American States (OAS). Takes place at 3–4 year intervals, with occasional special summits. Launched in 1994.

---

which lasts between five and seven days, is one of the best in this regard. Frequent summits at predetermined intervals are also more conducive to serious negotiation, because they are likely to arouse fewer public expectations and to have developed – provided informality is not overdone – clear and comprehensive rules of procedure. In this regard, the Franco–German summit, which in practice often meets as many as five or six times a year, is one of the best. Unfortunately, frequent summits in this category tend to be brief and long ones less frequent.

Whether serial summits are frequent or separated by a year or more, and whether they last for hours or days, they might contribute to a successful negotiation between the parties concerned for one or more of the following reasons:

- First, they educate leaders in international realities: they are forced to do their homework in order to avoid looking foolish among their peers, and they cannot avoid learning from the mouths of fellow leaders about the influences working on them.

- Second, they make package deals easier: sitting astride the apex of policy-making within their own administrations, heads of state and government are well-placed to make trades involving bureaucratically separate issue areas.
- Third, they set deadlines (see Chapter 4) for the completion of an existing negotiation, or stage of one, between the parties: because leaders might be publicly embarrassed by a failure to announce an agreement at a summit, their junior ministers and officials are under intense pressure to have effectively concluded much the greater part of the negotiation with their opposite numbers before the summit is held; in short, serial summits sustain diplomatic momentum.
- Fourth, if the negotiations have been brought to this stage, the summit – even if brief – might serve to break any remaining deadlocks by virtue of the authority of the assembled negotiators and their greater breadth of vision: the 'final court of appeal' function of the summit.

As for the other functions, serial summits are also the best suited to information gathering, including the gathering of information on personalities. Serial summiteers themselves stress this point; in 1992, Chancellor Kohl of Germany noted, in its support, that he had met President Mitterrand of France in excess of 80 times (Bower: 37). They are also probably the best for clarifying intentions, for these rarely appear more clearly than in the give–and-take of genuine negotiations.

On the other hand, precisely because it is the summit most suited to negotiation, the serial summit is perhaps least well suited to the promotion of friendly relations. Serious negotiation invariably generates tensions and these are almost bound to be greater at summits, as their critics have so frequently pointed out, since the protagonists can rarely pretend that their word is anything other than the last word of their governments. Besides, politicians tend to find it harder to resist point-scoring than professional negotiators, as Arab League summits are notorious for demonstrating. Summits where serious negotiation occurs also allow little time for the elaborate courtesies, observance of which is so important to the pursuit of friendly relations by the resident ambassador. Having said this, serial summits would not occur if there were not an appreciation of some significant overlap of interests or strong sense of cultural affinity among the participants. This will usually ensure that tensions are not permitted to become destructive, as the Franco–German summit and the CHOGMs demonstrate.

Also worth mentioning here is the SAARC summit that was held in Islamabad in 1988. This was the setting for a warm encounter between the Indian prime minister, Rajiv Gandhi, and the Pakistani prime minister, Benazir Bhutto, whose recent election had been widely welcomed in India.

The paradigm case of the serial summit is the French-inspired European Council, the regular conference of heads of state and government of the European Union that was designed, principally, to ensure that supranationalism in Europe did not get out of hand. This had its origins in informal summits starting in 1957, formally came into being in Paris in December 1974, and was finally embodied in the treaty regime of the then EC in the Single European Act in 1986. Despite a deliberate attempt to maintain flexibility and informality, clear rules of procedure have developed, some of which are to be found in documentary sources (Werts: 77) and some in custom and practice. Among the more important is the requirement that the Council shall meet at least twice a year, although in practice it is normally summoned three times, with ministers and members of the Commission also in attendance. A first draft of the agenda is prepared by the Committee of Permanent Representatives in Brussels but the final draft is submitted by the country holding the presidency; the agenda is only finally agreed, however, at the start of the meeting (Bulmer and Wessels: 51–3; Werts: 78–9). The chairman is the head of government of the country holding the presidency. The Council normally lasts for no more than 24 hours, starting at noon and ending at noon on the following day. In order to encourage frank exchanges, and although it can subsequently lead to arguments, no official minutes of the plenary sessions are recorded (Bulmer and Wessels: 57–8). These sessions are also intimate and restricted (ministers and officials are kept in a separate room), though 'not at all secret' since 'everybody goes out and tells great numbers of people exactly what they think has happened' (Jenkins: 75). After dinner on the first day, there is a very informal 'fireside chat' on general political questions beyond the formal agenda (Callaghan: 316–17; Werts: 80). Decision-making is by consensus (see Chapter 9).

What role has the European Council played? In theory, it was designed to promote frank exchanges of views, and to enable government heads to negotiate agreements on matters of high policy, especially those on which the Council of Ministers was deadlocked. In practice, the informal sessions have proved particularly useful, at least during some periods; they appear to have been vital, for example, in facilitating the establishment of the European Monetary System

(Bulmer and Wessels: 84). And, in general, the European Council has proved valuable in signalling to the world European solidarity on some key foreign policy questions. It must be admitted, however, that, as the scene of sometimes extremely tough negotiations in the plenary sessions, it has not been famous for its contribution to the promotion of friendly relations. Neither did this begin with the appearance of Margaret Thatcher in its ranks, and the bitter and protracted arguments that she stimulated in the 1980s over Britain's budgetary contributions. Even in Paris in 1974, when Britain was represented by Harold Wilson, the exchanges on this subject were 'long, argumentative and tense at times' (Callaghan: 315). But this is simply the price of seriousness.

Ad hoc summits

As with the serial summit, the usefulness of the *ad hoc* version in negotiation is, to some extent, a function of its length: the longer the better. The Camp David summit, for example, which took place in September 1978, lasted for a full 13 days, and the Wye River summit two decades later stretched from a planned four to eight days. On both occasions, extremely tough negotiations took place between the American, Israeli, and Arab leaders (and their senior advisers), and important breakthroughs were made; namely, the Camp David Accords and the Wye River Memorandum. In other words, these summits did not merely ratify an agreement made earlier. As *ad hoc* summits go, however, Camp David and Wye River were the exceptions rather than the rule. Most of them last no more than two or three days. Because of this, and because they also tend to generate more publicity than the serial summit, *ad hoc* meetings are unlikely to be so useful for negotiations during the meetings themselves.

But, precisely because this kind of summit is able to produce more publicity, it is well suited to gaining momentum for an ongoing negotiation, as when the G20 met for the first time at summit level in late 2008 and early 2009 (see Box 9.1) in order to energize the search for a consensus on the urgent steps needed to sort out the international financial chaos then reigning. Because there is no guarantee of a subsequent meeting to which an unresolved agenda item can be postponed, the *ad hoc* summit also represents a better deadline for a negotiation than the serial summit. For example, in May 1972, the prospect of the Nixon–Brezhnev summit in Moscow put huge pressure on the arms control negotiators of both sides to wrap up the first Strategic Arms Limitation Treaty in time for signature before Nixon had to return home.

Since *ad hoc* summits are characteristically designed, principally, for symbolic purposes rather than negotiation, it seems reasonable to suggest that, whether they have an emphasis on ceremonial functions or not, they are better suited to the promotion of friendly relations than the serial summit. In fact, many *ad hoc* summits are designed deliberately and openly for this purpose: the summit symbolizes this, and fosters it by providing a format that encourages relaxed encounters between the leaders. Good bilateral examples of such summits are provided by the meetings between President Clinton of the United States and President Hafez al-Assad of Syria in Geneva, in January 1994. A multilateral summit with heavy symbolic emphasis and the general aim of fostering increased economic and cultural ties between its participants was the two-day Ibero–American summit held in Mexico, in July 1991. A multilateral *ad hoc* summit designed for a quite different purpose can also be exploited in order to promote friendly bilateral relations, as when President Obama met the Russian president, Dmitri Medvedev, in the wings of the London summit of the G20 in April 2009.

As for clarifying intentions and gathering information, the qualifications of the *ad hoc* summit are a mixed blessing. On the one hand, the typically low emphasis on negotiation and high emphasis on photo-calls and ceremonial will reduce the opportunities for these purposes to be pursued. On the other, the more relaxed and less adversarial atmosphere might produce a frankness in the exchanges that suits them very well. As for raising the cases of any detained nationals, it is highly unlikely that the *ad hoc* summit will be an appropriate occasion for such a sensitive exercise. This will be especially so if nurturing an old friendship or putting the seal on a new one is the main object of the event.

An important and interesting category of *ad hoc* summits is the funeral of a major political figure attended by high-level delegations from the region concerned or, as is now very common, from all over the world (Berridge 1996). It is a special case, however, because it is more or less useless for the diplomatic purpose for which, it has been argued here, the typical *ad hoc* summit is principally conceived: generating significant diplomatic momentum on a major issue. This is partly because of its theme, and partly because of the unavoidable shortness of notice received by the countries sending delegations. Furthermore, funeral summits carry risks: existing diplomatic schedules are upset, and decisions on attendance and on level of attendance sometimes have to be made in the absence of perfect knowledge about what other states will be doing and of how the delegation will be received.

Nevertheless, 'working funerals' – which, at least by the 1960s, had fallen into a predictable pattern – are of considerable value to the world diplomatic system. This is partly because the shortness of notice available to the mourners has compensating advantages: it provides heads of state and government with a good excuse to break existing schedules in order to have urgent discussions on current problems without arousing public expectations; a decision to attend is unlikely to prove embarrassing as a result of changed circumstances in the short period that elapses before the funeral takes place; and, if attendance is likely to cause controversy, there is little time for domestic opposition to mobilize.

A working funeral is of special diplomatic significance if it is the funeral of an incumbent leader. This is because it is likely to be the first opportunity not only for foreign friends of the bereaved government to confirm their relationship with the new leadership, but also for its foreign rivals to explore the possibility of a change of heart. The leaders of Warsaw Pact satellite states always attended the funerals of Soviet leaders for the former purpose, while Western leaders attended them for the latter, at least in the 1980s. The funeral summit also provides a perfect cover for discreet consultations between foreign rivals seeking to keep their conflict within peaceful bounds, or striving for a way out of an impasse. Funerals of this kind are times of political truce.

Because there is so little time for preparation or for discussions during the event, funeral summits rarely serve for serious negotiation. Their functions are diplomatic signalling, promoting friendly relations (particularly between the mourners and the bereaved), clarifying intentions, and gathering intelligence.

The high-level exchange of views

The exchange of views, which is the final category of summit, is also usually *ad hoc*, but is a more modest affair. It is more likely to be bilateral than multilateral, and have a miscellaneous agenda, if it has an agenda at all, and a lower profile. Sometimes, it is nothing more than a courtesy call; for example, when a foreign leader visits London for medical treatment and is there met briefly by the prime minister (Young 2008: 122–5).

Heads of government who visit a number of countries on a foreign tour are usually engaged in this kind of activity, which is extremely common. For example, in September 1994 the British prime minister, John Major, accompanied by officials and businessmen, went on a week-long trip of this kind. It took in both the Gulf, where he had 'several hours of "very friendly" talks' with King Fahd of Saudi Arabia before proceeding to Abu Dhabi, and South Africa (*Financial Times*). Newly-elected American presidents have a particular weakness for this least ambitious form of summitry, or perhaps are just able to gratify it more readily.

Where new leaders are concerned, the educational argument for this kind of summitry is a strong one, though perhaps more in friendly relationships than adversarial ones. In the latter, there is hardly likely to be such frankness and, as illustrated by the famous Soviet–American summit encounter in Vienna in 1961, the pitfalls for the inexperienced are, in any case, more numerous. In the prior White House discussion on whether or not President Kennedy should seek a face-to-face talk with Nikita Khrushchev, the American ambassador to Moscow, Llewellyn Thompson, strongly supported the idea. His argument was that 'it was impossible for the new President to get at second hand the full flavour of what he was up against' (Schlesinger: 277). However, while the subsequent encounter was clearly educational for both leaders, Kennedy came to the conclusion that Khrushchev's own education had been poor, the latter having wrongly formed the impression that the new American president lacked the necessary resolve to defend Western positions.

The exchange-of-views summit is probably the best of all summits for cementing friendly relations. It also serves well in the promotion of trade, and in taking up serious cases of maltreatment of nationals or those involving the human rights of prominent individuals. It is not self-evident, however, despite its self-styling, that the exchange of views is necessarily better at clarifying intentions and gathering information than the serial summit, or even the average *ad hoc* summit. As for serious negotiations, this kind of summit can nudge continuing talks forward, and even rescue those deadlocked on a particular point, although it will not generally be up to the standard of the serial summit in the last regard or the *ad hoc* summit in the first.

Secrets of success

Chances sometimes have to be taken with summits, especially when the stakes are high. For example, the Americans had no firm guarantee that Nixon would be allowed to meet Mao before he left for China in 1972, and this was a gamble that courted humiliation (Macmillan: 8). But, as a rule, the key to the success of a summit is meticulous preparation by senior officials known as *sherpas*, a term that comes from the name for the locally hired bearers who assist mountaineers in the Himalayas. Assisted by *sous-sherpas*, the *sherpas* might even have the task of arranging a series of bilateral pre-summit summits. In the case of the G8 summits, these take place not only with the other participants, but also with important outsiders. However, if not staged properly, pre-summit summits can backfire. For example, if they include only a small number of the most powerful participants scheduled to attend the summit proper, some of those excluded can be angered. This happened when the leaders of Britain, France, and Germany met alone immediately prior to the European Council in Ghent in October 2001.

Where a summit dealing with a negotiation is concerned, the conventional wisdom is that the preparation should be meticulous – to the point of leaving the summiteers with little more to do than sign the agreement in front of the cameras. Although sometimes disregarded without mishap, as at the Reagan–Gorbachev summits at Geneva in 1985 and at Reykjavik in the following year (Shultz 1993: 596–607), the pre-cooking of agreements is obviously of great importance when the summit is of the highly delicate kind designed to seal a new friendship between erstwhile enemies, as in the case of the Nixon–Mao summit in February 1972. The famous Shanghai Communiqué, released at the end of President Nixon's visit, was substantially negotiated by Henry Kissinger on his own trip to China in the previous October, although it still took him a further 20 hours of negotiation in the wings of the summit to finalize it (Kissinger 1979: 781–4, 1074–87; Macmillan: ch. 19). Pre-cooking is also particularly important when the summit is a friendly encounter, but one that is only scheduled to last for a fleeting period – as in the case of the European Council.

The communiqué issued immediately after the summit should be prepared well in advance, but this is not all. Prior agreement, or agreement at the outset, on what might and might not be said to the media is another important requirement for successful summitry, as it is for any diplomatic encounter involving private discussion. A perfect example of what can happen when there is no script was provided by the joint press conference following the private meeting between Tony Blair and the Syrian leader, Bashar al-Assad, in Damascus at the end of October 2001. (Tony Blair was on a hurried tour of Middle East leaders designed to encourage support for the military action in Afghanistan and stimulate Israeli–Palestinian diplomacy.) To Mr Blair's obvious discomfort, his host condemned the bombing of Afghanistan, and stated that it was Israel and not Syria that was responsible for promoting state terrorism. The British prime minister was generally portrayed in the press as having been publicly humiliated.

There must also be detailed planning of the choreography of the summit. This means the pattern of meetings and events (such as visits, speeches, motorcades, 'walkabouts', joint press conferences, and so on), the mix depending on the character of the summit. Pre-planned choreography is always important, but is especially so if symbolism is expected to take precedence over substance, as at the Reagan–Gorbachev summit in Moscow in 1988. In preparation for this occasion, the White House planning group worked for three months to 'write a script that would resemble an American political campaign with strong emphasis on visual impressions'. Not surprisingly, the analogy that sprang to the mind of former B-movie film star Ronald Reagan was a Cecil B. De Mille epic (Whelan: 89). Among other requirements for successful summitry is not arousing excessive expectations. This might involve repeated prior statements that, say, a planned *ad hoc* summit will merely involve an 'exchange of views', which was the line taken by the Americans in the run-up to the Churchill–Eisenhower–Laniel summit at Bermuda in December 1953 (Young 1986: 901).

These secrets of success are necessary conditions; they are not sufficient ones. The best actors can fumble their lines when the curtain goes up, or simply fall ill. Churchill was unwell at the Bermuda summit, while the French prime minister, Laniel, took to his bed with a high temperature on the second day. Boris Yeltsin, President of the Russian Federation, apparently fast asleep, failed altogether to emerge from his Tupolev after it landed at Shannon airport in the Irish Republic in September 1994. What was going through the mind of the Irish prime minister, Albert Reynolds, who was waiting for his guest on the tarmac – complete with band, red carpet, and local dignitaries – is not difficult to imagine. Unforeseeable external events can also poison the atmosphere of a summit, or cause acute embarrassment. The shooting down over the Soviet Union of an American U-2 spy-plane two weeks before the opening of the East–West summit in Paris in May 1960 reduced this event to a fiasco. The occupation of Tiananmen Square in Beijing by pro-Democracy students prior to the Gorbachev–Deng summit in May 1989 turned this into a humiliation for the Chinese leadership: the programme had to be hastily revised and the Soviet leader brought into the Great Hall of the People through the back door (Cradock: 221). The Thai government had to use helicopters to rescue the leaders attending the 14th ASEAN summit in Pattaya in April 2009, following its abandonment after 'Red Shirt' activists successfully stormed the conference centre. In short, thorough preparation can minimize the risks of summitry, but not eliminate them.

Summary

Summitry might sometimes be highly damaging to diplomacy, and is always risky because of the publicity it attracts; also, it might serve only foreign or domestic propaganda purposes. Nevertheless, judiciously employed and carefully prepared, it can – and does – serve diplomatic purposes as well. This is especially true of the serial summit, an institution to which resort seems to have become reflexive following the establishment of an important international relationship. But the *ad hoc* summit and the high-level exchange of views are also of some importance to diplomacy, if only as devices to inject momentum into a stagnant negotiation. The pattern of summitry has changed in the past, and might change again. Nevertheless, there seems little reason to believe that it will go into a general decline as a mode of communication between states, as it did with the rise of the resident ambassador at the end of the Middle Ages. Television and democracy have seen to that.

Further reading

Albright, Madeleine, *Madam Secretary: A memoir* (Macmillan: London, 2003), ch. 19, on the Wye River summit, October 1998.

Ball, G., *Diplomacy for a Crowded World* (Bodley Head: London, 1976): ch. 3.

Bayne, Nicholas, *Hanging In There: The G7 and G8 summit in maturity and renewal* (Ashgate: Aldershot, 2000).

Berridge, G. R. (ed.), *Diplomatic Classics: Selected texts from Commynes to Vattel* (Palgrave Macmillan: Basingstoke/New York, 2004), selections from Commynes and Bynkershoek.

Bulmer, S. and W. Wessels, *The European Council: Decision-making in European politics* (Macmillan – now Palgrave: Basingstoke, 1987).

Carter, J., *Keeping Faith: Memoirs of a president* (Bantam: New York/London, 1982).

Clift, A. D., *With Presidents to the Summit* (George Mason University Press: Fairfax, VA, 1993).

Cohen, R., *Theatre of Power: The art of diplomatic signalling* (Longman: London/New York, 1987).

Dunn, David H. (ed.), *Diplomacy at the Highest Level: The evolution of international summitry* (Macmillan – now Palgrave: Basingstoke, 1996).

Eubank, K., *The Summit Conferences 1919–1960* (University of Oklahoma Press; Norman, OK, 1966).

Fairbanks, C., *The Allure of Summits* (Foreign Policy Institute: Washington, DC, 1988).

Frey, Linda S. and Marsha L. Frey, *The History of Diplomatic Immunity* (Ohio State University Press: Columbus, OH, 1999).

Gorbachev, Mikhail, *Memoirs*, trsl. by G. Peronansky and T. Varsavsky, first publ. 1995 (Bantam Books: London/New York, 1997).

Hajnal, Peter I., *The G7/G8 System: Evolution, role and documentation* (Ashgate: Aldershot, 1999).

Hodges, Michael R., J. J. Kirton and J. P. Daniels (eds), *The G8's Role in the New Millennium* (Ashgate: Aldershot, 1999).

Kirton, J. J., J. P. Daniels and A. Freytag (eds), *Guiding Global Order: G8 governance in the twenty-first century* (Ashgate: Aldershot, 2001).

Kissinger, H. A., *The White House Years* (Weidenfeld & Nicolson/Michael Joseph: London, 1979): 769, 781, 919–21.

Macmillan, Margaret, *Seize the Hour: When Nixon met Mao* (John Murray: London, 2006).

Nicolson, H., *Peacemaking 1919*, rev. edn (Constable: London, 1943).

Plischke, E., *Summit Diplomacy: Personal diplomacy of the United States presidents* (Greenwood Press: New York, 1974).

Post, J. M. and R. S. Robbins, *When Illness Strikes the Leader* (Yale University Press: New Haven/London, 1993).

Putnam, R., 'The Western Economic summits: a political interpretation', in C. Merlini, (ed.) *Economic Summits and Western Decision-making* (Croom Helm: London; St Martin's Press – now Palgrave: New York, 1984).

Putnam, R. and N. Bayne, *Hanging Together: Cooperation and conflict in the Seven Power summits*, 2nd edn (Sage: London, 1988).

Reynolds, David, *Summits: Six meetings that shaped the twentieth century* (Allen Lane: London, 2007).

Shultz, G. P., *Turmoil and Triumph: My years as Secretary of State* (Scribner's: New York, 1993): chs 30, 36, 46 and 49.

Thatcher, Margaret, *The Downing Street Years* (HarperCollins: London, 1993): ch. XVII, esp. the first two pages.

Weihmiller, G. R. and D. Doder, *US–Soviet Summits* (University Press of America: Lanham, NY/London, 1986).

Werts, J., *The European Council* (North-Holland: Amsterdam, 1992).

Whelan, J. G., *The Moscow Summit 1988* (Westview Press: Boulder, CO, 1990).

Yeltsin, B., *Midnight Diaries* (Phoenix: London, 2001): chs 8, 9, and 23.

Young, John W., *Twentieth-Century Diplomacy: A case study of British practice, 1963–1976* (Cambridge: Cambridge University Press, 2008): chs 6 and 7.

11
Public Diplomacy

Propaganda is the manipulation of public opinion through the mass media for political ends. It might be more or less honest, more or less subtle, and sometimes directed more at achieving long-term, rather than short-term, changes in opinion. Its target might be foreign public opinion, domestic public opinion, or both. Makers of propaganda have traditionally distinguished between white propaganda and black propaganda – the former admitting its source, while the latter does not. 'Public diplomacy' is the modern name for white propaganda directed chiefly at foreign publics. Why has it acquired this new name? Why are the activities it embraces now so popular? What contribution is made to them by foreign ministries and diplomats posted abroad?

Propaganda about propaganda

Propaganda directed abroad cannot be called 'propaganda' by governments because this term has long been associated with the systematic spreading of lies. What it needs, therefore, is a euphemism. But 'public diplomacy' was not the first euphemism for propaganda to be employed by governments; neither is it self-evident why it should currently be in fashion. How this came about is instructive, because there is an influential body of thought that maintains that public diplomacy is *not* propaganda but something quite new and altogether more enlightened.

Propaganda acquired a bad reputation in the first half of the twentieth century because in World War I, and especially in the hands of the totalitarian regimes that emerged afterwards, it was particularly slippery, strident, and mendacious. As a result, most governments, although forced to resort to methods that were, in principle, identical, baulked at the idea of *publicly* admitting that they were making propaganda. Instead, they claimed, what they were engaged in was 'information work'. Ministries of Information were created, especially during World War II, and although these tended not to outlast the duration, the inception of the Cold War in the late 1940s ensured that the residues they left were soon being used to build 'information services'. The result of this was that 'information sections', or 'information and cultural relations sections' (later known in the US Foreign Service collectively as 'public affairs sections'), together with their 'information officers', became an established feature of many embassies for the rest of the century; even the French employed *attachés d'information*. The United States Information Agency (USIA), with its arm's length relationship with the Department of State, which was the best-known supplier of such officers, was created in 1953. In the following year, a summary of the then still-confidential report of the Drogheda Committee on Britain's 'Overseas Information Services' – which was eventually so influential on British practice – was published (HCPP 1954). But the point is that no one involved in or discussing this *'information* work' was under any illusions that what they were really talking about was overseas *propaganda* (HCPP 1954: *passim*; Plischke: 149). The British prime minister, Winston Churchill, had no hesitation in describing even the cultural work of the British Council as propaganda, although others were sometimes more coy about this (National Archives, London).

The point is neatly illustrated by the memoirs of Sir Robert Marett, a British diplomat who specialized in propaganda and served as secretary to the Drogheda Committee. The sub-heading of his book is *An Inside View of Britain's Overseas Information Services*, but the first part is called 'An Introduction to Propaganda'. In describing his appointment as head of the Foreign Office's 'Information Policy Department' immediately after working for Drogheda, he even observed that he had achieved the 'doubtful distinction' of being the 'Dr. Goebbels of the Foreign Office' (p. 171). (Dr Joseph Goebbels was Hitler's notorious Minister for Public Enlightenment and Propaganda from 1933 until 1945.) In short, when it was publicly using a term such as 'information work', the political class knew that it was simply making propaganda about propaganda.

Referring to information work a decade later, the Plowden Report on the British foreign service observed that 'It is easy to see why it was necessary to adopt the more urbane label', though it regretted that the phrase lacked the 'sense of purpose and direction' conveyed by the term 'propaganda'. It added that information officers should not think that their task was merely to provide information to foreigners for its own sake. 'The Information Services', Plowden reminded its readers, 'grew out of the need, in two world wars, to help achieve political aims by means of propaganda' (HCPP 1964: para. 260).

It might be that the term 'information' had some success in camouflaging the propaganda activities of states such as Britain and the United States as far as their broad audiences were concerned, but it is unlikely to have fooled the foreign political classes. It also had other problems. Not only was there a worry that the label failed to convey a sufficient sense of political purpose to its practitioners, but also in some states, such as Turkey, it aroused suspicion of them: since 'information' suggested 'intelligence', it implied that their business was *gathering* information rather than imparting it – spying (Arndt: 28; Berridge 2009: 216). The consequence was that the term 'information work' gradually fell out of favour and a fresh euphemism was required.

In 1965, Edmund Gullion, a former US Foreign Service officer and then Dean of the Fletcher School of Law and Diplomacy, decided to press into service the vintage phrase 'public diplomacy', which was, up to this point, nothing more than a synonym for the 'open diplomacy' allegedly exemplified by the pre-war League of Nations. With its old echoes of this idealistic enterprise, 'public diplomacy' certainly generated better vibrations than 'propaganda', while, at the same time, suggesting it – because most observers of the League's successor, the United Nations, had come to the conclusion that open diplomacy was nothing more than propaganda anyway (Cull 2006b). Moreover, 'public diplomacy' does not suggest spying. The most important reason why this 'ill-defined portemanteau phrase' (Arndt: 480) eventually took off in the United States, however, was that its very vagueness served the purpose of those in Washington who wished to bring all of America's overseas propaganda activities under one roof – that of the US Information Agency. This was achieved in 1978, when – to the dismay of traditionalists – the USIA also assumed responsibility for US cultural diplomacy by absorbing the Department of State's Bureau of Educational and Cultural Affairs (Arndt: chs 23 and 24; Cull 2006b). Thus, ironically, did the allegedly more benign label 'public diplomacy' help to taint all agencies with the cruder style of propaganda: the 'poetry of diplomacy' in the US Foreign Service began to be heard less and less (Arndt: 546).

In the course of the 1990s, more states adopted the euphemism 'public diplomacy' to describe their propaganda operations and, today, it is more or less ubiquitous (although 'information' has by no means disappeared). But the term had been hijacked to give propaganda cosmetic surgery and to facilitate a successful campaign in American bureaucratic politics. It was not introduced to identify a new activity (Gullion, its author, knew this and would have preferred the term 'propaganda', but for its negative connotations). Neither does it now equate to a new activity, despite the popular view that public diplomacy 'at its best' is different from propaganda because it invites the absorption of as much influence from foreign publics as it seeks to achieve over them (Cull 2007). This might amount to nothing more than a claim that public diplomacy is a new *style* of propaganda, but sounds like a political doctrine. In this case, the answer has to be that listening to foreigners is one thing; giving equal weight to what they say is another. In the hard world of governments, 'public diplomacy' remains a euphemism for propaganda. This is obvious from what they do under its heading, as well as from how – despite the deep lake of semantic convolutions that they feel the need to fill and then wade through – they end up defining it (Wilton: 12; Carter of Coles: 8; US Advisory Commission on Public Diplomacy: 4).

The importance of public diplomacy

While one of the aims of conventional diplomacy is to exert direct influence on foreign governments, the aim of propaganda, or public diplomacy, is usually to do this *indirectly*; that is, by appealing over the heads of those governments to the people with influence upon them. In a tightly controlled authoritarian regime, these might be just 'the influential few', to borrow a phrase favoured by the Drogheda Committee; in a broadly based liberal democracy, it is likely to be the great mass of voters.

Propaganda has grown in importance since the start of World War I, albeit fitfully, because, after that time, the motives to reach for it strengthened while the means to employ it multiplied. The spread of democracy and total war both vastly increased the political importance of public opinion; then followed the emergence of ideology, a simplified, quasi-religious mode of political argument peculiarly suited to propaganda; and, finally, arrived the invention of nuclear weapons, which made too risky anything other than a 'war of words' between states incapable of serious diplomacy – as in the Cold War. In such circumstances, the appeal of being able to use propaganda to turn a foreign population against its own government on a key issue, or even to the point of overthrowing it, was enormous. And to all this was added a steady improvement in the means of delivery: first, via the printed word (and photograph) to increasingly literate populations; then, via short-wave radio broadcasting in indigenous languages, which reached the illiterate and is relatively cheap and virtually impossible to block; and, most recently, by television and the Internet.

In the course of the twentieth century, much was also learned about the ingredients of successful propaganda – notably, that it is best used to reinforce existing attitudes and stimulate action on the part of the already well-disposed, rather than to try to change entrenched opinions. There were sometimes doubts about its effectiveness, chiefly because of the methodological problems that have always dogged research into this subject, but these doubts were always overcome in the end (Berridge 1997: 138–43). This was generally a result of a consensus of informed opinion that propaganda had played a key role in certain dramatic developments. In recent years, these include the collapse of Communism in Eastern Europe, where broadcasting by Western radio stations is believed to have been critical; and the spread of Islamist thinking – not least, via the Internet, to Muslim communities in the West. Certainly, there is great fear of propaganda, which is why the Chinese government censors the Internet and the Iranian government did likewise during the turbulence in Tehran that began in June 2009.

In 1954, the Drogheda Committee probably summed up the view of those who assessed the value of propaganda most cautiously when it wrote that 'The effect of propaganda on the course of events is never likely to be more than marginal. But in certain circumstances it may be decisive in tipping the balance between diplomatic success and failure'. As a result, it concluded, 'The Information Services must today be regarded as part of the normal apparatus of the diplomacy of a Great Power' (HCPP 1954: 6–7). Since the notorious attacks on the Twin Towers of the World Trade Center in New York City on 11 September 2001, which drew attention so dramatically to the widespread hostility to the West in the Muslim world, this axiom has been taken to heart more than at any point since World War II: it has become a major instrument in the new, commanding conflict, the so-called 'War on Terror'.

'Public diplomacy' today, then, is not merely a fashionable phrase; it is also a fashionable practice – and a fashionable one over which to agonize. In 2002, the Wilton Review pronounced on it in Britain, but only two years later the government commissioned a further report on the subject, this time under the businessman and Labour life peer, Lord Carter of Coles, which appeared at the end of 2005 (neither appeared to have heard of the Drogheda Report, which was far more penetrating than either). But this was nothing compared with what was happening in the United States, where 25 reports had appeared in the previous two years (Carter of Coles: 68). In order to develop this epic rediscovery of the wheel, foreign ministries have generally been given the lead role.

The role of the MFA: player and coordinator

Ministries of foreign affairs, even of small states, commonly play a number of roles in connection with propaganda. Some of these are routine, well-known and uncontroversial:

- providing embassies with printed and other publicity materials for distribution (still in demand, despite spreading access to the Internet), and training for their press and public affairs officers
- dealing with foreign correspondents based in the capital (see Box 11.1)
- putting out their own propaganda directly, in recent years especially via their multi-language version websites, with Arabic pages increasingly popular on those of Western foreign ministries and even foreign ministers' personal blogs, and
- perhaps funding associated broadcasting organizations and cultural and educational bodies such as the Goethe-Institut (Germany), the Alliance Française (France), the Cervantes Institute (Spain), the Dante Alighieri Society (Italy), the Camões Institute (Portugal), and the British Council (Britain), whose audiences are, in the main, the *next* generation of decision-makers and opinion-leaders.

Box 11.1   'News management': dealing with foreign correspondents

Making sure that foreign correspondents see things from the 'correct perspective' is particularly important because, as the Wilton Review noted in 2002, there are good grounds for believing that their articles have a greater impact in their home countries than 'any of our [*sic*!] other public diplomacy outputs'. News management normally includes the provision of official briefings on current events, helping to arrange interviews with ministers and officials, and laying on tours. It might even, as at the 'Foreign Press Centers' in Washington and New York (the former opened in 1946, and the latter in 1968), extend to the provision of computer work stations and other facilities. The number of foreign correspondents based in Western capitals has increased greatly in recent years. In 2005, the Carter Review estimated that there were over 2000 foreign correspondents in London. The Israeli MFA is believed to be particularly effective in dealing with foreign correspondents, as also is the Quai d'Orsay. The Information Department of the Chinese MFA opened an 'International Press Center' in May 2000.

Sources: Wilton: 11, 20; Carter of Coles 2005: 52–4; US Department of State; www.

Some of these tasks are also far from new. News management, at least on an organized and systematic basis, goes back only to World War I, but one favourite device goes back to the early nineteenth century. This is the selective publication by foreign ministries of documents from their archives. These were not only carefully chosen, but also sometimes 'corrected' – a practice for which, in Britain, Lord Salisbury was notorious (Roberts: 509). It even became quite common for 'secret' diplomatic despatches to be drafted with a view to their possible later publication, the real messages being confined to 'private letters'. The one-off publications containing these selections were called 'Blue Books' in Britain, 'Yellow Books' in France, 'White Books' in Germany, and so on. The US State Department favoured what was, for a considerable time, an annual publication, the *Foreign Relations of the United States*, which first appeared in 1861 (Hamilton: 49).

Foreign ministries, or functionally equivalent bodies under other names, also have public diplomacy tasks that are sometimes more controversial at home and raise serious public policy questions. These include the elaboration of public diplomacy strategy and relating it to foreign policy priorities; the monitoring of implementation and measuring of performance; and the coordination of the activities of the various bodies engaged in propaganda to minimise duplication of effort and ensure that they are in tune with the strategy.

It is especially in liberal-democratic states – that is, in those where individual liberties from state control exist independently of broadly based democratic institutions, and where such liberties remain strong – that foreign ministry coordination of public diplomacy raises awkward questions. This is because, in such states, some of the most effective propaganda – gentle, stimulating, honest as far as it goes, and associated with the provision of valuable services to its audiences – has usually been conducted by bodies with a marked degree of independence from state control. The paradigm cases are the BBC World Service (since March 2008, including BBC Arabic Television) and the British Council, which, despite their financial dependence on the Foreign Office, have generally been able to maintain editorial independence and day-to-day operational independence, respectively; in the United States, the Fulbright Programme has traditionally had a similar status. Moreover, it is, in large part, precisely because of their arm's length relationship with government that they have always been so effective.

The problem for the liberal-democracies is how to improve coordination without undermining the credibility of the arm's length public diplomacy bodies. This is not surprising, since there is a very thin line between coordination and 'direction'. In the last few years, the British government's answer to this has been to create a Public Diplomacy Board representing the Foreign Office, the British Council and – as an observer – the BBC World Service. It is chaired by a Foreign Office minister but is supposed to have a 'strong independent vice-chair', and is supported by a unit within the Foreign Office that is, in effect, its executive arm. The Public Diplomacy Board – which is supplemented by an advisory board on which other organizations are represented – is responsible for agreeing strategy, advising on resource allocation, and performance measurement. Similar steps have been attempted in the United States, where already, in 1978, the previously separate oversight commissions on 'Information' and 'Educational Exchange' established under the Smith–Mundt Act of 1948 had been merged into the politicized, if bipartisan, United States Advisory Commission on Public Diplomacy, and (as noted) USIA took over cultural diplomacy as well. In 1999, albeit chiefly for reasons of economy, USIA itself was absorbed by the Department of State and a new position of 'under secretary of state for public diplomacy' created, while the former agency's area offices were rather awkwardly integrated into the appropriate geographical bureaus (US Advisory Commission on Public Diplomacy: 26–7). Oversight of the Voice of America (VOA) was also transferred from USIA to a 'politically appointed' Broadcasting Board of Governors (Cull 2006a). In both Britain and the United States, some nervousness (at a minimum) on the part of cultural diplomatists has been generated by this trend.

The role of the embassy

When asked by a member of the Select Committee on Foreign Affairs of the House of Commons to comment on views expressed to it in support of more public diplomacy, Sir John Kerr, former British ambassador in Washington and then permanent under-secretary in the Foreign Office, replied:

> I think it is a very elegant re-invention of the wheel. Embassies have always had such a role. While they exist to talk privately to governments, they also exist to talk to people and populations at large, and that is *probably the modern ambassador's principal function, to be on television, to be on the radio, to accept all the platforms.* ... We are not shut away but we never really were (FAC: para. 119, emphasis added).

Sir John Kerr was right, and it is not difficult to find early examples to illustrate his point; neither do they always feature eccentric ambassadors acting without instructions.

Sir Henry Wotton, British resident ambassador in Venice at the beginning of the seventeenth century, distributed Protestant publications among members of the political elite as a key part of his attempt to stir up the republic against the Pope; it is true that he seems not to have been acting on written instructions, but he knew that he could rely on the sympathy of James I (Smith 1907: 89–90). To take another example, at the end of the eighteenth century, the new French minister plenipotentiary to the United States, Citizen Charles-Edmond Genet, was formally despatched from Paris as primarily a 'revolutionary missionary to the American people', rather than as an envoy in the ordinary way to its government, and he behaved accordingly, determined to 'excite, display, and exploit American enthusiasm for the French Revolution' (O'Brien: ch. 5). Nevertheless, as in the case of foreign ministries, it was the twentieth century before embassies became routinely involved in public diplomacy, and only in recent years that, as Sir John Kerr maintained, it has become arguably the principal role of the ambassador, as opposed to the embassy generally.

Having said this, the ability of an ambassador to engage in public diplomacy varies with the political culture of the receiving state and the sensitivities of the government of the day. This is especially true when there is a risk that the ambassador's propaganda might be construed as interference in the domestic affairs of the state concerned. In a totalitarian state such as North Korea, where diplomats are very tightly controlled and even the telephone directory is a state secret (Hoare: 116–21), it is inconceivable that an ambassador would be either willing or able to make direct appeals to the public on questions of any kind. Even in France, remarked Sir Nicholas Henderson, a former British ambassador to that country, 'it would be thought odd and might prove counter-productive with the French government for a foreign diplomat in Paris to appear to be advancing his country's cause in public'. But in the liberal democracies, as a rule, the ambassador is able to adopt a propaganda role with considerable freedom. In Washington, to which Henderson was moved in 1979, it was quite different, he noted: 'It would be regarded there as a sign of lack of conviction in his country's case if an Ambassador did not go out of his way to promote it publicly' (Henderson: 287–8). Henderson famously did just this, putting the British point of view directly to the American people on television on a number of issues of considerable sensitivity in Washington, notably

Northern Ireland and the Falklands crisis; it is generally believed that he had considerable success. Ambassadors from authoritarian regimes enjoy the same rights. For example, during the Gulf War in early 1991, Iraq's ambassadors in Europe and the United States were at the forefront of Baghdad's propaganda campaign. This is perhaps one reason why Saddam Hussein did not sever diplomatic relations with the Coalition powers until three weeks after the outbreak of the war (Taylor: 97–8, 106, 181).

Resident ambassadors are well-placed to engage in public diplomacy, because they are attractive to the local media as interviewees and to a variety of local bodies as speakers. In the absence of a high-ranking visitor from home, they are the most authoritative representatives of their governments. They are also likely to have mastered the sound-bite and the after-dinner address. It is improbable that they will make any great fuss about having to appear at an inconvenient time. And they will expect neither a fee nor payment of their expenses.

But the ambassador is by no means the only member of the embassy with a public diplomacy role. Even small embassies usually have one officer who is required to devote at least some time to handling the local media and trying to coordinate the activities of local representatives of any public diplomacy 'partners'. Such a person used to be known – and sometimes still is – as the 'press attaché', but is now, more often than not, known as an 'information officer'. Larger embassies might have a whole section devoted to public diplomacy, usually relying heavily on locally engaged staff. They also often have responsibility for cultural relations: in this case they are known in US embassies as the 'public affairs section', as already mentioned; and, in British embassies, as the 'press and public affairs section'. The Danish embassy in Washington has a 'public diplomacy and communication section'. These sections are not always as large as the recent enthusiasm for public diplomacy might lead us to expect, because some diplomatic services believe that the embassy's other sections are best placed to conduct their own public diplomacy – the commercial section should handle commercial publicity, and so on. The Wilton Review formed the impression that information activities could sometimes form as much as 50 per cent of a British embassy's work (Wilton: 17).

An information officer's role does not only involve distributing publicity material, but also 'working the media'; that is, persuading local journalists to run friendly stories: this is the counterpart activity of what the foreign ministry should be doing at home with foreign correspondents (Box 11.1). In the past, this has involved bribing individual journalists and subsidizing local newspapers, and it would be surprising if the same sort of thing does not go on in some states today. One of the reasons why the British embassy in Turkey retained a major presence in Istanbul after it was forced – along with other embassies – gradually to shift its presence to Ankara in the 1920s, and also why the ambassador continued to spend a great deal of time in the former capital, was that this was where the editors and leader writers of the major Turkish newspapers were still located.

The work of an embassy's information officers is particularly prone to bursts of frenetic activity; some of them anticipated, some of them not. In the former category falls that provoked by the long-planned arrival of high-level visitors from home, which must be preceded with the sort of advance publicity that will ensure their enthusiastic reception, and be accompanied by solicitous attention to the needs of the local media for interviews, photo-opportunities and background briefings during their stay. In short, the information section must ensure that a glow of warmth and approval is left behind after the visitors' departure, and so assist other aspects of the embassy's work. In the 'bursts of unanticipated activity' falls that required, for example, by a furious explosion on the part of the local media, perhaps accompanied by hostile demonstrations in the streets, at criticism of some aspect of the host country's domestic habits by the press at home. Information sections often find themselves fire-fighting for this and other reasons. The sudden increase of the workload of information officers in Denmark's embassies, especially in Muslim states, following publication of the cartoons of the Prophet Muhammad in a Danish newspaper in early 2006, is not difficult to imagine.

It will be apparent that, in contrast to the long-term outlook of cultural attachés or cultural affairs officers, the horizon of the embassy's information officers is much more proximate: their task is the manipulation of public attitudes in the following hours, days and weeks, and is obviously political. Because cultural diplomats have a quite different style of operation, and usually wish to avoid the impression of having any kind of political agenda at all, there has – at least, where they are members of bodies such as the British Council – always been some resistance to the idea of serving under the embassy's roof. Those sharing this view maintain that a separate physical presence not only makes them more approachable, but also makes it more probable that they will be able to remain even if the embassy is forced to depart. However, the 'coordinators' reply that appointing them to the embassy as cultural attachés makes coordination easier. They also point out that, in practice, it does not do significant harm to the reputation of the educational bodies – because foreign publics are aware that they are sponsored by the sending state anyway, that putting them under the embassy roof is more economical than having to maintain (and guard) separate premises for them, and that it gives them diplomatic privileges and immunities that might well turn out to be valuable in unstable states. In recent years the calls to coordination and economy have been difficult for the 'culturalists' to resist. A compromise solution is to give them diplomatic rank, but still permit them to operate from separate premises, although this has given the British Council offices in Russia little protection from severe police harassment in recent years.

Summary

'Public diplomacy' is what we call our propaganda; 'propaganda' is what the other side does. It remains true that this activity, the aim of which is to influence foreign governments by trying to win over their own people, varies enormously in both its character and its targets. Renewed emphasis has been given to it in the West in recent years, chiefly because of fear of the consequences of mounting popular hostility in the Muslim world. The lead role in public diplomacy is frequently given to foreign ministries. For ambassadors, it is probably now their most important duty – although, for the rest of the embassy staff, only one among many.

Further reading

Arndt, Richard T., *The First Resort of Kings: American cultural diplomacy in the twentieth century* (Potomac Books: Washington, DC, 2005).

Berridge, G. R., *International Politics: States, power and conflict since 1945*, 3rd edn (Pearson Education: Harlow, 1997): ch. 8.

Carter of Coles, Lord, *Public Diplomacy Review*, December 2005 [www].

Childs, J. Rives, *American Foreign Service* (Holt: New York, 1948): ch. 12.

Cull, Nicholas J., ' "Public Diplomacy" before Gullion: the evolution of a phrase', USC Center on Public Diplomacy [www].

Cull, Nicholas J., 'Public diplomacy: seven lessons for its future from its past' [www].

Cull, Nicholas J., ' "The Perfect War": US public diplomacy and international broadcasting during Desert Shield and Desert Storm, 1990/1991' [www].

Cull, Nicholas J., *The Cold War and the United States Information Agency: American propaganda and public diplomacy, 1945–1989* (Cambridge University Press: Cambridge, 2008).

HCPP, Cmd. 9138, April 1954: *Summary of the Report of the Independent Committee of Enquiry into the Overseas Information Services* ['the Drogheda Report'].

Hamilton, Keith, 'Historical diplomacy: foreign ministries and the management of the past', in Jovan Kurbalija (ed.), *Knowledge and Diplomacy* (DiploFoundation: Malta, 1999).

Marett, Sir Robert, *Through the Back Door: An inside view of Britain's Overseas Information Services* (Pergamon Press: Oxford, 1968): chs 13–15.

Melissen, Jan, *The New Public Diplomacy: Soft power in international relations* (Palgrave: Basingstoke, 2006).

Plischke, Elmer, *Conduct of American Diplomacy*, 3rd edn (Van Nostrand: Princeton, NJ, 1967): 149–50.

Taylor, Philip M., *Munitions of the Mind: A history of propaganda from the ancient world to the present era*, 3rd edn (Manchester University Press: Manchester, 2003).

Wilton, Christopher, Jonathan Griffin, Andrew Fotheringham, *Changing Perceptions: Review of public diplomacy* ['Wilton Review'], 2002 [www].

12
Telecommunications

From ancient times until well into the nineteenth century, all messages, including diplomatic messages, were carried by hand. Even at the beginning of the twenty-first century, diplomatic couriers are still employed for the delivery of certain top-secret packages (Angell). But over the past century and a half, diplomatic messages have been increasingly carried by telecommunication: any mode of communication over a long distance (*tele* is Greek for 'far') that requires human agency only in the sending and reception of the message that it contains and not, as with a courier, in its conveyance. This chapter will consider the advantages and disadvantages of the different kinds of telecommunication. It will also give some emphasis to crisis diplomacy, because it is in this activity that telecommunication is often held to be of greatest value, and it is certainly here that it has received the greatest attention.

The communication by drums and smoke-signals that originated in ancient times, and the optical telegraph or semaphore systems introduced in Europe in the late eighteenth century, were forms of telecommunication. Nevertheless, it did not make a major impact on diplomacy until the introduction of the electric telegraph towards the middle of the nineteenth century. Soon, using submarine as well as land cables, written messages sent by telegraph cut delivery times over some routes from weeks to hours, although they were insecure and so needed to be enciphered, and for a long time were also expensive and prone to garbling. The invention of radio telegraphy in the 1890s improved this medium further, although it remained insecure. In the early twentieth century, it became possible to deliver the spoken word over vast distances by telephone (available in the late nineteenth century only over short distances) and short-wave radio. Since World War II, further well-known refinements have been added, among them fax, electronic mail, instant messaging, mobile phones, and multi-media video-conferencing; and other exciting developments in information and communications technologies (ICTs) are no doubt in the pipeline.

Worries over security have traditionally caused governments to employ the latest form of telecommunication only with great caution – and after considerable hesitation. Nevertheless, eventually the appeal of these various means of communication has generally won the day, and the appeal of none has been greater than that of the telephone, especially in a crisis.

Telephone diplomacy flourishes

Telephone diplomacy has serious drawbacks, some of which are common to most forms of telecommunication. For one thing, it foregoes all forms of non-verbal communication. The use of body language, dress, venue, and setting – by means of which, in a personal encounter, a summiteer or diplomat can add nuance or emphasis to an oral message, or even *say* one thing but *mean* another – are all foregone in telephone diplomacy. A corollary of this is that, compared with a personal visit by a foreign minister, with all its attendant preparations, a telephone call is far less effective in forcing officials to focus on the questions at issue. It also passes up the opportunity, should this be advantageous, to generate news coverage for a message. These points were both made by critics of Colin Powell, US secretary of state from 2001 until 2005, who undertook far fewer foreign trips than his predecessors and relied instead more on the telephone, sometimes making as many as 100 calls a day (*Washington Post* 2003).

Furthermore, telephone conversations cannot be scripted: the issues that come up are not entirely predictable and remarks made spontaneously might not convey exactly the meaning intended, even if simultaneous translation is not needed. A particular danger that flows from this, as well as from the immediacy of the exchange, is that there is 'no time for reflection or consultation' (Satow: vol. I, 157). This might have one of two results, neither of which is desirable: either the receiver of the call is bounced into a hasty decision on what might well be a matter of vital importance; or the receiver refuses to make an immediate decision – thereby creating resentment on the part of the caller because the gambit has failed, and on part of the receiver because it has been attempted (Thatcher 1995: 230).

Things said over the telephone cannot be unsaid, either, and there is no telling to what use an adversary might put a suitably edited tape-recording of a conversation. Written messages that subsequently prove embarrassing might plausibly be dismissed as forgeries but this is more difficult with taped conversations, as President Nixon found to his cost during the Watergate affair in the early 1970s. While there might be disadvantages to the recording of a telephone conversation, a disadvantage might also attach to its absence: a subsequent difference of opinion as to what was actually said (Shultz 1997: 6). In a relationship where there is mistrust, a profound cultural gap, and only a limited understanding of the rival's machinery of government, there can also be no confidence that a promise to pass on a message has been acted upon, or even that the person at the other end of the line is who they say they are. The last risk is not merely hypothetical. President George W. Bush once had an extended telephone conversation with a person purporting to be President Hashemi-Rafsanjani that was later traced back to the Iranian Ministry of Intelligence and Security; some time later a 16-year-old Icelandic high school student pretending to be the president of Iceland and passing background security questions by getting the answers from Wikipedia, got as far as President George W. Bush's secretary.

Different time zones and congested schedules can also create serious logistical difficulties for use of the telephone, especially at head of state and government level: 'preparing a phone call can sometimes take days', remarks a former senior minister and ambassador of Saudi Arabia (Algosaibi: 238). If a call is arranged at this level, there are also circumstances in which the choice of the medium – irrespective of what is said by means of it – might have the effect of inducing a crisis atmosphere when the opposite effect is what is intended. It appears to have been fear of this that, after some debate in the Situation Room, induced President George W. Bush to leave to traditional channels resolution of the dispute provoked by the collision over the South China Sea between an American EP-3 spy plane and a Chinese jet fighter in April 2001, rather than telephone his Chinese opposite number, Jiang Zemin (*Guardian* 2001a). Finally, unless exceptional precautions are taken, telephone diplomacy is vulnerable to eavesdropping by the sophisticated and well-resourced SIGINT agencies of the major powers. The UN secretary general has fallen victim to this (Boutros-Ghali 1999: 276–7), and there has been much publicity about the electronic interception of the communications of permanent missions at the UN in New York.

But telephone diplomacy has such appeal that great efforts have been taken to minimise these risks, and the remaining ones are courted every day. Unlike the various forms of written telecommunications, the telephone is easier to use and does not involve squinting at a desk-top computer screen or hand-held device, or require manual dexterity; it can also send signals by means of tone of voice and volume. The telephone is, above all, more *personal*, which means that it is more flattering to the recipient; by contrast, written messages, especially at the highest level, are usually drafted by someone else and recognized as such. The telephone also provides considerable certainty that a message has got through and, because it rarely generates a verbatim transcript, is deniable if this should prove to be expedient. It also makes possible the *immediate* correction of a misunderstanding or *immediate* adjustment of a statement that has given unintended offence (provided this is realized), so that neither is allowed to fester. Finally, the telephone provides the opportunity to extract an *immediate* response from the party at the other end of the line – and many people find it more difficult to say 'no' over the telephone than in a written response. Thus, the possibility of being bounced into a hasty decision might be a danger to one party, but the corollary is that it is an attractive opportunity to the other.

At head of state and government level, advisers can prepare talking points and take notes (Patterson: 57–9); and internal regulations of government can – and do – expressly forbid the treatment of classified issues on the telephone at the sub-political level. Technical steps can also be taken to assure the security of sensitive messages and, in any case, much of the information contained in telephone calls is out of date long before hostile intelligence agencies can track, digest, and circulate it to their customers. It is chiefly for all of these reasons that political leaders and senior government officials, both in foreign ministries and OGDs, attach such importance to using the telephone in maintaining their overseas communications.

Telephone diplomacy, despite its appeal, is more appropriate in some circumstances, and in some relationships, than in others. Its advantages are particularly apparent during fast moving situations and major international crises, although less so for making contact with an adversary than with allies and other friends, whether to orchestrate their response to a crisis or sort out a serious problem among them. In either case, 'conference calls' can be employed.

Madeleine Albright claims to have been the first to use a conference call, while US secretary of state at the time of the NATO air war against Serb forces during the Kosovo conflict in 1999. It was the best means, she believed, of coordinating the actions and statements of the alliance, which in all had 19 members (Albright: 409, 412). Unavoidably using the more traditional method in the run-up to the Gulf War at the beginning of 1991, the US President, George H. W. Bush, used the telephone to contact the Malaysian prime minister in a Tokyo restaurant in order to secure his support for a vital Security Council resolution. Between the opening of this crisis in August 1990 and the end of the year, Bush exchanged 40 telephone calls with another leader whose support was even more vital to him in this crisis, Turgut Özal, the president of Turkey (Stearns: 11). On the morning of Good Friday, 10 April 1998, when the Northern Ireland talks in Belfast were on the verge of an historic breakthrough (see Chapter 4), US president, Bill Clinton, made personal calls to many of the key participants, urging them to grasp the moment. 'The calls were very helpful', says the US mediator, as almost certainly they were (Mitchell: 178).

A particularly vivid account of the effective use of the telephone in an intra-alliance crisis is provided in the memoirs of James Callaghan, British foreign secretary in the mid-1970s. Here, he describes in some detail the many calls he exchanged in the hours immediately following the entry of Turkey's forces into Cyprus on 20 July 1974, which led to an immediate threat of war with Greece. This was a crisis in which Britain could not avoid playing a key role because not only was Cyprus a member of the Commonwealth, but also Britain was one of the three guarantors of its constitution, independence, and territorial integrity under the Treaty of Guarantee of 1960. The other two guarantors were fellow NATO allies Greece and Turkey. Callaghan wished to obtain an immediate ceasefire and instigate talks between the Greeks and the Turks, for which he needed American assistance. In the course of 'mad activity' on 21 July, Callaghan spoke on two occasions each to the Turkish president, the Greek foreign minister, and the French foreign minister (acting for the European Community). He also spoke to the Austrian chancellor, Bruno Kreisky, about the possibility of using Vienna as the venue for the talks. And he spoke to US secretary of state, Henry Kissinger, 'about nine or ten times'. By means of these 'almost continuous telephone exchanges', amplified massively by the fact that Kissinger was also calling both the Greeks and the Turks, shortly before midnight Callaghan learned that the Turks had finally accepted a ceasefire effective from 14.00 hours on the following day. Talks between the foreign ministers of the three guarantor powers began three days after that (Callaghan: 342–6).

A further example of the use of the telephone in an intra-alliance crisis is provided by the calls exchanged in October 1983 on the White House–10 Downing Street 'hotline' (Box 12.1). The first was made by the British prime minister, Margaret Thatcher, and was designed to underline the importance of a written message that had just been dispatched imploring the American president, Ronald Reagan, not to invade the Commonwealth state of Grenada. (Only the previous day, the British foreign secretary had publicly stated that he had no knowledge of any American intention to intervene in Grenada. A subsequent invasion of a Commonwealth state by Britain's closest ally, without consultation, would make Mrs Thatcher look weak and foolish.) As it turned out, her telephone diplomacy was ineffective – it was already too late. However, the story was different with the call that she received back from Ronald Reagan the following day. The president began with a gallant and disarming preamble, which was just as well because, on her own admission, the Iron Lady was 'not in the sunniest of moods'. He then apologized for the embarrassment that had been caused and explained the practical considerations that had made full consultation impossible. This clearly had a soothing effect on Mrs Thatcher. 'There was not much I felt able to say', she records in her memoirs, 'and so I more or less held my peace, but I was glad to have received the telephone call' (Thatcher 1995: 331–3). This exchange over the hotline was the more effective because, despite the closeness of these two leaders, it was at that time still rarely used (see Box 12.1).

More examples of both sorts accumulate every day: Tony Blair keeping in touch on the Lebanon crisis with allies and friends during his holiday in the Caribbean in August 2006; President-elect Barack Obama phoning the German, French, and British leaders about the global financial crisis immediately after his election victory in November 2008; the foreign ministers of China, Japan, and South Korea having to resort to the telephone over the mini-crisis provoked by North Korea's missile launch in April 2009 after the summit they were attending in Thailand

---

Box 12.1   The White House–10 Downing Street hotline

This telephone hotline was probably set up in the early 1960s. In an interview enquiry in 1993, Mrs Thatcher, the then prime minister, was asked whether it was used very often. She replied: 'No, I don't think these things ought to be used very often. But I sometimes received a very welcome call at difficult times from Ronald Reagan, who was very, very thoughtful' (Thatcher 1993: 10). This was consistent with the traditional Whitehall view that personal, top-level exchanges of this sort should be regarded as 'the diplomatic weapon of last resort'. However, times were changing. In 1998, Bill Clinton and Tony Blair are recorded as having spoken on the phone on average once a week (Patterson: 57).

had to be abandoned (see Chapter 10); in the same month, Italian prime minister Silvio Berlusconi missing a NATO group photograph to take a call on his mobile from his Turkish counterpart about the election of the alliance's next secretary-general; and so on.

In all of the above examples, what is apparent is that the telephone excelled as an instrument for achieving rapid personal exchanges between friendly states when urgent decisions were essential. The absence of language barriers, and confidence that any slips of the tongue or ill-considered statements would be treated charitably, also favoured use of the telephone. The last point is particularly important, and is one reason why the telephone is only rarely a feature of diplomacy between hostile states. It is true that a 'hotline' between the White House and the Kremlin was established following the alarm caused by the Cuban missile crisis in October 1962 but – contrary to the popular impression fostered by films such as *Dr Strangelove* – this was not a telephone connection but a direct telegraph link, designed chiefly to help cope with the consequences of accidental or unauthorized use of nuclear weapons. Letters delivered via ambassadors were the normal medium of direct communication between the rival superpowers during the Cold War.

Telephone diplomacy might be a rarity in the delicate diplomacy between hostile states, but it is certainly not unknown. It also seems to be growing in popularity as statesmen become more used to it and so reach for it almost reflexively. President Reagan employed it with his Syrian counterpart in 1985, albeit not apparently with much success (see Box 12.2). It appears to be used more fruitfully following a reduction in tension caused by some natural disaster or secured by other means, and when the moment needs to be seized quickly. For example, a North Korea–South Korea telephone hotline was installed following

---

Box 12.2　The Reagan–Assad exchange

In July 1985, President Reagan placed a telephone call to President Assad of Syria, a Soviet-backed state regarded in Washington as a sponsor of terrorism. He thanked him for his role in ending the crisis provoked by the hijacking to Beirut of a TWA airliner, and urged him to use his influence to secure the release of the remaining American kidnap victims being held in Lebanon. The president added, however, that he wanted Assad to end his support for terrorism. Not surprisingly, the conversation was 'stiff and cold' (Shultz 1993: 667–8). 'He got a little feisty', the President subsequently recorded in his memoirs, 'and suggested I was threatening to attack Lebanon' (Reagan: 497).

the improvement in relations marked by the summit meeting in June 2000, and reportedly used to good effect for several years afterwards (Lim Dong-won); calls exchanged between US deputy secretary of state Richard Armitage and Iran's UN ambassador, Mohammad Javad Zarif, helped facilitate acceptance by Tehran of the offer of American aid at the time of the earthquake in Bam in December 2003; and an impetus to an improvement in the deeply embittered relations between Islamabad and New Delhi was provided by a telephone call made to the Indian prime minister by his Pakistani counterpart on 28 April 2003, after the former had made a speech ten days earlier in which he promised the hand of friendship.

Tony Blair, British prime minister from 1997 until 2007, was particularly ready to use the telephone in such circumstances. 'Blessed with a fluent tongue and great personal charm', determined to make the world a better place, and confident that he could persuade to his point of view even the most unlikely persons (Reynolds: 381–3), he is credited, among other achievements, with employing his telephone to win a point with that legendary thorn in the side of the West, Colonel Qadhafi of Libya. According to evidence given to SIAC by the British ambassador at Tripoli, it was the prime minister's personal telephone call to the Libyan leader in August 2005 that led to the swiftness with which the sought-after 'No Torture' agreement was concluded between the two states (see Chapter 6). Tony Blair's confidence had, no doubt, been earlier reinforced by the remarkable conversation he had held with the Iranian president, Mohammad Khatami, from his aircraft en route to New York following the 9/11 attacks in 2001. Perhaps it is since this time, and especially in view of Iran's fear of an American attack in recent years, that its foreign ministry has become adept at reaching out to other ministries by telephone; numerous examples of this activity are easily located on the Internet.

Video-conferencing stalls

Video-conferencing, in principle, allows any number of persons at remote locations, provided they have compatible facilities, to see and hear each other in real time and, so, hold a conference without having to go to the trouble and expense of travelling to a distant venue. It is, therefore, in some ways a significant advance on a telephone conference call, and has for some time been a mouth-watering prospect to the prophets of virtual diplomacy. Its great advantage is that the visual images it produces enable body language to be conveyed more readily. Smiles – forced or genuine – and nods of agreement can clearly be witnessed, as can frowns, glares, yawns, bored expressions, rolling eyes, slumped shoulders, fingers drumming on table tops, shaking heads, and lips curling with contempt. As at real conferences, it is also possible to look for clues to the health of other parties in their appearance, movement, and mannerisms: facial tics indicating high levels of stress are, no doubt, readily discerned on high definition screens. Something of the influence of particular individuals might also be read into their physical proximity to a lead negotiator, and the gestures and comments exchanged between them. Video-conferencing is also becoming increasingly sophisticated, with larger screens and more versatile software, as well as high definition images; and it is becoming cheaper.

But the technical problems associated with video-conferencing remain considerable, and its fundamental limitations as a vehicle of either bilateral or multilateral diplomacy immense. Among the former are the poor quality of 'multicasting' – linking persons at multiple locations – and the impossibility of producing eye contact. But, even if these problems are eventually solved, the fact remains that video-conferencing will never be able to replicate the advantages of the personal encounter.

The participants in a video conference will always miss the physical dimension of body language – for example, the handshake or embrace – and, in some cultures, physical touch and bodily closeness are particularly important (Cohen 1987: ch. 5). Video conferences are also known to be intimidating because of the awareness of being 'on camera'; politicians are used to this, but most officials are not. Furthermore, unlike a real conference, they provide no opportunity to relieve the tension inevitably associated with some diplomatic encounters by gracious social ritual and acts of hospitality. Video conferences also provide no opportunities for corridor diplomacy; that is, for informal personal contacts, where the real breakthroughs in negotiations are sometimes made and useful information gleaned. And, by leaving delegations at home, these so-called conferences also leave them under the immediate influence of their constituencies and, thus, in the position in which they are least likely to adopt an accommodating outlook; to this extent they are actually anti-diplomatic.

In the light of these drawbacks, it is not surprising that even Gordon Smith, one of the best known apostles of virtual diplomacy, believes that negotiations 'are best done face to face', and that 'video does not work very well unless the parties know each other and the stakes are relatively minor' (Smith 1999: 21). On this, there seems broad agreement, and there is little evidence at all that video-conferencing has so far been prominently employed in serious negotiation. A trawl of the website of the Canadian foreign ministry, which has long prided itself at being at the forefront of space-age diplomacy, seems to confirm this. In connection with negotiations for an agreement to coordinate enforcement activities between the Canadian and Japanese authorities responsible for regulating commercial competition, there is a reference to the employment of several video-conferencing sessions in 2003, following negotiations *in Ottawa* in the previous November – but that is it. This seems to exemplify the role of video-conferencing in the negotiations between friendly states with the resources to support it: supplementing face-to-face negotiations, especially in the follow-up stage (see Chapter 6), when there is often an emphasis on information exchange, technicalities, and the need for reassurance. Tony Blair used video-conferencing, especially for his regular communications with George W. Bush, who had a video-conference room at his ranch at Crawford in central Texas, as well as in the White House; Blair's successor, Gordon Brown, did likewise.

None of this is to deny that video-conferencing might – and does – serve other useful diplomatic purposes. Some foreign ministries use it to engage with groups at home in order to garner their support, as well as to provide more intimate contact with their embassies abroad. Some of these embassies, such as the Canadian embassies in Berlin and New Delhi, use it to assist their public diplomacy. Some international organizations, including the UN, also use it for internal meetings. But all of this is quite different from using video-conferencing to conduct negotiations between governments.

Other means multiply

One reason why video-conferencing has failed to take off is probably the extraordinary progress that has taken place in other areas of telecommunication, and not only in the mobile phone technology and text messaging that is now so cheap and ubiquitous. Radio and television broadcasters (with 24-hour news channels at their disposal) now reach wider audiences, not least by streaming over the Internet. So do foreign ministry websites, which are now more informative, available in more languages, easier to use, and more numerous. These media can be used for direct communication between states, as well as for communication with their peoples (see Chapter 11).

In a crisis, radio and television channels and foreign ministry websites are particularly valuable if, for example, an urgent 'no change in policy' message needs to be sent to a large number of allied states simultaneously. The fact that the commitment has been made publicly also gives added reassurance. If all other channels of communication with a rival state or alliance have collapsed, broadcast communications might be indispensable. With its capacity to present visual images of political leaders, ministerial spokespersons, and ambassadors, television broadcasts and webcasts streamed over the Internet are particularly useful because – as with video-conferencing – they can send non-verbal, as well as verbal, messages. Also, there is little risk that these messages will be missed, because certain official monitoring services pick up foreign broadcasts, together with the content of other open source media; they then translate and summarize them with an eye to the special interests of customers in the governments that support them, and those abroad who are friends or are willing to pay. The best known are the Foreign Broadcast Information Service (FBIS) of the United States and the BBC Monitoring Service, which work in partnership.

Finally, it is necessary to emphasize the impact of electronic mail and the text messaging (SMS) with which it is progressively converging. This has now, more or less, replaced the telegram or cable, and – via Wi-Fi hotspots and, especially, the BlackBerry – has the capacity to place diplomats in continuous contact virtually anywhere. It appears to have been only relatively recently, however, that there has been sufficient confidence in its security – when especially enhanced – to permit its use at head of state and government level. Bill Clinton tested the medium with a message to the Swedish prime minister, Carl Bildt, on 16 February 1994 (Patterson: 59). Later, however, there were reports that Israeli intelligence had tapped into his emails, and the Bush White House developed an acute allergy to electronic mail; George W. Bush never used emails at all (*Washington Post* 2007). This changed with the inauguration, in January 2009, of President Barack Obama, who wears a BlackBerry on his hip, albeit one with special features, a highly restricted address list and frequently changed personal address. The secretary of state, Hillary Clinton, also uses a BlackBerry (*New York Times* 2009). Whether either of them uses emails for their personal diplomacy, however, is unclear. They probably still prefer the telephone.

Electronic mail and text messaging have brought their own perils, some of which – for example, the risk of impulsive decision-making – are identical to those of telephone diplomacy. However, email probably presents a more serious threat to security. Messages can be accidentally forwarded too easily, and the 'reply to all' facility with a distribution list of thousands is a particular hazard. The latter is not only a particularly clear security threat, but can also create a perfect email storm with the capacity to capsize a whole service. In January 2009, just such an event caused the US Department of State to threaten employees worldwide with disciplinary action in the event of its careless use. (This threat was issued by means of a cable.) The temptation to diplomats of some countries with poor government email services to use, instead, free web-based services such as Gmail, Yahoo and Hotmail for official business on ministry computers can also be difficult to resist. This is a security threat because of the risk of importing viruses and spyware, and led the Indian foreign ministry to ban it in February 2009. And then there are weak passwords and poorly understood encryption systems, which can easily render email accounts public knowledge. In 2007, such failings were responsible for embarrassing numerous governments – including those of Russia, India, China and Iran – when the login credentials of many email accounts at embassies were published on the Internet by a Swedish hacker (the password for the Iranian embassy in Tunisia was – you guessed it – 'Tunisia'). Because it makes it so easy for everyone to have their say, this kind of communications technology also weakens, or (depending on your point of view) makes more democratic, the authority structure in foreign ministries and embassies.

Summary

Direct telecommunication between governments is now a very important channel for the conduct of diplomacy, both in crises and more normal times, despite its risks and limitations. In crises, the telephone is especially valued by allied and friendly states, not least at head of state and government level. Here, it seems to be used chiefly as a vehicle for providing reassurance and intelligence, urging support, explaining attitudes, and agreeing joint responses. Adversaries in a crisis are more likely to use written telecommunication, although use of the telephone might be essential when an opportunity to improve relations is a fleeting one. Video-conferencing has had little impact on the world of serious international negotiations, while, in routine diplomacy, email is now the written mode of telecommunication of choice.

Further reading

Bruckner, Sandra, 'Video Conferencing: The next best thing to being there', *State Magazine*, December 2000 [www].
Callaghan, James, *Time and Chance* (Collins: London, 1987): 344–6.

Cohen, Raymond, *Theatre of Power: The art of diplomatic signalling* (Longman: London/New York, 1987): ch. 5.

Dobrynin, Anatoly, *In Confidence: Moscow's ambassador to America's six Cold War presidents (1962–86)* (University of Washington Press: Seattle, 2001): 96–8.

International Telecommunication Union, 'History' and 'Landmarks' [www].

Johnson, Joe, 'Wiring State: A progress report', *Foreign Service Journal*, December 2005 [www].

Johnson, Lyndon Baines, *The Vantage Point: Perspectives of the presidency, 1963–1968* (Weidenfeld & Nicolson: London, 1972): ch. 13, mainly: 287–8, 297–304.

Jones, R. A., *The British Diplomatic Service 1815–1914* (Smythe: London, 1983): ch. 7.

Kennedy, P. M., 'Imperial cable communications and strategy, 1870–1914', *English Historical Review*, Volume 86, October 1971: 728–52.

Kissinger, Henry A., *Years of Upheaval* (Weidenfeld & Nicolson/Michael Joseph: London, 1982): chs 11 and 12.

May, Ernest R., 'The news media and diplomacy', in Gordon A. Craig and Francis L. Loewenheim (eds), *The Diplomats 1939–1979* (Princeton University Press: Princeton, NJ, 1994).

McNamara, Robert, *Blundering Into Disaster: Surviving the first century of the nuclear age* (Pantheon: New York, 1986): 10–13.

Nickles, David Paull, *Under the Wire: How the telegraph changed diplomacy* (Harvard University Press: Cambridge, MA/London, 2003).

Patterson, Jr., Bradley H., *The White House Staff: Inside the West Wing and beyond* (Brookings: Washington, DC, 2000): 57–9.

Rawnsley, Gary D., *Radio Diplomacy and Propaganda: The BBC and VOA in international politics, 1956–64* (Macmillan – now Palgrave: Basingstoke, 1996).

Rawnsley, Gary D., 'Monitored broadcasts and diplomacy', in J. Melissen (ed.), *Innovation in Diplomatic Practice* (Macmillan – now Palgrave: Basingstoke, 1999).

Smith, Gerard C., *Disarming Diplomat: The memoirs of Gerard C. Smith, arms control negotiator* (Madison: New York, 1996): 107–9, 174–5.

United States Institute of Peace, *Virtual Diplomacy Initiative* [www].

Yeltsin, Boris, *Midnight Diaries* (Phoenix: London, 2001): ch. 16.

Part III

Diplomacy without Diplomatic Relations

Introduction to Part III

In some bilateral relationships, ordinary communications – including those usually maintained by means of ordinary embassies – cannot be employed because the parties are not in diplomatic relations (see Introduction to Part II). This might be because one party is not recognized by the other as a *state*, frequently because it has seceded from another by means with worrying implications for international norms and the integrity of other states, or because priority attaches to good relations with its parent. The Turkish Republic of Northern Cyprus (TRNC) has found this to be its near-universal experience since it announced its establishment in 1983; this has also been the fate of the two Republics of Abkhazia and South Ossetia since their own declarations of statehood in August 2008; and it has been the partial fate of the Republic of Kosovo following its declaration of independence from Serbia in February 2008. Diplomatic relations might also be absent because one party is not recognized by the other as the *government* of the state over which it claims to rule, even though the state itself does enjoy recognition. Although this is now less common than it used to be (Young 2008: 199–207), this was the misfortune of the PRC for many years, notably at the hands of the United States: from 1949 until 1979 the United States recognized China as a state but insisted on recognizing, as its legitimate government, the regime of the anti-Communist Kuomintang (the Republic of China) although, in practice, the writ of the latter ran little beyond the island of Taiwan. Finally, diplomatic relations might not exist because one party, while continuing to recognize the other as a state and not denying the legitimacy of its government, has simply *severed* those relations, whether as a protest at some policy, as a more general expression of distaste for its regime, or because of an outbreak of fighting.

However, even if states go to war, they usually wish to prevent the fighting from escalating out of control, especially in this age of weapons of mass destruction. They normally desire to restrict its geographical extent as well, secure the humane treatment of prisoners of war, and eventually edge towards a restoration of peace and, in due course, normality. If, in war, there is an urgent need for a minimum of diplomatic communication, the requirement for it might be no less urgent in fractured relations still below this threshold – because there is still time to prevent the parties crossing it. In 2009, the relationship between the United States and Iran was very much an example of this sort of situation.

When diplomatic relations are in abeyance but the parties maintain an interest in communicating with each other, this may be achieved by a variety of means, some of which have already been touched upon; for example, telecommunications (see Chapter 12), contacts in the diplomatic corps of third states where both have embassies (Chapter 7), and meetings in the wings of international organizations of which they are both members (Chapter 9). The final part of the book will discuss three other, more important methods: disguised embassies, special envoys, and mediation by different kinds of third party. Which is the best means, or combination of means, to employ? Aside from consideration of the personalities involved, which could be decisive, the answer to this cardinal question depends chiefly on the reasons for the absence of diplomatic relations, the nature of the interests at stake in preserving contact, and whether diplomatic relations have only just collapsed or are already in prospect of restoration. These considerations will be much to the forefront in the following chapters.

13
Disguised Embassies

Regular, flag-flying embassies might well disappear when diplomatic relations are severed, but diplomatic functions might still be performed by as many as four kinds of irregular resident mission – some more irregular, and therefore more heavily disguised, than others. These are interests sections, consulates, representative offices, and front missions – the last being analogous to the 'front organizations', typically businesses of one sort or another, employed to conceal espionage activities during the Cold War. This chapter will consider the advantages and disadvantages of each of these disguised embassies, and why one is preferred to another in different circumstances. It will also consider whether the differences between formally accredited embassies and at least some of these missions (especially interests sections and representative offices) are merely nominal.

Interests sections

The interests section is a 'refinement' of the old institution of the protecting power (Wylie: 8), which originated in the sixteenth century with the successful assertion by Christian rulers – notably His Most Christian Majesty, the King of France – of the right to protect co-religionists of any nationality in 'heathen' lands such as the Ottoman Empire. In the nineteenth century, the need for diplomatic protection was increased by the great expansion in trade and travel, and the growing tendency to expel enemy consuls on the outbreak of war. Protecting powers to rival France were not slow to come forward. Apart from considerations of religious and racial solidarity, prestige accrued to any state able to demonstrate its influence by assuming this responsibility. States with neutralist traditions, such as Switzerland and Sweden, became especially active as protecting powers, although Austria (a permanent neutral after 1955), Belgium, Spain and – especially in the Americas – the United States have also been important. The practice was duly codified in the Vienna Convention on Diplomatic Relations, 1961 (see Box 13.1).

Although the institution of the protecting power certainly proved useful, it had drawbacks. For one thing, its embassy could not be expected to have any special familiarity with the interests of the protected power, especially if they were complicated. For another, the protecting power could not be expected to look upon the interests of the protected power as equivalent to its own, for the very good reason that these would not necessarily be in harmony. Finally, employing a protecting power was also attended by the general drawbacks of relying on a third state (see Chapter 15), as well as by the possibility of having to pay it a political price to take on what could well prove to be a delicate, even dangerous, job. When the US embassy in Kampala was forced to close for security reasons in 1973, the protection of American interests in Uganda by the West German ambassador was only secured after protracted and difficult negotiations (Keeley).

In view of the drawbacks of protecting powers, therefore – and perhaps also because the role was beginning to be seen as a growing burden by the increasingly stretched diplomatic services of the time – the original institution was significantly modified when weak, new states began routinely to sever diplomatic relations for largely symbolic reasons in

---

Box 13.1   Protecting powers and the Vienna Convention on Diplomatic Relations, 1961

Article 45
If diplomatic relations are broken off between two States, or if a mission is permanently or temporarily recalled:

(a) the receiving State must, even in case of armed conflict, respect and protect the premises of the mission, together with its property and archives;
(b) the sending State may entrust the custody of the premises of the mission, together with its property and archives, to a third State acceptable to the receiving State;
(c) the sending State may entrust the protection of its interests and those of its nationals to a third State acceptable to the receiving State.

Article 46
A sending State may with the prior consent of a receiving State, and at the request of a third State not represented in the receiving State, undertake the temporary protection of the interests of the third State and of its nationals.

the 1960s. The practice quickly developed of formally closing embassies but – with the assent of the host state – arranging for a handful of diplomats to be left behind who would be attached to the embassy of a protecting power. (Where the animosity was too great or conditions were too dangerous, the old system still had to be used. For example, the Polish embassy in Baghdad had no clutch of American diplomats to help it protect US interests in Iraq after the outbreak of the Gulf War in 1991.) The beauty of the new practice was that it permitted resident diplomacy to continue while, simultaneously, making it possible to claim that relations with an unsavoury government, or a government currently pursuing an unsavoury policy, had been 'severed'. The burden placed on the protecting power was also reduced, and any hostility redirected to its own embassy perhaps diluted – and probably removed altogether – if the diplomats composing the interests section continued to work, as became quite common, in their own embassy building. This is not a hypothetical risk, as we shall see.

An interests section, then, is a group of diplomats of one state working under the flag of a second on the territory of a third. The first ones were established by West Germany in Cairo and Egypt in Bonn in May 1965, when the Egyptians broke diplomatic relations with the Germans in retaliation for the decision of the latter to open them with Israel. (Similar sections had been seen in World War I, but were staffed by consuls, Berridge 2009: 124–8.) Shortly afterwards, Britain was allowed to adopt the same practice in order to maintain contact with the more important of the nine states that broke off relations with London in protest at the refusal of the Wilson government to put down, by force, the rebellion in Southern Rhodesia. Some of these states, which also included Egypt, reduced their embassies or high commissions in London to interests sections.

The interests section then spread rapidly as its advantages became apparent. It was first used by the United States in the aftermath of the Six Day War in the Middle East in 1967, when a number of Arab states severed relations with Washington, alleging that it had supported Israel's attack on Egypt. Interests sections also appeared in Washington; in 2009, there were only two, although they were highly significant – one belonging to Iran, based in the embassy of Pakistan, and the other belonging to Cuba. The new device also proved particularly useful to Israel, especially in Africa, where over 20 states severed relations with it at the time of the Yom Kippur War in 1973 (Klieman: 63–4).

Although, at first, a reaction to a break in diplomatic relations, interests sections have also been used since as a tentative first step towards their restoration following a long period in which there was no sustained, direct contact – in popular terms, as a half-way house to an embassy. For example, the United States had severed relations with Cuba in January 1961 but, during a brief thaw in 1977, a Cuban interests section was allowed to open in the Czech embassy in Washington and a US interests section in the Swiss embassy in Havana. The Cuban section was bombed by anti-Castro Cuban exiles in July 1978, and no further improvement in US–Cuban relations occurred, but the interests sections remained in place. (In 1991, the Swiss also took over the sheltering of the Cubans in Washington after the Czechs, whose new government disliked them, kicked them out – *New York Times* 1991).

More immediately productive was the introduction of interests sections into the Soviet–South African relationship. This had been severed in 1955, but Moscow and Pretoria had strong common interests in the economic sphere, especially in controlled gold and diamond marketing, and changes in both countries at the end of the 1980s began to make normal diplomatic contact once more conceivable. The Soviet government, moreover, had decided to encourage the African National Congress to negotiate with the South African government: as a result, under an agreement of February 1991, the two states exchanged interests sections, both enjoying the protection of an Austrian embassy. These became embassies in the following year, although it was a Russian rather than Soviet embassy that was welcomed by the South Africans.

Interests sections might have become popular since the mid-1960s, and on the upside as well as the downside of diplomatic relations (James 1992). But are they really – as American diplomats with experience of work in them sometimes claim – embassies in all but name? The answer to this is 'no', although they sometimes come very close to it. How close they come depends on the degree of animosity prevailing at the time of the break and the importance of the interests likely to be damaged by a break taken to extremes.

Although they are legally a section of the embassy of the protecting power, interests sections generally operate under a somewhat restrictive interpretation of diplomatic privileges and immunities. Set out in the agreements with the protecting power and the host state under which they are established, these usually include specific numerical limits on staff, prohibitions of certain sections (typically, the more sensitive ones, such as political and defence), and a requirement for prior approval of all individual appointments (*agrément*) rather than only for the head of mission (Bergus: 70; Lowe: 473; Kear 2001: 80). But there might be great variations in the details of these agreements and how they are interpreted in practice.

In an extreme case, when relations are broken as a result of a bitter bilateral dispute, any interests sections established are normally very stunted affairs, with severe limits on what they can do. For example, the 19-strong British embassy in Argentina was replaced, at the time of the Falklands War, by an interests section containing only two British diplomats, while, two years later, the 18-strong British embassy in Libya was replaced by an interests section similarly reduced. US interests sections have had similar experiences. The American embassy in Cairo was the biggest US mission in the Middle East at the time of the Six Day War in 1967, occupying premises and grounds that gave it an atmosphere 'something like a university campus'. However the interests section that replaced it was initially limited to a mere four diplomats and, by 1970, it had been allowed to grow to an establishment of no more than sixteen (Bergus: 70–1).

What this drastic scaling-down in personnel means is a large reduction in the numbers of specialist personnel and, thus, a severe limit on what the interests section can be expected to achieve. This was clearly seen in the case of the interests section established in May 1991 by the Iraqis in their former chancery building in Washington, by then under Algerian protection, following the earlier fight with Saddam Hussein over Kuwait. The section would be allowed only three Iraqi nationals (two diplomats and one of administrative and technical rank) and was designed, the Department of State emphasized, merely to 'facilitate maintenance of minimal communications between the United States and Iraq and provide basic consular services' (US Department of State: 347).

At the same time, an atmosphere of political crisis will normally generate not only a huge increase in workload (especially consular, if there is a large expatriate community over which to watch), but also a severe reduction in the local cooperation that the interests section can expect. Trouble can easily be made for it, and its staff rendered relatively ineffective, by refusing the appointment of individuals known to be hostile or, simply, too effective. Formal restrictions are also routinely placed on what an interests section may be permitted to do, which will usually provoke retaliatory action. For example, the agreement of 1991 permitting an Iraqi interests section in Washington also specified that no Iraqi member was to be allowed to travel, without special permission, beyond a 25-mile zone of free movement. Direct access to government departments might also be limited. Thus, the tiny British interests section in the Swiss embassy in Buenos Aires was boycotted by the Argentine foreign ministry for at least the first 18 months after the Falklands War (*Times* 1983). And even the US interests sections in Algiers (1969–74) and Iraq (1980–84) were only able to secure mid-level contacts with the host governments (Eagleton: 92–6). The typical experience of an interests section in an actively hostile environment, albeit one exacerbated by American provocation (OIG 2007: 1, 24), is summed up by that of the US interests section in Cuba (USINT):

> The COM [Chief of Mission] and DCM [Deputy Chief of Mission] must deal with an implacably hostile government ... in the absence of many formal authorities available to an Ambassador at an ordinary embassy. Official contact in Havana is minimal; with rare exceptions, officers cannot travel outside city precincts. The Cuban government obstructs or violates the terms of agreement for operating USINT and its Cuban counterpart in Washington (OIG 2007: 7).

On the other hand, interests sections set up in more benign circumstances, such as a thaw in hitherto frozen relations or the aftermath of a purely symbolic break, are likely to resemble a regular embassy much more closely. When Egypt reluctantly severed relations with Britain over Southern Rhodesia in December 1965, large numbers of staff were permitted to remain in the new interests sections; the political section of the British embassy in Cairo was closed, but the counsellor was allowed to stay on under cover of responsibility for consular affairs; and, in London, even two assistant military attachés were permitted to stay put in the guise of 'medical advisers' (Kear 2001: 77–9). A similar state of affairs appears to have obtained in the interests sections employed to cope with the symbolic severance of relations with Egypt by most Arab states following the Camp David accords in 1978. And the US interests section in Havana might not have been operating in benign circumstances recently, but things were better when it was created in 1977; moreover, the Cubans recognize that it carries a heavy consular burden. The result is that, while it operates under heavy restrictions, it is huge – with 51 US direct-hire staff and almost 300 locally engaged support staff recorded in 2007 (OIG 2007: 5). In 2009, there were 25 diplomatic staff at the Cuban interests section in Washington.

Whether small or large, heavily restricted in movements and official access or as free in these respects as any regular embassy, interests sections are a most useful means of preserving, or initiating, resident bilateral diplomacy in the absence of diplomatic relations. Since July 2008, there has been periodic speculation that the United States would install its own diplomats in the Swiss embassy in Tehran, where Swiss diplomats have – in the style of old – been responsible for protecting American interests since 1981.

Consulates

There is a long tradition of employing consulates as the usual device for conducting resident diplomacy in the absence of diplomatic relations, although there was uncertainty over its legality until this was confirmed by the VCCR in 1963 (see Box 13.2). Fortified by its provision, subsequently adopted in other important consular conventions, the encouragement of friendly relations is a normal consular function (Lee and Quigley: 541–3). In the same way as interests sections, therefore, consular posts might take over diplomatic functions following a breach in diplomatic relations, or be established as a first step towards their restoration. For most states, this has only been an occasional ploy in recent years, but it was a common one for South Africa during the period of its greatest, apartheid-inflicted, diplomatic isolation. But why should states still occasionally prefer to talk to their enemies via consulates now that interests sections are available? For, as the first part of this chapter has been at pains to stress, this new institution has made it

---

Box 13.2 Diplomatic acts and the Vienna Convention on Consular Relations, 1963

Article 2
Establishment of consular relations

1. The establishment of consular relations between States takes place by mutual consent.
2. The consent given to the establishment of diplomatic relations between two States implies, unless otherwise stated, consent to the establishment of consular relations.
3. The severance of diplomatic relations shall not ipso facto [by virtue of that fact] involve the severance of consular relations...

Article 17
1. In a State where the sending State has no diplomatic mission and is not represented by a diplomatic mission of a third State, a consular officer may, with the consent of the receiving State, and without affecting his consular status, be authorized to perform diplomatic acts. The performance of such acts by a consular officer shall not confer upon him any right to claim diplomatic privileges and immunities.

possible to leave existing *diplomatic* officers securely in place following a breach in diplomatic relations.

One advantage of using the older device of a consular post, rather than an interests section sheltered by a protecting power, is the avoidance of the general drawbacks of relying on a third party: indebtedness, possible misunderstandings, the need to share at least some secrets, and so on. Another is that the typically unostentatious and often grubby consular post, popularly identified with visa work and relief for destitute back-packers, is unlikely to smack of high politics to the general public and, thus, to draw attention; by contrast, the interests section is known to be more political and even, more often than not, left in the former embassy building. It is salutary in this connection that, in 1988, the US administration resisted Congressional pressure to open an interests section in Hanoi on the grounds that it would represent the establishment of a US diplomatic presence in Vietnam and be seen as 'a major political victory by Hanoi' (House of Representatives: 41).

A further advantage of using consular posts, at least for states with greater resources, is that they sometimes come in multiples; spread around the country, they are better placed than the interests section to gather intelligence. With the general integration of the consular and diplomatic services that occurred in the course of the twentieth century (see Chapter 8), consular officers are also now much more likely to have had previous diplomatic experience and, thus, to be able to cope with any diplomatic tasks thrust upon them. Furthermore, while the assumption of diplomatic functions does not confer *diplomatic* privileges and immunities on consular officers (see Boxes 8.1 and 13.2), the gap between those enjoyed by diplomats and those grudgingly given to consuls has narrowed – so, in practice, this is not a great handicap.

Finally, it is important to note that consular representation can also be a convenient method of conducting limited relations in the special case of unrecognized states, when these states were created out of provinces of larger states in which external powers happened already to have consulates. This is possible because of the international norm, albeit rather shaky and perforce carefully worded by Satow (note my emphasis), that 'neither the retaining nor the replacing of consular officials *necessarily* constitute recognition' (Satow: 213). Here, an important example in the late twentieth century is provided by North Vietnam, which was effectively sliced off from the rest of Vietnam following the Geneva Conference in 1954. The British government, among others, had a long-established consular post in Hanoi (and in Haiphong) which, despite its primitive conditions and frequent humiliations, was retained throughout the Vietnam War, when it was a valued source of intelligence to pass on to the United States (Kear 1999). Various states, including Britain, also used their consular posts in Elisabethville to conduct highly important and sensitive communications with the government of the unrecognized and short-lived secessionist state of Katanga between 1960 and early 1963, although this got them into hot water with the central government of the Congo Republic in Léopoldville. Today, nine states conduct their relations with the Palestinian National Authority in the West Bank and Gaza, as well as with the local authorities in Jerusalem, by means of their consulates, which have been long-established in the holy city (see Box 13.3).

A similar, although not identical, case is provided by the British consulate at Tamsui (today, Danshui) in the Chinese province of Taiwan. The establishment of this long pre-dated the establishment by the Communists of the PRC government in Peking in 1949, and the retreat of the Nationalist government of the 'Republic of China' (ROC) to Taiwan. Britain recognized the PRC government as the legitimate government of China in January 1950 but, over the Communist objection

---

Box 13.3   The consulates in Jerusalem

The peculiar position of the consulates in Jerusalem – which, in effect, handle relations with the Palestinian Authority – was neatly summarised in a UN report in 1997:

> Particular mention should also be made of the continued presence in Jerusalem of an international *sui generis* consular corps, commonly referred to as the 'Consular Corps of the Corpus Separatum'. Nine States have maintained consulates in Jerusalem (East and West) without, however, recognizing any sovereignty over the City. Unlike consuls serving in Israel, the consuls of those States do not present a consular letter of authorization to the Foreign Ministry and do not receive accreditation by the President of Israel. They do not pay taxes and have no official relations with Israeli authorities. In their activities, they respect common protocol rules designed to prevent any appearance of recognition of sovereign claims to the City.

The nine states are Belgium, France, Greece, Italy, Spain, Sweden, Turkey, UK, and USA.

Source: *The Status of Jerusalem* (United Nations: New York, 1997). Prepared for, and under the guidance of, the Committee on the Exercise of the Inalienable Rights of the Palestinian People.

that it implied recognition of the ROC, the consulate at Tamsui – which, in the nineteenth century, had been Taiwan's main port and is close to its capital, Taipeh – remained in place, albeit formally accredited to the provincial authorities rather than the ROC. The Tamsui consulate was also given a subordinate vice-consulate in Taipeh, described as an 'Office of the Tamsui Consulate', and was used to maintain unofficial political relations with the ROC until 13 March 1972, when it was closed (HCPP 1993: 11). Its role and peculiar position is well illustrated by a short item in *The Times*:

> PROTEST ON SHELLING OF BRITISH SHIP
> Taipeh, Aug. 30. – Britain to-day protested to the Chinese Nationalists against the shelling of the British freighter Inchkilda off Foochow last week. The British Consulate at Tamsui, near Taipeh, handed the protest Note to the provincial government of Formosa [Taiwan], instead of to General Chiang Kai-Shek's Foreign Ministry because the United Kingdom has no diplomatic relations with the Nationalists (*Times* 1954).

As a rider to this example, it must be admitted that the Tamsui consul's unofficial function as the political representative of Britain on Taiwan was not physically well-disguised by the building in which he was housed. This was a hill-top, red fort at the mouth of the Tamsui River built by the Spanish in the seventeenth century, with a colonial-style, red-brick residence attached in 1891. It also had a prominent flagpole displaying the Union Jack, which was twice pulled down by Nationalist protesters following Britain's recognition of the Communist government (*Times* 1951).

Representative offices

In some circumstances – typically, when businesslike relations between two governments are desired, but one continues to grant recognition to a rival of the other – interests sections cannot be employed and consular posts are problematical. For example, when the governments of the United States and the PRC wanted to consolidate their *rapprochement* in 1973, interests sections could not be contemplated because their employment would have amounted to a denial of a firmly-held American position: that Chinese interests in the United States were already protected by the ROC's Washington embassy. As for consular posts, Chou En-lai, the PRC prime minister, regarded these as insufficiently political to advertise the new Sino–American relationship and, thus, inadequate for the purpose of deterring any Soviet attack (Kissinger 1982: 61). In such circumstances, an increasingly common expedient is now the representative office, sometimes also known as a 'liaison office'. This is a mission that looks and operates much like an embassy, the only difference being its informality.

According to Henry Kissinger, the liaison offices exchanged between the United States and the PRC were embassies in all but name. 'Their personnel would have diplomatic immunity; they would have their own secure communications; their chiefs would be treated as ambassadors and they would conduct all exchanges between the two governments. They would not become part of the official diplomatic corps,' he adds, 'but this had its advantages since it permitted special treatment without offending the established protocol orders'. Both countries sent senior and trusted diplomats to head these offices. According to Kissinger, the establishment of diplomatic relations with the PRC on 1 January 1979 produced nothing more than an entirely nominal change to the resident missions in Beijing and Washington (Kissinger 1982: 62–3).

Representative offices have proved particularly useful to so-called international pariahs, as well as to entities struggling for recognition: the TRNC; Taiwan, although many of Taipei's are called the 'Taipeh Economic and Cultural Office' or, in the United States, where its *de facto* consulates in state capitals have the same title, the 'Taipeh Economic and Cultural Representative Office'; the Palestinian National Authority, which hosts numerous representative offices in Ramallah, Jericho, and Gaza, as well as sending its own abroad; and – in the past – the Republic of South Africa. Unlike interests sections, representative offices do not have the disadvantages of reliance on a third party and, in contrast to the position of consular posts, nothing – except dislike – stands in the way of giving their staff and premises the somewhat stronger privileges and immunities enjoyed by diplomatic missions.

Front missions

Front missions are the most heavily disguised of the irregular resident missions: on the surface, altogether innocent of diplomatic purpose – but, beneath it, pursuing their political work with zeal. Distinct from the representative office, by virtue of their genuine cover function, front missions come in all shapes and sizes. Trade missions or commercial offices are an old favourite, and a natural ploy for a trading state. This was the device by which the PRC and Japan maintained representation in each other's capitals prior to normalization in 1972 (Beer: 170–1), and that employed at the end of the 1950s by Britain as a half-way house to the restoration of diplomatic relations with Egypt following the Suez crisis (Parsons: 41–2). It was also used by Britain to preserve relations with Taiwan, a very important trading partner, after it was obliged to close the Tamsui consulate in 1972. A few years after this, the Anglo–Taiwan Trade Committee (ATTC) was established and, in 1989, it acquired a visa handling unit. This was a front mission that might have been heavily disguised relative to other kinds of irregular resident mission, but it was thinly disguised relative to other front missions: by 1992 its entire senior staff, including its 'Director', were British Diplomatic Service officers 'on secondment' (HCPP 1993: 11, 14 Annex A). Israel, and Taiwan itself, have also made widespread use of commercial offices for diplomatic purposes, as did South Africa during the apartheid era.

Information or tourist offices, travel agencies, scientific missions, and cultural affairs offices are also favourite covers for diplomatic activity (Berridge 1994: 53–8; Peterson 1997: 117–18). In the late 1960s and early 1970s, the North Vietnamese disguised their diplomats in London, who were well known to the Foreign Office, as journalists (Young 2008: 215–16). The Holy See's apostolic delegate, whose mission in a foreign country is formally (and largely) religious, has also served as a saintly cover for diplomacy in states where the Vatican was unable to accredit *a nuncio* or *pro-nuncio*. The apostolic delegate served this purpose in Britain until 1979, and in the United States until as late as 1984 (Berridge 1994: 54–6).

Some front missions have gathered so many responsibilities of the kind commonly associated with diplomatic posts that, apart from their names, they are little different from representative offices. For example, in 1993 the privately-managed Anglo–Taiwan Education Centre was taken over by the British Council and merged with the ATTC to form the 'British Trade and Cultural Office'.

Front missions are of greatest value where visible relations between unfriendly powers could lead to embarrassment on one or both sides. However, precisely because they have to preserve their cover by pursuing work that is normally important in its own right, their time and resources remaining for diplomatic activity might be comparatively slender. Furthermore, while the staff of some trade missions gained partial immunities after 1945 (Peterson 1997: 117), it seems unlikely that – with some important exceptions – many front missions enjoy anything like full diplomatic, or even consular, immunities. This means that their staff must be unusually circumspect in their activities. Their access to local officials is also likely to be restricted and might have to be conducted through intermediaries (Cross: 257–8).

Summary

A state may refuse to recognize another as a state, or refuse to recognize its government as the legitimate government of that state. While maintaining recognition in both senses, it might also simply refuse to have anything to do with it; that is, sever diplomatic relations. In any of these eventualities, regular embassies cannot be maintained. If the parties wish to preserve some degree of communication by resident means, therefore, alternatives have to be found that can achieve the purpose without undue embarrassment. These are interests sections, consulates, representative offices, and front missions – disguised embassies. However, their similarities to regular embassies beneath their covers should not be exaggerated. All labour under handicaps that embassies do not experience, except perhaps for the average representative office.

Further reading

Berridge, G. R., *Talking to the Enemy: How states without 'diplomatic relations' communicate* (Macmillan – now Palgrave: Basingstoke, 1994): chs 1 and 3.

Cross, Charles T., *Born a Foreigner: A memoir of the American presence in Asia* (Rowman & Littlefield: Lanham, MD, 1999): ch. 19, on Taiwan.

Franklin, W. M., *Protection of Foreign Interests: A study in diplomatic and consular practice* (US Government Printing Office: Washington, DC, 1947).

Hertz, Martin F. (ed.), *The Consular Dimension of Diplomacy* (University Press of America: Lanham, MD, 1983).

James, Alan, 'Diplomatic relations and contacts', *British Yearbook of International Law 1991*, Volume 62 (Clarendon Press: Oxford, 1992): 347–87.

Kear, Simon, 'The British Consulate-General in Hanoi, 1954–73', *Diplomacy and Statecraft*, 10(1), March, 1999: 215–39.

Kear, Simon, 'Diplomatic innovation: Nasser and the origins of the interests section', *Diplomacy and Statecraft*, 12(3), September, 2001: 65–86.

Kissinger, Henry A., *Years of Upheaval* (Weidenfeld & Nicolson: London, 1982): 60–3.

Lee, Luke T. and John Quigley, *Consular Law and Practice*, 3rd edn (Oxford University Press: Oxford, 2008): ch. 36.

Lowe, V., 'Diplomatic law: protecting powers', *International and Comparative Law Quarterly*, 39(2), April, 1990.

Melissen, Jan (ed.), *Innovation in Diplomatic Practice* (Macmillan – now Palgrave: Basingstoke, 1999): ch. 13.

Newsom, David E. (ed.), *Diplomacy under a Foreign Flag: The protecting power and the interests section* (Hurst: London, 1990; St Martin's Press – now Palgrave: New York, 1990, for the Institute for the Study of Diplomacy).

OIG, *Report of Inspection: U.S. Interests Section Havana, Cuba*, July 2007 [www].

Peterson, M. J., *Recognition of Governments: Legal doctrine and state practice, 1815–1995* (Macmillan – now Palgrave: Basingstoke, 1997): ch. 7.

Rawnsley, Gary D., *Taiwan's Informal Diplomacy and Propaganda* (Palgrave: Basingstoke, 2000).

Shaw, M. N., *International Law*, 6th edn (Cambridge University Press: Cambridge/New York, 2008): ch. 9, on recognition.

Sullivan, Joseph G. (ed.), *Embassies Under Siege* (Brassey's for the Institute for the Study of Diplomacy: Washington, DC, 1995).

Whiteman, M. M., 'Diplomatic missions and embassy, protection of interests by third states', *Digest of International Law* (1970): 450–1.

Wylie, Neville, 'Protecting powers in a changing world', *Politorbis*, 40(1), 2006: 6–14 [www].

Young, John W., *Twentieth-Century Diplomacy: A case study of British practice, 1963–1976* (Cambridge: Cambridge University Press, 2008): ch. 9.

14
Special Missions

Special missions, or special envoys, are persons sent abroad to conduct diplomacy with a limited purpose for a limited time. Their employment was the normal manner of conducting relations between friendly rulers until resident diplomacy began to take root during the late fifteenth century, and advances in air travel led to its resurgence for this purpose in the anxious days preceding and following the outbreak of World War II; since then, the resurgence has been spectacular. Special missions are particularly valuable to the diplomacy between hostile states, not least in breaking the ice between them – as when the American national security adviser, Henry Kissinger, flew secretly to Beijing, the capital of the PRC, in July 1971. What are the advantages of special missions used in the absence of diplomatic relations? How are they variously composed? When should they be sent in public, and when in secret?

The advantages of special missions

Special envoys come in many guises, but they all have some characteristics in common, including a common legal regime. It is possible, therefore, to identify the advantages that all of them share, and it is as well to do this to begin with.

The employment of special envoys in diplomacy between hostile states has numerous benefits, whether they are designed to supplement activity by disguised embassies or play a larger role in their absence:

- First, they provide maximum security for the secrecy of a message, which, in the circumstances, might be of considerable sensitivity; in this respect their function is identical to that of a diplomatic courier

- Second, their use to bear a message underlines the importance attached to it by the sending state, and makes it more likely that it will command respect
- Third, because special envoys will generally be in closer touch with opinion at home, they are well placed to make a concession if this should be required
- Fourth, the members of special missions usually have some special knowledge.

The procedures of special missions, and the privileges and immunities of their members, were clarified and marginally reinforced in the second half of the twentieth century. The Convention on Special Missions adopted by the UN General Assembly on 8 December 1969, which was unfinished business for the ILC in the codification and development of diplomatic law, entered into force on 21 June 1985, albeit with a narrow base of support, because it was seen as a Third World instrument. It made clear that special missions can be sent even though neither diplomatic nor consular relations exist between the states concerned. It also stated that the privileges and immunities given to the members of such missions are identical with those given to the staff of regular embassies in the VCDR, 1961, except in two main regards: first, the inviolability of the premises temporarily occupied by them is qualified by a 'fire clause', as with consulates; and, second, the prior agreement of the receiving state must be obtained to both the size and – as with interests sections – named members of a special mission.

In order that, in a hostile relationship, a receiving state might be allowed to insist that the members of a special mission should have unusually limited privileges and immunities (North Korea contemplating the prospect of a special mission from the United States comes to mind), and that a sending state should be permitted to go along with this if it feels that this would be better than no mission at all, the Convention on Special Missions also made clear that its rules were residuary rather than mandatory, a default setting: they are rules from which states are free to derogate by mutual agreement and that only apply when they omit to do this. The functions of a special mission, it added, must be determined by mutual consent. It was also silent on the question of special missions to and from an authority not constituting a state. Thus did the Convention, either by deliberate act or oversight, not place this diplomatic method in a legal straight-jacket but, rather, permit it great flexibility.

The variety of special missions

Special missions vary in form at least as much as disguised embassies, but they can be classified fairly simply by their political weight and nature of appointment. There are four main kinds: unofficial envoys (high- and low-level); and official envoys (high- and low-level).

Unofficial envoys

Unofficial envoys are recruited from outside government or, at least, from outside the foreign policy and military establishments, and are informally – albeit *authoritatively* – tasked. If they are high-level envoys – typically friends or political cronies of government leaders – they are commonly known as 'personal envoys'. They represent a tactic long-favoured by American presidents, but their use is by no means unique to the United States. In the 1960s, the British prime minister, Harold Wilson, sent his close political ally, Harold Davies, on a peace mission to North Vietnam (Young 2008: 100) and, for almost a decade, one of Wilson's successors, Tony Blair, used Lord Levy as his personal envoy to the Middle East (see Box 14.1). Low-level unofficial envoys are usually known as 'private envoys'. Good examples of these are Landrum Bolling, the private American citizen used by Jimmy Carter to make contact with the PLO in September 1977 (Quandt: 101–2), and Ya'acov Nimrodi, the private Israeli arms dealer employed by the Israeli prime minister, Shimon Peres, to respond to feelers (carried by agents of similar standing) from moderates inside the Iranian government in 1985 (Segev: 2–3). In the twenty years prior to the normalization of relations between the PRC and Japan in 1972, both high- and low-level unofficial envoys were the most marked feature of the 'private diplomacy' by which Tokyo had been forced to engage China in order to satisfy the Americans and the Chinese Nationalists; some of the most important of these were pro-Beijing members of the Diet (Johnson: 405–7).

Unofficial envoys, whether personal or private, have the great advantage of flexibility and are, therefore, the kind of envoy often employed on the most sensitive missions. As we have seen, they can be chosen from any walk of life; they can also be given any rank or title, or none at all; and their instructions and credentials can take any form desired (Wriston: 220). If they are rich, like Lord Levy, so much the better: they can pay their own travel expenses and fly off at the drop of a hat, at the same time deflecting any criticism that they are an unnecessary drain on the public exchequer. Among unofficial envoys, personal envoys have the great advantage of being known to enjoy the complete confidence

---

Box 14.1 About Lord Levy: Tony Blair's Personal Envoy to the Middle East and Latin America

Lord Levy, a multi-millionaire businessman, was the Labour Party's chief fund-raiser and a close friend of Tony Blair, whom he partnered at tennis. By reason of his great success in delivering funds for the party he was popularly known as 'Lord Cashpoint', and subsequent to his appointment as the PM's personal envoy in 1999 as 'Lord Fix-it' (unfortunately he never did). It was reported in 2007 that he had made 121 visits to 24 states, including 24 to the Palestinian National Authority (*Mail Online*, 4 January 2007). The following written exchange between Tony Blair and the Conservative frontbench spokesman on foreign affairs, Cheryl Gillan, on 5 February 2001, illustrates some interesting points about such envoys.

Mrs. Gillan: To ask the Prime Minister...concerning messages carried by Lord Levy, for what reason such messages could not be carried by Ministers and diplomats.

The Prime Minister: The purpose of asking Lord Levy to convey such messages as my personal envoy was to signal my personal interest in our relations with the countries. He was accompanied throughout by our ambassadors to the countries concerned and by a Foreign and Commonwealth Office official.

...

Mrs. Gillan: To ask the Prime Minister ... what his policy is on the payment of travel expenses by Lord Levy while travelling as his personal envoy

...

The Prime Minister: Lord Levy has always paid his own travel expenses when travelling as my personal envoy.

Source: Hansard 2001.

---

of the leadership that has despatched them and, thus, of being able to command maximum attention, although a high-level reception is not automatic and still needs to be negotiated prior to departure. Personal envoys also convey the maximum degree of flattery to the recipient of the message, and generate the conviction that any message returned will go direct to the top.

If flattery is not desired and disavowal is an important option in the event that a secret mission is exposed, the more peripheral figure of the private envoy will normally be preferred, even though establishing the credentials of this individual might be more difficult. This was probably one of the motives for choosing Bolling as the US emissary to the PLO, and was certainly the reason why Peres used Nimrodi to deal with the Iranians: 'he chose a private merchant so that he could deny any connection with the matter should there be a snafu or early revelation' (Segev: 23).

Unofficial envoys have the additional advantage that they can be used by political leaders to by-pass the foreign service of their own country. They may want to do this for any number of reasons: to take the credit for any diplomatic breakthrough themselves; or because they regard the foreign service as politically hostile, incapable of radical thinking, prone to leaking or just plain incompetent. At the end of the 1960s, the South African prime minister, John Vorster, employed Eschel Rhoodie, secretary of the Department of Information, as a personal envoy in his adventurous diplomacy in West Africa and elsewhere, because he was convinced that the Department of Foreign Affairs lacked imagination and was paralyzed by an obsession with protocol (Rhoodie).

There is usually a price to be paid for the use of unofficial envoys, particularly personal ones. They tend to create resentment in the foreign ministry at home and if – as is often the case – it has not been kept fully in the picture, problems might occur in implementing any new policy agreed. Personal envoys might also make serious mistakes if they act in the absence of professional scrutiny. This is a dilemma, because giving them foreign ministry minders, as in the case of Lord Levy (see Box 14.1), might defeat the object of sending them in the first place.

Official envoys

The more common type of high-level envoy is the official species; that is, those recruited from within the political establishment and formally appointed. It is only in exceptional circumstances that presidents or prime ministers themselves visit states with which their governments do not have diplomatic relations, as when President Nixon made his epic journey to Beijing in February 1972. Instead, it is senior political advisers or civil servants – who, despite their elevation, are often not well-known to the press and can 'carry out the most delicate mission without drawing attention' – who are usually selected (Young 2008: 101). If they are in, or not far from, the inner circle of a leader or foreign minister, they will also carry similar weight to a personal envoy, without the same liability to make mistakes or cause disaffection in the bureaucracy – the misadventures of Colonel Oliver North and the national security adviser Robert McFarlane in the Iran-Contra affair in the mid-1980s notwithstanding (*Tower Commission Report*: vii).

A more typical high-level official envoy was Harold Beeley, the quiet, pragmatic Arabist in the British Diplomatic Service, who had been previously ambassador at Cairo and, in 1967, was treading water as representative to the UN disarmament conference in Geneva. In October, he was whisked away from Switzerland and sent for 'path-finding talks' with the Egyptian leader, Nasser; in December, Anglo–Egyptian diplomatic relations were restored, with Beeley himself once more ambassador (*Guardian* 2001b; Young 2008: 210). Some high-level official envoys soon become well-known to the press precisely because of the international dramas in which they have been involved. Henry Kissinger was one such individual, but more on him later.

In addition to foreign affairs officials, typical sources of high-level official envoys include senior intelligence officers, generals, war heroes, retired ministers, and – although not in Zimbabwe – opposition politicians (Young 2008: 105–7).

Some high-level official envoys are appointed as roving ambassadors, or 'ambassadors-at-large'. As with some personal envoys, these are individuals given the task of visiting a number of countries, usually within the same region. In the past, roving ambassadors were often employed to explain the policies of a new government suspicious of the loyalties of the diplomats it had inherited, and it would be surprising if they were not still sometimes used for this purpose. Normally diplomats of great experience and seniority ('seasoned' is the adjective commonly applied), they are more often today a feature of the diplomacy of a major power that wants to promote a settlement of a regional conflict, and be seen to be doing so. They are in a position to coordinate the broad approach needed but for which the ambassadors accredited to individual states in the region are not suited, and a president or foreign minister has neither the time nor grasp of the necessary detail (Fullilove: 15, 18). Such trouble-shooters cannot be too fastidious about the people they meet.

The multi-lingual US General, Vernon A. ('Dick') Walters, is a famous example of a roving ambassador, having been formally ambassador-at-large for President Reagan from 1981 until 1985, and still involved in special missions afterwards. One of these, in July 1987, was to Syria, from which the United States had withdrawn its ambassador in the previous year, although diplomatic relations had not been severed (Berridge 1994: 108); the ambassador was returned in December. Malcolm MacDonald, a veteran politician and diplomat, was a British envoy of the same kind who helped to negotiate the restoration of diplomatic relations between Britain and a number of East African states in the late 1960s (Young 2008: 102–4, 211–12).

One of the first moves of newly-elected President Obama, in January 2009, was to appoint two key roving ambassadors: George Mitchell, the 75-year old former Senate majority leader who played such an important role in ending Northern Ireland's troubles in 1998–99, as his 'Special Envoy for Middle East Peace'; and Richard Holbrooke, who so successfully banged heads together in the former Yugoslavia in 1995, as 'Special Representative for Afghanistan and Pakistan'. At the end of February 2009, another roving ambassador was appointed by the Obama administration. This was Stephen Bosworth, Dean of the Fletcher School of Law and Diplomacy at Tufts University in Massachusetts and previously ambassador to South Korea, who was made 'Special Representative for North Korea Policy' only weeks after returning from a 'private trip' to Pyongyang. Without even a disguised embassy in the North Korean capital (the Swedish embassy looks after US interests without the benefit of any American diplomats on its staff), and having to rely chiefly on contacts via the North Korean mission to the UN (the 'New York channel'), the United States has a clear need for a high-level official envoy able to visit Pyongyang.

Low-level official envoys sent to unfriendly regimes, or to meet their counterparts in third countries, tend to surface – if they ever surface at all – only when government archives are opened up many years after the event. This is because they are used for the most delicate, initial contacts and are often secret service officers. 'Low-level' officials – who, in practice, are probably more often middle-level – are used because of their relative invisibility and because, if revealed, the significance of their missions can nevertheless be more plausibly played down. They can even be disavowed altogether, although less convincingly than private envoys. On the other hand, they are easier to control.

Rumours about special missions conducted by unnamed, low-level officials – urged by insiders, actively planned, or actually in progress – often circulate and are occasionally confirmed. For example, James Dobbins, the Bush administration's first Special Envoy for Afghanistan, has recorded that low-level contacts were employed to try to keep the post-9/11 improvement in US–Iranian relations alive, although they were infrequent and inconclusive (*Washington Post* 2004). Then, amid much talk of a new era of diplomatic engagement with Tehran, it was persuasively reported in early January 2009 that members of President-elect Obama's transition team were urging him to 'initiate low-level or clandestine approaches' to the Iranian-backed Islamist organization, Hamas, regarded by the United States government as a terrorist group (*Guardian* 2009). Two months later, in the course of an interview on BBC Radio 4, the British foreign secretary, David Miliband, publicly confirmed that Britain had 'sanctioned low-level contacts' with the political wing of Hezbollah (*Al Arabiya*).

It would be surprising if, in addition to secret service officers, embassy personnel at first or second secretary level dealing with subjects where otherwise hostile states find common ground – for example, in the distribution of humanitarian aid or combating illegal narcotics- and people-trafficking – do not find themselves parts of special missions. One of these was divulged in 1989, when the first secretary at the British embassy in Bangkok was sent to Cambodia to discuss the distribution of humanitarian aid within the country with the Vietnamese-backed government of Hun Sen, which Britain refused to recognize (Berridge 1994: 106). The now numerous DLOs and ILOs in embassies in the Balkans and the Middle East – where Iran has such a massive problem with heroin flowing out of Afghanistan, and stages an annual conference for DLOs from states willing to attend – seem very likely candidates (Berridge 2009: 255–61).

To go secretly or openly?

When special missions are employed in diplomacy between hostile states, they are often despatched in secret – especially when contacts are at an early stage. Indeed, because they are professionals in the business of disguised travelling and secret communications, as well as reflexively discreet, senior secret service officers are themselves commonly employed in this capacity (Geldenhuys: 147–9; Heikal: 72–3; Klieman: 48–9), and it was a source of regret to the Tower Commission that the CIA was not used to run the arms-for-hostages initiative into Iran in the mid-1980s (*Tower Commission Report*: vii).

The first reason for the preference for secret emissaries is the avoidance of sabotage. Public knowledge that a special mission to a hostile state is planned, especially if it is a high-level one rumoured to be seeking a *rapprochement*, is likely to spread alarm among factions at home and allied governments abroad whose interests are locked into the *status quo*. Advance warning of what is afoot permits them time to marshal their forces against it and nip it in the bud. The fear of an outcry from die-hard anti-Communists at home (especially in the well-organized, pro-Taiwan 'China lobby'), as well as vigorous opposition from Japan and Taiwan itself, was the given reason for the intense secrecy cloaking Henry Kissinger's first mission to Beijing in July 1971 in order to explore the possibility of a summit spectacular between President Nixon and Chairman Mao (Kissinger 1979: 725; MacMillan: 179–80). The anxiety to avoid sabotage has also been behind the employment of secret envoys in contacts between Israel and its Arab neighbours, a tradition that goes back to the activities of the Arab experts of the Jewish Agency before World War II, notably Elias Sasson (Shlaim: 11–12).

The second reason for sending a special envoy in secret is the need to avoid the damage to one's prestige that might result from appearing to the world as a supplicant at the seat of the rival's power. Any power in decline will be readily persuaded by this argument, and – although it was not admitted – was probably another reason for the American insistence on the secrecy of Kissinger's first visit to Beijing. If secrecy is impossible or for other reasons inadvisable, another way of minimizing the risk to prestige is for special envoys from both states to meet on neutral ground – for example, in Geneva, where the US secretary of state, James Baker, met his Iraqi counterpart, Tariq Aziz, in a televised last-minute attempt to avert fighting in the Gulf in April 1991; or at working funerals (see Chapter 10); or in the setting of the diplomatic corps of a third state, as when, in the early 1970s, Henry Kissinger flew to Paris to meet the Chinese ambassador, and Le Duc Tho of North Vietnam flew there to meet Kissinger.

The third reason for despatching special envoys in secret, at least where the object is the ambitious one of exploring a general *rapprochement*, is to make it easier to 'reverse course quickly'. In his memoirs, Kissinger speculates that China's apprehension of the US desire that his first trip should be made in secret might have been prompted by the suspicion that this sort of thinking was behind it (Kissinger 1979: 724). When a special mission arrives, it might soon become apparent that there is not the degree of common ground that had been hoped for, and that the best course is to abort amid expressions of mutual regret – thereby leaving the door open for another attempt in the not too distant future. However, if the mission is public knowledge, a quick return might cause expressions of mutual regret to be replaced by mutual recriminations at the failure, thereby closing the door on diplomacy for the foreseeable future. Alternatively, the public hopes riding on the mission's success and the fear of being seen to have squandered an investment, might lead the mission to clutch at straws and make unwise concessions.

There are also reasons for despatching envoys in secret that have nothing to do with diplomatic considerations; they are rooted, instead, in either the personalities or domestic political needs of the sending government. It is, for example, notorious that Richard Nixon also had re-election on his mind when he insisted on the secrecy of Kissinger's first visit to the PRC. Secrecy right through to the end of the trip meant that he could produce a *coup de théâtre* by springing the news of it on the world on Kissinger's return, and also ensure that as much public attention as possible was focused on his own plans to visit China (Ball: 22).

When the risk of sabotage and loss of prestige is judged to be minimal – perhaps because a previous secret trip had been successful, as with Kissinger's visit to China in July 1971 – the advantages of publicly announcing a special mission and, indeed, encouraging maximum media coverage, might become overwhelming. Kissinger's second visit to Beijing, in October 1971, was made openly. The Chinese appear to have been more insistent with regard to openness on this occasion. In any case, it would have been difficult for the Americans to conceal because their party needed to be much larger, and it flew in Air Force One in order to familiarize the Chinese with its handling in preparation for the president's own arrival (MacMillan: 205).

The United States also publicly sent numerous special missions headed by high-ranking official envoys to the Socialist Republic of Vietnam in the years prior to the restoration of diplomatic relations in 1995. Among these were the former chairman of the joint chiefs of staff, General John Vessey, and assistant secretary of state for East Asian and Pacific affairs, Winston Lord, who alone had made five trips to Hanoi in the first Clinton administration (Lord). This enabled the administration to advertise its efforts on the highly emotional Prisoners of War/Missing in Action question, while simultaneously maintaining the formal diplomatic isolation of Vietnam (Berridge 1994: 56–8). In April 2002, and again in January 2003, South Korea publicly sent a high-level official envoy, Lim Dong-won, to North Korea in an attempt both to highlight its attachment to, and to keep alive (at a time when it seemed imperilled) Seoul's 'Sunshine Policy'.

Special missions are sometimes announced beforehand because, while secrecy might be preferred, there is no faith in either the determination or the capacity of the other side to preserve it. In such circumstances, it is generally best to have one's own justification of the mission made known, especially to one's friends, as soon as possible. In the interests of balancing the need for decisive action with that of carrying allies, secrecy before the mission and publicity immediately afterwards is probably the optimal course. This was Kissinger's tactic with regard to the November 1973 mission to Morocco of General Walters, by then deputy director of the CIA but still America's most notable 'expert at discreet missions', where he met an emissary of the PLO. 'Though the meeting in Rabat was supposed to be secret,' says Kissinger, 'it was potentially too explosive to risk its uncontrolled leakage to other countries. Moreover, if word spread only through the Arab gossip mill, it would take on a more dramatic significance than we intended, disquieting especially those countries on whose support we relied for a moderate evolution. I therefore informed Hussein, Sadat, and Boumedienne, and later discussed it with Asad. Brent Scowcroft briefed [Israeli] Ambassador Dinitz' (Kissinger 1982: 628–9). The release of information about Kissinger's own earlier secret mission to China, in July 1971, was less well contrived, with temporarily unfortunate consequences for relations between the United States and its allies, especially Japan.

So-called pariah states – such as the TRNC and North Korea, and those on the US Department of State's list of 'State Sponsors of Terrorism' (in 2009 Cuba, Iran, Sudan, and Syria) – are nearly always anxious both to despatch and to receive special envoys in public. It advertises their own commitment to good international behaviour, and so is a regular rebuke to those who have made them outcasts; and it advertises the fact that they are weighty players with which the world has no alternative but to deal. If they are not widely recognized, either as states or as legitimate governments, the public despatch and receipt of special envoys might also grant them a degree of *de facto* admission to this blessed status. While all of this is going on, their enemies become demoralized. These reasons explain why the white South African government, pursuing its policy of 'dialogue' with black Africa in increasingly difficult circumstances, was so delighted to receive a public special envoy from the Ivory Coast in October 1971. And also why the Sudanese regime of the hunted president, Omar al-Bashir (see Box 10.1), took a degree of comfort from the widely reported arrival in April 2009 in Khartoum – where the US embassy has had no ambassador since 1998 – of President Obama's close friend and Special Envoy to Sudan, retired Air Force general, Scott Gration, in order to 'engage' it on the question of Darfur.

Summary

Special missions come in many guises but, compared with embassies, they all have a limited purpose and a limited time-span, and experience a more permissive legal regime. They also share the same advantages, albeit in varying degrees. Personal envoys are perhaps the most suitable in underlining the personal interest of a president or prime minister in a particular foreign policy approach, although high-level *official* envoys can do likewise without the liability of the former to make mistakes and prompt bureaucratic disaffection – at least, to the same degree. This is why high-level official envoys are more common. Low-level envoys, who are relatively invisible, are best for the most delicate, initial contacts. Private envoys are the most easily disavowed if discovered, while official envoys – often secret service officers – are most easily controlled. In the conduct of diplomacy without diplomatic relations, special missions are especially valuable in the absence of disguised embassies.

Further reading

Bartos, M., 'Fourth Report on Special Missions', *Yearbook of the International Law Commission*, (1967), Volume II, UN Doc. A/CN. 4/SER A/ 1967/ Add. 1.

Berridge, G. R., *Talking to the Enemy: How states without 'diplomatic relations' communicate* (1994): ch. 6.

Convention on Special Missions, 8 December 1969, United Nations, *Treaty Series*, 1400 (UN: 2005) [www].

Farnsworth, Eric, 'Back to smart diplomacy', *Poder 360*, September 2008 [www].

Fullilove, M., 'All the presidents' men', *Foreign Affairs*, March/April 2005: 13–18.

James, A., 'Diplomatic relations and contacts', *British Year Book of International Law 1991* (Clarendon Press: Oxford, 1992): 347–87.

Jennings, Sir Robert and Sir Arthur Watts (eds), *Oppenheim's International Law*, 9th edn, Volume I (Longman: Harlow, Essex, 1992): 1125–31.

Johnson, Chalmers, 'The patterns of Japanese relations with China, 1952–1982', *Pacific Affairs*, 59(3), Autumn, 1986.

Macmillan, Margaret, *Seize the Hour: When Nixon met Mao* (John Murray: London, 2006): chs 12 and 13.

Roberts, Sir Ivor (ed), *Satow's Diplomatic Practice*, 6th edn (Oxford University Press: Oxford, 2009): ch. 13.

Ryan, Michael H., 'The status of agents on special mission in customary international law', *Canadian Yearbook of International Law*, 16, 1978.

Wriston, H. M., 'The Secretary of State abroad', *Foreign Affairs*, 34(4), 1956.

Wriston, H. M., 'The special envoy', *Foreign Affairs*, 38(2), 1960.

Yearbook of the International Law Commission (1967), II: 344–68 [www].

Young, John W., 'The Wilson government and the Davies peace mission to North Vietnam', *Review of International Studies*, 24, 1998: 545–62.

Young, John W., *Twentieth-Century Diplomacy: A case study of British practice, 1963–1976* (Cambridge: Cambridge University Press, 2008): ch. 5.

15
Mediation

Mediation, which has a long and generally honourable record in the history of diplomacy, is by definition multilateral and might occur, as in the momentous talks on the Middle East at Camp David in September 1978, at the summit. To this extent, it raises questions identical to those discussed in Chapters 9 and 10. But mediation warrants separate treatment because it raises separate questions and is so important. It is particularly necessary in long, bitter disputes in which the parties are unable to compromise without seriously jeopardizing the domestic positions of their leaders. It is usually needed the more when the parties retain the most profound distrust of each other's intentions, where cultural differences present an additional barrier to communication, and where at least one of the parties refuses to recognize the other.

The presence of mediation in international conflicts, and also in civil wars, is extensive, although only occasionally does it attract great attention: some form of *official* mediation alone was enjoyed by 255 of the 310 conflicts between 1945 and 1974 (Princen: 5). At the beginning of the twenty-first century, it seems even more difficult to find conflicts in which intermediaries – unofficial, as well as official – are not participating in one way or another. What does mediation involve? What motivates the mediator? What are the intermediary's ideal attributes? Should the start of a mediation effort wait until the time for a settlement is ripe? And what are the drawbacks of involving third parties in disputes? These are the questions that this chapter will consider.

The nature of mediation

Mediation is a special kind of negotiation designed to promote the settlement of a conflict. In this negotiation, a distinctive role is played by a third party; that is, one not directly involved in the dispute in question. The third party must have a special characteristic, in addition to an inclination to behave in a special way. To be precise, it must be substantially *impartial* in the dispute – at least, once the negotiation has started and on the issue actually on the agenda. Certainly, the third party must want a settlement, but *any* settlement with which the parties themselves will be happy. As to its role, in a mediation – which is not to be confused with being a 'facilitator' or provider of 'good offices' (see Box 15.1) – the third party searches actively for a settlement and, for this reason, is sometimes described as a 'full partner' in the negotiations. Typically, this means drawing up an agenda, calling and chairing negotiating sessions, proposing solutions, and – where the third party is a powerful state – employing threats and promises in order to promote resolution. In short, mediation is the active search for a negotiated settlement to an international or intra-state conflict by an impartial third party.

Providing good offices might be more passive than mediation, but is sometimes its starting point. It is, moreover, by no means merely a question of providing the parties with a channel of communications and, perhaps, a secure and comfortable venue for their talks. Ideally,

---

Box 15.1   Good offices

A third party acting as a facilitator or provider of good offices has a more limited role than a mediator, usually involving no more than helping to bring the parties in conflict into direct negotiations. At this point it withdraws, although it will usually remain in the wings in case the talks threaten to founder and it is needed again. In short, its role is limited to the prenegotiations stage. Modern social-psychological versions of this traditional approach emphasize that an enduring settlement is one at which the parties must arrive themselves, and reflect basic attitude changes. It is quite common for a good offices mission to turn into a mediation, but the activities remain distinct. Unfortunately, this does not prevent many mediations from being described as missions of 'good offices', and the separate chapters on 'Good Offices' and 'Mediation' disappeared from the later editions of *Satow's Guide to Diplomatic Practice*. Mediation should also be distinguished from *conciliation*. This is the attempt to resolve a dispute by having it examined in depth by an independent commission of inquiry or conciliation commission. This then offers its recommendations for a settlement, which are non-binding. Conciliation had a short heyday in the period between World Wars I and II. *Arbitration* is the same as conciliation, except that the recommendation is binding. It is akin to, but not the same as, judicial settlement.

the third party will also assist with the interpretation of messages and be able to show one or both parties how the style, as well as the content, of a message from one party can be made more palatable to the other. It should also provide reassurance to each party that the other means what it says and is sincere in seeking a negotiated settlement. This seems to have been at least one of the roles played by the government of General de Gaulle in the earliest stage of the Sino–American *rapprochement* in 1969. The French leader was a figure who still enjoyed enormous international respect and whose reassurances, in consequence, were trusted (Nixon: 370–4; Hersh: 351–2).

Via the communications they have exchanged through the facilitator, the parties to a conflict might conclude that there is a basis for negotiation between them. In this eventuality, the third party might be required to facilitate this by arranging for a neutral venue for the talks. (This is not essential: in the final Iranian hostages negotiations in 1980, the Americans shuttled between Washington and Algiers, the Algerians shuttled between Algiers, Tehran and Washington, and the Iranians stayed at home.) This might be on its own territory, or it might be elsewhere. During the Angola/Namibia negotiations in 1988, which were mediated by the United States, meetings were held in London, Cape Verde, Brazzaville, Geneva, and Cairo, as well as in New York. The Israeli–Syrian talks in early 2000, also mediated by the United States, were held at Sheperdstown in West Virginia, and then shifted to Turkey in 2008 following Ankara's assumption of the role of third party. Talks mediated by the UN are commonly held at its headquarters in New York or Geneva.

Having brought the parties together, the subsequent role of the third party depends on a variety of factors. These include its own motives, influence, diplomatic skill, and standing with the parties; and whether or not the latter have been brought to a stage where they can bear it to be known that they are talking face to face with their enemies.

A third party might lack significant influence with the rivals and find that, in any case, they are by now prepared to talk directly. This was the case in the Sino–American *rapprochement* in the early 1970s, in which Pakistan had emerged as the most important provider of good offices and then withdrew to the wings. Conversely, the influence of the third party over the antagonists might be considerable, especially if it has the support of other important players. Furthermore, the parties in dispute might not only find it impossible to meet without the face-saving presence of the third party, but also require a constant stiffening of their resolve to continue talking. In such circumstances, third parties – by this point, full-blown mediators – have the chief responsibility for driving the negotiations forwards. To reassure the rivals that calamity will not follow non-compliance with any agreement reached, the mediator might also provide tangible guarantees – a vital feature of American mediation in the Arab–Israeli conflict in the 1970s (Touval 1982: chs 9 and 10). The mediator might make a final contribution to face-saving on the part of one or both of the antagonists by going along with an agreement that suggests, by its packaging, that the concessions it contains have been granted to the mediator rather than to the opponent. In the Iranian hostages negotiations in 1980, for example, the final agreement took the form of a 'Declaration of the Government of the Democratic and Popular Republic of Algeria' – *not* of an 'Agreement between Iran and the United States'.

Different mediators and different motives

Mediators resemble those brokers in the worlds of commerce and finance who act as middlemen between clients in order to turn a profit (*FRUS*: 532; Touval 1982: 321). In early modern Europe, resident ambassadors were given handsome and valuable personal gifts by foreign monarchs grateful for their assistance in helping to bring peace to their conflicts. This was especially good business for ambassadors in Constantinople, where diamond snuff boxes and sable furs often changed hands in the constant cycle of war and peacemaking between Ottoman Sultan and Russian Tsar and Sultan and Habsburg Emperor. Today, the nature of the profit sought by mediators still depends on who they are and what kind of dispute they are trying to mediate, but ambassadors seeking the role for personal gain are no longer prominent among them. First, then, who are today's mediators? It is most useful to divide them simply into official and unofficial categories, or into 'track one' and 'track two'. (The attempt to identify additional tracks under the aegis of the concept of 'multitrack diplomacy' trivializes the key distinction between states and the rest, and merely confuses matters.)

Track one

The most important mediators in international relations are states – whether acting singly or collectively, or via the international organizations (such as the United Nations) that are largely their creatures. The major powers, which held a virtual monopoly over mediation until the twentieth century, generally pursue it for one or more of the following main reasons.

First, and generally foremost, they seek the mediator's mantle in order to defuse crises that threaten the global stability, including global economic stability, in which they have such an important stake. These were certainly major considerations prompting most administrations in the United States to make a settlement of the Arab–Israeli conflict a high priority after the Yom Kippur War in October 1973. For this not only strained US–Soviet *détente*, but also produced such a massive increase in the price of oil that the economies of the West were severely rocked.

Second, the major powers see mediation as a means of generally raising their prestige. It is to the interest of a great prince, wrote Callières, to procure peace between quarrelling sovereigns 'by the authority of his mediation. Nothing', he concluded, 'is more proper to raise the reputation of his power, and to make it respected by all nations' (Callières: 73). This is as true today as when it was written in the early eighteenth century, and is seen immediately in the potential of a successful mediation to extend a major power's network of dependent clients into areas where previously it had not been great. This prompted Soviet mediation in the India–Pakistan conflict at Tashkent in January 1966, at a time when both of these South Asian powers were disgruntled with the West, and 'must have made Lord Curzon turn in his grave' (Trevelyan 1971: 200). It was also behind the American role in the Angola/Namibia negotiations that were finally brought to success at the end of 1988 (Berridge 1989). In 2008 and early 2009, the French president, Nicolas Sarkozy – his policy justified by holding the rotating EU presidency for only part of this period – was transparently keen to extend French influence by mediation exercises in Georgia and the Middle East. Callières would have understood Sarkozy only too well.

Finally, in order to maintain internal solidarity and pre-empt offers of 'assistance' from outside, the major powers always think it prudent to mediate in conflicts within alliances or looser associations of states in which they play leading roles. In some cases, this inclination is reinforced by a lingering sense of imperial responsibility and ethnic lobbying at home. These have been key factors leading the United States and Britain to interest themselves in the Cyprus dispute, which involves two of the most important members of NATO's southern flank – Turkey and Greece. Britain also has legal guarantor obligations towards the Republic of Cyprus – which hosts important NATO military and SIGINT installations, and is a member of the Commonwealth. Considerations of in-group solidarity and leadership have also, no doubt, been behind Britain's long-standing attempts to mediate in the dispute over Kashmir between India and Pakistan – prominent Commonwealth members.

The major powers, however, are not the only kind of state that involve themselves in mediation efforts. Middle powers – such as Turkey, leading between Syria and Israel in 2008, as already mentioned; and South Africa in the Zimbabwe crisis that came to a head in the same year – periodically play this role for reasons similar to those that lead to its adoption by the major powers, not the least their interest in regional stability and extending their influence. Among the middle powers, however, Switzerland and Austria should be mentioned as special cases by virtue of their permanent neutrality.

Having joined the EU in 1995, and shortly afterwards NATO's Partnership for Peace, Austria's status of permanent neutrality is now questionable, and even Switzerland's has been slightly diluted following its entry into the United Nations in September 2002. Nevertheless, their reputations still provide them with an outstanding qualification to provide good offices or engage in international mediation. Both Vienna and Geneva have been the venues of much sensitive diplomacy, and Geneva hosts the European headquarters of the UN. In 1979, at considerable cost to the Austrian taxpayer, a new International Centre for the use of UN agencies was opened in Vienna. And both Switzerland and Austria are frequently employed by states in conflict as protecting powers – which, in practice, is usually a mediating role, although in theory it is not (see Chapter 13). It is true that with a particularly purist conception of neutrality, and aware that genuine mediation involves the kind of active diplomacy that risks the charge of bias, Switzerland has tended to confine itself to the provision of good offices, as in its discreet promotion of low-level contacts between Israel and Syria in 2004–07 (*Haaretz*). By contrast, Austria has prided itself on its 'active neutrality', especially during the period when it was led by Dr Bruno Kreisky (see Box 15.2).

However, permanent neutrality provides Austria and Switzerland with a motive, as well as an opportunity, to provide good offices and play the role of mediator. This is the need to deflect the free-rider criticism of their neutrality. By their unusual diplomatic exertions in the cause of peace, they are able to take the edge off the complaint that, in the same way that non-unionized workers take the pay rises secured by trade unions without paying their dues, they enjoy the security provided by NATO without contributing to its military strength.

Small states, too, sometimes mediate in international conflicts, including those involving far larger states than themselves. A case in point is the mediation of Algeria in the hostages crisis between the United States and Iran at the beginning of the 1980s. Algeria was interested in both

---

Box 15.2 Dr Bruno Kreisky

Kreisky, a Jewish but anti-Zionist Socialist, was Austrian minister of foreign affairs from 1959 until 1966, and federal chancellor from 1970 until 1983. He took a strong interest in the Arab–Israeli conflict in the mid-1970s, and was the first Western statesman to recognize the PLO, allowing it to open an information office in Vienna. In 1977, he also hosted a famous encounter in the city between South African prime minister, John Vorster, and US vice-president, Walter Mondale, and later visited Tehran on behalf of the Socialist International in an unsuccessful attempt to break the impasse in the hostages crisis (Stadler: 16–17). According to Henry Kissinger, Kreisky was 'shrewd and perceptive ... [and] ... had parlayed his country's formal neutrality into a position of influence beyond its strength, often by interpreting the motives of competing countries to each other' (Kissinger 1979: 1204).

---

the huge prestige that successful mediation in this most serious crisis would bring in its train, and the increased influence in Tehran and Washington that it would produce. Another interesting example under this head is the Holy See, for which mediation is a spiritual duty as well as a political requirement – although, for much the greater part of the post-war period, Communism and religious divisions together severely restricted the mediating capacity of the Vatican diplomatic service. Not in diplomatic relations with any Communist state (including the PRC) until the end of the 1980s, and refusing to recognize the State of Israel, the Holy See was as much in need of mediation itself as it was available as a provider. In practice, its activities under this heading were confined to the Catholic world, as, for example, in Pope John Paul II's mediation of the Beagle Channel dispute between Argentina and Chile – diplomacy that began in 1979 and culminated successfully six years later.

Finally, it is important to note that states also mediate in international and intra-state conflicts under the authority of the charters of the international organizations they have established. As well as the United Nations, these include regional bodies such as the OAS and the AU. With councils dominated by their weightiest members, it is hardly surprising that the interests of the latter should be most influential in shaping the mediations in which these intergovernmental bodies are involved. Nevertheless, their secretariats are not entirely puppets. The secretary-general of the UN, for example, now has some limited capacity to engage in independent mediation. This derives, in part, from the tradition going back to the Middle East crisis of 1956, in which the Security Council gave the then secretary-general, Dag Hammarskjöld, the right to use his discretion in seeking fulfilment of the purposes and principles of the UN Charter and the Council's decisions (Bailey and Daws: 119–20; De Soto: 350). It is reinforced by the express and implied provisions of the Charter, especially Article 99 (see Box 15.3). Successive secretaries-general have pointed out that they cannot form an opinion of the sort envisaged in this article without the ability to appoint staff, authorize research, make visits, and engage in diplomatic consultations (Bailey and Daws: 111–13).

It is because track one mediators stand to earn a profit from brokering a settlement to a conflict – whether in cash or in kind, and whether it

---

Box 15.3   Mediation in the UN Charter

Article 33
1. The parties to any dispute, the continuance of which is likely to endanger the maintenance of international peace and security, shall, first of all, seek a solution by negotiation, enquiry, mediation, conciliation, arbitration, judicial settlement, resort to regional agencies or arrangements, or other peaceful means of their own choice.
2. The Security Council shall, when it deems necessary, call upon the parties to settle their disputes by such means...

Article 36
1. The Security Council may, at any stage of a dispute of the nature referred to in Article 33 or of a situation of like nature, recommend appropriate procedures or methods of adjustment.

Article 37
1. Should the parties to a dispute of the nature referred to in Article 33 fail to settle it by the means indicated in that Article, they shall refer it to the Security Council.
2. If the Security Council deems that the continuance of the dispute is in fact likely to endanger the maintenance of international peace and security, it shall decide whether to take action under Article 36 or to recommend such terms of settlement as it may consider appropriate.

Article 38
Without prejudice to the provisions of Articles 33 to 37, the Security Council may, if all the parties to any dispute so request, make recommendations to the parties with a view to a pacific settlement of the dispute...

Article 99
The Secretary-General may bring to the attention of the Security Council any matter which in his opinion may threaten the maintenance of international peace and security.

arrives indirectly in the shape of increased prestige or directly from the erstwhile antagonists – that states and others have an incentive to dispense with them as soon as possible. Payments for mediation services can be considerable. For example, the Americans found themselves having to 'tilt' to Pakistan in the latter's conflict with India in the early 1970s partly by way of payment of a debt to Yahya Khan for acting as intermediary in the early approaches to Beijing. Using mediators also causes delays in communications between rivals, increases the number of foreigners who share their secrets, and carries the risk that messages might be garbled in transmission. Not surprisingly, as early as mid-1970 both Nixon and Kissinger were anxious 'to get rid of all the middlemen' in their developing relationship with China (Kissinger 1979: 722–3; Hersh: 364). More often than not, however, this is not easy.

Track two

Mediation by private individuals and NGOs was known in the United States as 'citizen diplomacy' until it was christened 'track two' by the American diplomat, Joseph Montville, in 1981. It has increased rapidly over recent decades. Prominent among private individuals engaged in these activities are well-connected businessmen such as the legendary Armand Hammer (Box 15.4) and 'Tiny' Rowland, the former managing director of the mining-finance house, Lonrho, whose diplomatic playground was central Africa. Such people are prompted by any mixture of corporate interests, political ambitions, and charitable instincts – and, perhaps, just by a simple desire to show off. Among NGOs, religious bodies have long been important, and new ones are still emerging. The Quakers, with their strong pacifist leaning, have been energetic in this work since the seventeenth century, while the Rome-based religious order of Sant'Egidio came to prominence for its role in the ending of the civil war in Mozambique in the early 1990s. However, secular NGOs dedicated to conflict prevention and resolution, as it is known in trade jargon, are now also extremely numerous. Sometimes referred to as track two professionals, these include such bodies as the very effective Carter Center, set up by former US president Jimmy Carter, and Conciliation Resources in London.

Multiparty mediation

So far, and despite occasional hints to the contrary, it has been assumed that mediation is an activity carried out by a single party. However, the involvement of more than one mediator in the attempt to settle a conflict, including those in both track one and track two, is now so

---

Box 15.4   Armand Hammer: citizen-diplomat

Hammer, who died in 1990, was an American tycoon whose Russian father had emigrated to the United States in the late nineteenth century. During the Cold War he received much carefully engineered publicity for his attempts as a citizen-diplomat to promote East–West *détente*, although less so for his efforts on behalf of Soviet Jews at the instigation of Israel. Exploiting to the full his huge experience of the Soviet Union, his vast wealth, and his remorseless energy, Hammer seemed to open doors in Moscow that others found closed. He certainly had political achievements to his credit. However, there were many in the US Department of State who did not trust him, and some of his efforts on behalf of East–West *détente* were rendered superfluous by the fact that diplomatic relations between the superpowers were never actually broken off (Hammer; Weinberg; Blumay and Edwards).

---

common as probably to be the norm. It is the more necessary to be clear about the very different kinds of diplomatic operation that are grouped under the broad label of multiparty mediation, for it might be simultaneous or sequential, coordinated or uncoordinated.

When two or more parties are trying *simultaneously* to facilitate or mediate the settlement of a conflict but make no attempt to coordinate their activities, it is usually because they are in competition: rival brokers seeking the sole contract. This was the situation in the early stages of the Sino–American *rapprochement* at the beginning of the 1970s. But, sometimes, the parties anxious to mediate a solution to a conflict are willing – indeed, eager – to coordinate their actions. In this case, the result is sometimes described as 'collective mediation' and the coordinating body involved – in which responsibility is formally shared – as a 'contact group'. Typically having four or five members, one of the most important contact groups in recent years is the Contact Group on Bosnia, which was created in April 1994 and was revived in an attempt to grapple with the Kosovo crisis in 1999. It consisted of Germany, France, Russia, Britain, and the United States. When there are only two mediators – as, for example, in the original UN/EU mission to broker a settlement in Bosnia – the designation 'joint mediation' is more common. A joint effort of this sort between the UN and the regional organization with the closest interest in the dispute concerned was the model proposed by the then UN Secretary-General (Boutros-Ghali 1992: ch. vii).

As for *sequential* multiparty mediation, this is predicated on the notion that conflicts have life cycles with levels of violence that rise and then fall, and that certain kinds of mediator are more appropriate to one stage in this cycle than another. Only one mediator is active in the conflict at any one time, but – as in a relay race – makes a deliberate 'hand-over' to one thought more suitable to the new stage considered imminent (Crocker *et al.*: 10). This sort of mediation was seen in Haiti in the early 1990s, where responsibility started with the OAS, then passed to the UN, and finally – when the threat of real force seemed necessary – came to rest with the United States (McDougall). It is important to stress, however, that not all mediations in which different parties take turns to try to settle a conflict are examples of this species of multiparty mediation. There is, for example, no evidence that the attempt to mediate a settlement between Israel and Syria – first by the United States in 2000, then by Switzerland in 2004–07, and finally by Turkey in 2008 – was in any way orchestrated.

The ideal mediator

The attributes of the ideal mediator vary according to the nature of a conflict. For example, the Holy See is, in principle, well-suited to the mediation of a conflict between two Catholic states, provided the exertion of material power over them is not required. Small states might be appropriate as mediators between major powers, since the latter will not feel threatened by them. The UN often seems best for the mediation of conflicts that appear intractable but are of relatively marginal concern to the major powers. Track two NGOs might well have a role in the settlement of a conflict in which at least one of the parties believes that track one intervention would give too much legitimacy to its rival, or in which the major powers would dearly like to see progress but, for one reason or another, cannot risk direct involvement themselves. As for the major powers, and at the risk of appearing tautological, they are usually the best-suited to the mediation of conflicts that are amenable only to power.

It also seems likely that the ideal mediator might vary with the stage of the conflict cycle, as remarked in the discussion of sequential multiparty mediation (p. 244), or with the stage of the mediation. It is a common observation that a track two party might have a key role in the prenegotiation stage of a mediation, but must stand down in favour of a more muscular track one party once the mediation is properly launched. This is an oversimplification, as the Oslo channel (which produced the historic agreement between Israel and the PLO in September 1993) and other mediations have demonstrated. Be that as it may, whatever the nature of the conflict or the stage that it has reached, all mediators should have certain common characteristics in addition to routine diplomatic skills, which include the ability to generate 'creative formulas' (Crocker 1999: 243).

All mediators should be perceived as impartial on the specific issues dividing the parties to a conflict; have influence, if not more effective power, relative to them; possess the ability to devote sustained attention to their dispute; and be propelled by a strong incentive to achieve a durable settlement.

Mediation, by definition, requires a third party that is impartial on the issue of the moment, even if the parties to the conflict are not, in general, held in equal affection. Impartiality enables the third party to be trusted by both parties. This is important if they are to believe that the mediator will convey messages between them without distortion, that its reassurances about their mutual sincerity are well-founded, and that their confidences will be kept. It is also important if they are to believe that any compromises it proposes are of equal benefit to both, and that it will implement any guarantees if this is required by any defaulting on the settlement achieved – irrespective of which party is guilty. It is true that a third party with close ties to only one of the antagonists might be attractive as a mediator to the other because the role will require the third party to draw away somewhat from its traditional relationship. This might also strengthen the hand of such a mediator, once the mediation has started, by enabling it to play on the fears of desertion of the one and the hopes of consolidating a new friendship on the part of the other (Touval 1982). The fact remains, however, that the party not hitherto enjoying friendly relations with the third party is only likely to accept it as a mediator on two conditions. It must believe, first, that it will be impartial on the issue actually on the table and, second, that it is able to deliver its traditional friend. It was on these conditions that the Egyptians accepted American mediation with the Israelis in the late 1970s. The notion of a biased intermediary (Touval 1982: 10–16; Ross: 228–9) is a contradiction in terms.

What next of the value to the mediator of influence or more effective power relative to the parties? This might not be of great importance if the 'mediation' is in the good offices stage, provided ripeness does not need engineering. However, it is clearly vital to a genuine mediation, when the parties will probably need cajoling to a settlement; it is even more so if it is necessary to provide guarantees against the consequences of any subsequent non-compliance with its terms. Mediator influence has many sources. It might derive from a record of past success and the lack of alternative mediators acceptable to both parties at a critical point, which seems to have helped Algeria during the Iranian hostages negotiations. It might even derive from spiritual authority, as in the case of the Holy See. It seems most effective, however, when it is based on the ability to manipulate tangible rewards and sanctions, including increased or reduced levels of economic and military aid. Thus, Jimmy Carter said that he was wary of 'buying peace' in the Camp David negotiations between Egypt and Israel – but he did. Israel received US$3 billion in concessional loans to fund the building of new airfields in the Negev to compensate for those they would have to surrender in Sinai (Quandt: 241); while by 1980–81, the year following signature of the Egypt–Israel Peace Treaty, Egypt was the top recipient of US official development assistance (Berridge 1997: table 7.2).

Whatever the source of the mediator's influence relative to the parties, it will also be increased to the extent that it is allied to that of other states or track two bodies pushing in the same direction. For example, America's influence in the Angola/Namibia negotiations in 1988 was clearly enhanced by the support of a considerable list of states – among them the Soviet Union, Britain, Portugal, and the African Front Line States – together with members of the UN and OAU secretariats (Crocker 1999: 229–39). If, as in this case, the external patrons of the parties to the conflict are all on the list, the latters' game is usually up. If a settlement is achieved against this background, it also increases the cost of any subsequent default by multiplying the ranks of those who will be directly affronted by it. It is important to add that, in principle, the same effect – maximizing power relative to the parties – can be achieved by multiparty mediation in the form of a contact group. However, in practice, the disadvantages of this form of mediation tend to weaken it, as we shall see later. Track two bodies now often acknowledge that their own efforts are most effective when conducted in support of those of track one, although this is usually difficult to organize. In Sudan, it has not been especially effective (Dixon and Simmons).

It is important, too, that the mediator should be able to give continuous attention to a conflict, possibly over many years. The conflicts that require mediation are the most intractable, and intractable conflicts are not settled overnight. Continuous involvement produces familiarity with the problem and key personalities, enables relationships of personal trust to develop that reinforce calculations of interest, and fosters a routine that reduces the likelihood of false expectations being generated. It also makes possible procedural breakthroughs, and even breakthroughs of principle – which, in turn, make seizing a propitious moment for settlement that much easier. This is where track two diplomats and the secretariats of international organizations, notably the UN, tend to have the edge over states, especially in the mediation of disputes where major power interest is, at most, moderate. This applies even to stable political regimes such as that of the United States. Such states might have foreign ministries capable of pursuing consistent policies over long periods, but electoral cycles (as well as a constantly changing international context) tend to condemn their mediations to being episodic rather than continuous affairs. This has been a marked feature of American mediation in the Middle East. It is fair to note, however, that Chester Crocker, the US assistant secretary of state for African affairs who successfully negotiated the Angola/Namibia Accords of December 1988, was able to devote the full period of both Reagan administrations to the task. Not surprisingly, Crocker himself emphasizes the value of continuity in his memoir of this negotiation (Crocker 1992: 468–70).

Finally, the ideal mediator should have a strong incentive to obtain a settlement and, thus, not be easily discouraged by setbacks (Ross: 230–1). Mediators, as already noted, have different motives, but one of these is enhancing prestige. It is for this reason that the ideal mediator, while being able to rely on the support of 'friends', is also usually not one who shares formal responsibility for the negotiation with them. The clear allocation of responsibility to one party alone is uniquely energizing. This is because not only will it take all the blame for failure, but also all the credit for success. By contrast, where responsibility is formally divided, as in a contact group, individual third parties can pass on the blame for failure and will have to share the credit for any success. Their incentive to make settlement of the conflict a high priority is thereby reduced. It is, thus, perhaps no accident that the real breakthroughs tend to come when one of the members of a contact group seizes the reins of the mediation itself, frees itself of the need to work within a consensus, and puts its prestige directly on the line. This is well-illustrated by the success of American mediation in south-western Africa in the late 1980s, subsequent to Washington's withdrawal from the Western Contact Group on Namibia. It is also demonstrated by its even more spectacular success at Dayton, Ohio, in November 1995, following President Clinton's decision to take the lead in Bosnian diplomacy from the Bosnia Contact Group.

It will, thus, be clear that the attributes of the ideal mediator are one thing; the attributes of the ideal mediation are another. Single mediation, albeit assisted by 'friends', is better than simultaneous multiparty mediation. In some conflicts, for example that in Haiti already mentioned, the most effective mediation might be one conducted by an orchestrated sequence of different, single mediators – sequential multi-party mediation.

The ripe moment

Provided there is to hand an ideal mediator appropriate to a particular dispute, mediation is most likely to succeed in the circumstance in which any negotiation is most likely to succeed. This is when the antagonists have both arrived at the conclusion that they will probably be better off with a settlement than without one – when, in other words, the situation is 'ripe' for a settlement. (This can be engineered by a prospective mediator, especially if it is a major power; for example, by manipulating the flow of arms to a client that is a party to the dispute.) But does this mean that no move to launch a mediation should be contemplated before this point is reached?

There is a view that any attempt to launch a mediation before the time is propitious will not only fail, but also make matters worse. That this – barring a miracle – will guarantee failure is undeniable. However, why a 'premature' attempt at mediation should also be *counter-productive* is not self-evident, and is positively disputed by many scholars (Rubin). In fact, so-called premature mediation need not always exacerbate a conflict; it depends on the form the diplomacy takes and the goals those bent on this course set themselves. If the former is low-key (track two, for example) and the latter modest, there is no reason to suppose that the situation will deteriorate if and when the negotiations stall, and certainly not that it will become more difficult to resolve. On the contrary, useful advances on procedure, in the building of trust, and even on broad principle might be made that will make seizing the opportunity that much easier when the time really is ripe for substantive negotiations (Crocker 1992: 471; Ross: 220). Besides, diagnosing 'ripe moments' is not exactly a scientific exercise, and it is not always possible to tell if these circumstances exist until they are put to the test; that is, by negotiation. The very fact that such a move is made can, itself, also affect the degree of ripeness for settlement.

It remains true that if a mediation launched in unpropitious circumstances is ambitious and conducted with much fanfare, and if in consequence it fails, then it can be counter-productive. The leaders and domestic groups on which political support for negotiations rests will be at least temporarily discredited, the view that the conflict is intractable will be strengthened, and one or both of the parties to the conflict might take provocative measures in reaction to the failure.

In any event, having secured the agreement of the parties – however reluctantly – to collaborate with its efforts, the mediator also needs to judge whether it is best to seek a comprehensive solution to the dispute, or approach it in a step-by-step manner. Since conflicts would not require mediation if they were not very deep, it is often best to adopt the latter approach. This emphasizes the need to build both trust and momentum by confining the initial negotiations to subjects of only limited political implications, such as the disengagement of military forces. Besides this, the mediator needs to employ a judicious combination of carrots and sticks, together with deadlines and press manipulation in order to sustain diplomatic momentum (see Chapter 4). A fair share of luck is also needed. This is because a local incident can sour the atmosphere at a critical juncture, while the eruption of a major international crisis can, at best, distract attention from the dispute in question and, at worst, seriously alter the calculation of interests on which one or more of the parties – including the mediator – had previously agreed to proceed. Certain diplomatic breakthroughs in the 1990s – notably, the Israel–PLO agreement in 1993, and the Bosnian peace settlement at Dayton, Ohio, two years later – show that mediation can produce handsome dividends, even if they do not always last forever. More recently, the limited truces obtained by Egypt in the fighting between Israel and Hamas in Gaza in 2008 and early 2009 show that it can produce dividends worth having, even if they are less eye-catching and not ideal.

Summary

Mediation is the active search for a negotiated settlement to an international or intra-state conflict by an impartial third party. Mediators come in all shapes and sizes, as well as singly and in groups. The attributes of the ideal mediator vary with the nature of the conflict in question and, sometimes, with the stage reached by the conflict or the mediation itself. However, all mediators should be perceived as impartial once the mediation is in progress. They should also have influence – if not more effective power – relative to the parties, the ability to devote sustained attention to the dispute in question, and a strong incentive to achieve a durable settlement. This incentive will usually be the greater if one third party alone has sole responsibility for the mediation, because this means that its prestige, as well as the more specific policy goals in which it is interested, will be at stake. Mediation is often needed and often accepted; but it is often refused as well, and, if accepted, sometimes discarded at the first opportunity. The lure of direct talks, even at a high political price, is usually strong.

Further reading

Abbas, Mahmoud ['Abu Mazen'], *Through Secret Channels – The Road to Oslo* (Garnet: Reading, 1995): esp. chs 6–8.

Albright, Madeleine, *Madam Secretary: A memoir* (Macmillan: London, 2003), ch. 19, on the Wye River summit, October 1998.

Bailey, Sydney D. and Sam Daws, *The Procedure of the UN Security Council*, 3rd edn (Clarendon Press: Oxford, 1998): ch. 3 (1), 'Secretary-General'.

Bercovitch, J. (ed), *Studies in International Mediation* (Palgrave Macmillan: Basingstoke, 2002).

Bercovitch, J. and Scott Sigmund Gartner (eds), *International Conflict Mediation: New approaches and findings* (Routledge: London, 2008).

Berman, Maureen R. and Joseph E. Johnson (eds), *Unofficial Diplomats* (Columbia University Press: New York, 1977).

Berridge, G. R., *Return to the UN: UN diplomacy in regional conflicts* (Macmillan – now Palgrave: Basingstoke, 1991).

Berridge, G. R. (ed.), *Diplomatic Classics: Selected texts from Commynes to Vattel* (Palgrave Macmillan: Basingstoke/New York; Peking University Press: Beijing, 2004), index refs. 'mediation'.

Bourantonis, D. and M. Evriviades (eds), *A United Nations for the Twenty-First Century* (Kluwer Law International: The Hague/London/Boston, 1996): esp. pt II.

Boutros-Ghali, B., *An Agenda for Peace: Preventive diplomacy, peacemaking and peace-keeping* (United Nations: New York, 1992).

Boutros-Ghali, B., *Unvanquished: A U.S.–U.N. saga* (I. B. Tauris: London/New York, 1999).

Brinkley, D., 'Jimmy Carter's modest quest for global peace', *Foreign Affairs*, November/December 1995: 90–100.

Christopher, W. and Paul H. Kreisberg (eds), *American Hostages in Iran: The conduct of a crisis* (Yale University Press: New Haven/London, 1985).

Cohen, Herman J., *Intervening in Africa: Superpower peacemaking in a troubled continent* (Macmillan – now Palgrave: Basingstoke, 2000).

Corbin, Jane, *Gaza First: The secret Norway channel to peace between Israel and the PLO* (Bloomsbury: London, 1994).

Crocker, C. A., *High Noon in Southern Africa: Making peace in a rough neighbourhood* (Norton: New York/London, 1992).

Crocker, C. A., F. O. Hampson and P. Aall (eds), *Herding Cats: Multiparty mediation in a complex world* (US Institute of Peace Press: Washington, DC, 1999).

Druckman, D. and C. Mitchell (eds), *Flexibility in International Negotiation and Mediation* (Sage: London, 1995): chs by Bates and Mitchell, and Touval.

Heikal, Mohamed, *Secret Channels* (HarperCollins: London, 1996): esp. chs 11–15.

Holbrooke, Richard, *To End a War* (Random House: New York, 1998).

Hume, Cameron, *Ending Mozambique's War: The role of mediation and good offices* (US Institute of Peace Press: Washington, DC, 1994).

Jones, Deiniol L., *Cosmopolitan Mediation? Conflict resolution and the Oslo Accords* (Manchester University Press: Manchester, 1999).

Kriesberg, L. and S. T. Thorson (eds), *Timing the De-Escalation of International Conflicts* (Syracuse University Press: Syracuse, NY, 1991).

Lindsley, L., 'The Beagle Channel settlement: Vatican mediation resolves a century-old dispute', *Journal of Church and State*, 29(3), 1987.

Mitchell, George J., *Making Peace* (Heinemann: London, 1999), on the Good Friday agreement.

Owen, David, *Balkan Odyssey* (Indigo: London, 1996).

Princen, T., *Intermediaries in International Conflict* (Princeton University Press: Princeton, NJ, 1992).

Pruitt, D. (1997), 'Ripeness theory and the Oslo talks', *International Negotiation*, 2(2).

Quandt, W. B., *Camp David: Peacemaking and politics* (Brookings Institution: Washington, DC, 1986).

Roberts, A. and B. Kingsbury (eds), *United Nations, Divided World*, 2nd edn (Clarendon Press: Oxford, 1993): chs 5 and 6.

Ross, Dennis, *Statecraft: And how to restore America's standing in the world* (Farrar, Strauss: New York, 2007): chs 10 and 11.

Rouhana, N. and H. C. Kelman, 'Promoting joint thinking in international conflicts', *Journal of Social Issues*, 50(1), 1994: 157–78.

Rubin, B., J. Ginat, and M. Ma'oz (eds), *From War to Peace: Arab–Israeli relations, 1973–1993* (Sussex Academic Press: Brighton, 1994): esp. pts I and III.

Schaffer, Howard B., *Ellsworth Bunker: Global troubleshooter, Vietnam hawk* (University of North Carolina Press: Chapel Hill/London, 2003).

Touval, S., *The Peace Brokers: Mediators in the Arab–Israeli conflict, 1948–1979* (Princeton University Press: Princeton, NJ, 1982).

Touval, Saadia and I. William Zartman (eds), *International Mediation in Theory and Practice* (Westview: Boulder, CO/London, 1985): esp. chs by Sick and Thornton.

Watkins, Michael and K. Lundberg, 'Getting to the table in Oslo: driving forces and channel factors', *Negotiation Journal*, 14(2), 1998: 1156–136.

Zartman, I. W. and S. Touval, 'International mediation: conflict resolution and power politics', *Journal of Social Issues*, 41(2), 1985: 27–45.

Conclusion: the Counter-Revolution in Diplomatic Practice

In examining the different functions of diplomacy and how they are pursued, this book has traced in some detail what elsewhere I have called a 'counter-revolution in diplomatic practice' (Berridge 2005). As a broad trend, this rejuvenation of some of the key features of traditional diplomacy has gone unnoticed – partly because it has been masked by the attachment of new labels to old procedures, and partly because the novel has a greater fascination than the tried and tested. For those who care to look, however, the evidence of this counter-revolution is unmistakeable.

There has emerged a quiet, almost resigned acceptance that resident embassies are not the anachronism they were thought to be in the 1960s and 1970s but, rather, are still the state's first line of defence abroad, a key vehicle for routine negotiations, essential support to special envoys, and nearest thing to a mind-reader bolted onto the side of a host government. With the great increase in the flow of people across frontiers, the value of consular services has also been rediscovered, and the old institution of the honorary consul, or consular agent, has received a powerful shot in the arm. Propaganda – with which diplomats have often been uneasy, but with which they came to terms in the middle of the twentieth century – has been reinvented, and even returned to war-time proportions; to describe this as 'public diplomacy' and allege that it is something new is just to make free with the most transparent of marketing ploys. As the importance of coordinating foreign activities – among them, propaganda – has been rediscovered, so, too, has the foreign ministry bounced back, or a functionally equivalent body placed over its shell. Summitry has also played its part in the counter-revolution, for its serial – as opposed to its *ad hoc* – form has become by far its most important; this, as with the new respect for the resident mission, signifies further recognition of the value of *continuous* contact between states – a cardinal principle of the old, French system of diplomacy. Greater reliance on special envoys is a return to a medieval reflex. In multilateral diplomacy, the twentieth century's experiment with taking decisions by voting after a public debate has been liquidated by the rejuvenation of secret negotiation, among the many benefits of which is a working Great Power concert called the UN Security Council. As for the so-called 'new actors in diplomacy' – in particular, the international NGOs – they are neither new nor diplomats: they are either free-booting amateurs, or para-diplomats with valuable but limited usefulness and no special immunities, and, in either case, long pre-date the appearance of the professional diplomat. The main point here, though, is that the more experienced track two 'diplomats' now appreciate that, to make a real contribution to diplomacy, they must work with, and not parallel to, the professionals.

It is true that the counter-revolution in diplomatic practice that I have described is only a partial one. For example, 'consensus decision-making' employs a blend of old tricks and a few new ones that, in sum, represents a new version of secret negotiation in multilateral diplomacy; and special envoys are now transported so quickly that this change might be said to represent a change of kind. Besides, planes are not being grounded, secure telephones are not being disconnected, and BlackBerrys are not being dropped into bins: there *is* innovation in diplomacy. But innovation is one thing; the complete transformation often claimed as a fact or heralded as imminent is quite another.

What we have witnessed in recent years, the great growth in multilateral diplomacy notwithstanding, is not the complete transformation of diplomacy but, rather, the more intelligent application of new technology and new devices to support tried and tested methods, with the added advantage that this has helped to integrate the many poor and weak states rather better into the world diplomatic system. What we have now is neither an old nor a new diplomacy but, instead, a blend of the two, which has produced a mature diplomacy. It is also one that is fortified by a respected legal regime.

This development is just as well because, while power remains dispersed between states – while there remains, in other words, a states-system – international diplomacy, bilateral or multilateral, direct or indirect, at the summit or below, remains essential. This much is particularly obvious from the inventiveness that has gone into preserving resident diplomacy, even when diplomatic relations do not exist. Only diplomacy can produce the enormous advantages obtainable from the cooperative pursuit of common interests, and prevent violence from being employed to settle remaining arguments over conflicting interests. When violence breaks out, nevertheless, diplomacy remains essential if the worst excesses are to be limited and if, in addition, the ground is to be prepared against the inevitable day of exhaustion and revised ambition.

References

Adair, E. R. (1929) *The Exterritoriality of Ambassadors in the Sixteenth and Seventeenth Centuries* (Longman: London).

Acheson, D. (1969) *Present at the Creation: My years in the State Department* (Norton: New York).

Adelman, K. L. (1989) *The Great Universal Embrace: Arms summitry – a skeptic's view* (Simon & Schuster: New York).

Ahmad, Z. H. (1999) 'Malaysia', in B. Hocking (ed.), *Foreign Ministries: Change and adaptation* (Macmillan – now Palgrave Macmillan: Basingstoke).

Albright, Madeleine (2003) *Madam Secretary: A memoir* (Macmillan: London).

Alexander, Michael (2005) ed. and introduced by Keith Hamilton, *Managing the Cold War: A view from the front line*, (RUSI: London).

Algosaibi, G. A. (1999) *Yes, (Saudi) Minister! A life in administration* (London: Centre of Arab Studies).

Anderson, M. S. (1993) *The Rise of Modern Diplomacy* (Longman: London/New York).

Angell, James B. (2007) 'DS rides the iron rooster', *Foreign Service Journal*, July–August [www].

Arndt, Richard T. (2005) *The First Resort of Kings: American cultural diplomacy in the twentieth century* (Potomac Books: Washington, DC, 2005).

Ashrawi, Hanan (1995) *This Side of Peace: A personal account* (Simon & Schuster: New York/London).

Aurisch, K. L. (1989) 'The art of preparing a multilateral conference', *Negotiation Journal*, 5(3).

Avalon Project (no date) *The Versailles Treaty, June 28, 1919* [www].

Bailey, S. D. and S. Daws (1998) *The Procedure of the UN Security Council*, 3rd edn (Clarendon Press: Oxford).

Baker, James A. (1999) 'The road to Madrid', in C. A. Crocker, F. O. Hampson and P. R. Aall (eds), *Herding Cats: Multiparty mediation in a complex world* (USIP: Washington, DC).

Ball, G. (1976) *Diplomacy for a Crowded World* (Bodley Head: London).

Beer, Lawrence W. (1969) 'Some dimensions of Japan's present and potential relations with Communist China', *Asian Survey*, 9(3), March.

Bergus, D. C. (1990) 'U.S. diplomacy under the flag of Spain, Cairo, 1967–74', in D. D. Newsom (ed.), *Diplomacy Under a Foreign Flag* (Hurst: London; St Martin's Press – now Palgrave Macmillan: New York).

Berridge, G. R. (1987) *The Politics of the South Africa Run: European shipping and Pretoria* (Clarendon Press: Oxford).

Berridge, G. R. (1989) 'Diplomacy and the Angola/Namibia Accords', *International Affairs*, 65(3).

Berridge, G. R. (1991) *Return to the UN: UN diplomacy in regional conflicts* (Macmillan – now Palgrave Macmillan: Basingstoke).

Berridge, G. R. (1992) *South Africa, the Colonial Powers and 'African Defence': The rise and fall of the white entente, 1948–60* (Macmillan – now Palgrave Macmillan: Basingstoke).

Berridge, G. R. (1994) *Talking to the Enemy: How states without 'diplomatic relations' communicate* (Macmillan – now Palgrave Macmillan: Basingstoke).

Berridge, G. R. (1996) 'Funeral summits', in David H. Dunn (ed.), *Diplomacy at the Highest Level: The evolution of international summitry* (Macmillan – now Palgrave Macmillan: Basingstoke).

Berridge, G. R. (1997) *International Politics: States, power and conflict since 1945*, 3rd edn (Prentice Hall/Harvester Wheatsheaf: Hemel Hempstead).

Berridge, G. R. (2004) *Diplomatic Classics: Selected texts from Commynes to Vattel* (Palgrave Macmillan: Basingstoke/New York).

Berridge, G. R. (2005) 'The counter-revolution in diplomatic practice', *Quaderni di Scienza Politica*, 1, April.

Berridge, G. R. (2007) 'The origins of the diplomatic corps: Rome to Constantinople', in P. Sharp and G. Wiseman (eds), *The Diplomatic Corps as an Institution of International Society* (Palgrave Macmillan: Basingstoke).

Berridge, G. R. (2009) *British Diplomacy in Turkey, 1583 to the Present: A study in the evolution of the resident embassy* (Martinus Nijhoff: Leiden).

Berridge, G. R. and N. Gallo (1999) 'The role of the diplomatic corps: the US–North Korea talks in Beijing, 1988–94', in J. Melissen (ed.), *Innovation in Diplomatic Practice* (Macmillan – now Palgrave Macmillan: Basingstoke).

Berridge, G. R. and Alan James (2003) *A Dictionary of Diplomacy*, 2nd edn (Palgrave Macmillan: Basingstoke/New York).

Berridge, G. R., Maurice Keens-Soper and T. G. Otte (2001) *Diplomatic Theory from Machiavelli to Kissinger* (Palgrave Macmillan: Basingstoke/New York).

Binnendijk, H. (ed.) (1987) *National Negotiating Styles* (Center for the Study of Foreign Affairs, Foreign Service Institute, US Department of State: Washington, DC).

Blix, Hans (2004) *Disarming Iraq* (Bloomsbury: London).

Blumay, C. and H. Edwards (1992) *The Dark Side of Power* (Simon & Schuster: New York).

Boutros-Ghali, B. (1992) *An Agenda for Peace: Preventive diplomacy, peacemaking and peacekeeping* (United Nations: New York).

Boutros-Ghali, B. (1999) *Unvanquished: A U.S.–U.N. saga* (I. B. Tauris: London/ New York).

Bower, D. (1994) 'Summit and symbol: Franco-German relations and diplomacy at the top', unpublished dissertation (University of Leicester).

Bradshaw, K. and D. Pring (1973) *Parliament and Congress* (Quartet: London).

Brown, J. (1988) 'Diplomatic immunity – state practice under the Vienna Convention', *International and Comparative Law Quarterly*, 37(1).

Brzezinski, Z. (1983) *Power and Principle: Memoirs of the National Security Adviser 1977–1981* (Farrar, Straus & Giroux: New York).

Bull, H. (1977) *The Anarchical Society: A study of order in world politics* (Macmillan – now Palgrave Macmillan: Basingstoke).

Bulmer, S. and W. Wessels (1987) *The European Council: Decision-making in European politics* (Macmillan – now Palgrave Macmillan: Basingstoke).

Busk, Sir Douglas (1967) *The Craft of Diplomacy: How to run a diplomatic service* (Praeger: New York).

Buzan, B. (1981) 'Negotiating by consensus: developments in technique at the United Nations Conference on the Law of the Sea', *American Journal of International Law*, 72(2).

Callaghan, J. (1987) *Time and Chance* (Collins: London).

Callières, F. de (1994) *The Art of Diplomacy*, ed. by H. M. A. Keens-Soper and K. Schweizer (University Press of America: Lanham/New York/London).

Carter, J. (1982) *Keeping Faith: Memoirs of a president* (Bantam: New York).

Carter of Coles, Lord (2005) *Public Diplomacy Review* [www].

Cohen, R. (1987) *Theatre of Power: The art of diplomatic signalling* (Longman: London/New York).

Cohen, R. (1997) *Negotiating across Cultures: International communication in an interdependent world*, rev. edn (US Institute of Peace Press: Washington, DC).

Cohen, R. and R. Westbrook (eds) (2000), *Amarna Diplomacy: The beginnings of international relations* (The Johns Hopkins University Press: Baltimore and London).

Coles, J. (2000) *Making Foreign Policy: A certain idea of Britain* (Murray: London).

CPRS (1977) *Review of Overseas Representation* (HMSO: London).

Cradock, P. (1994) *Experiences of China* (Murray: London).

Crocker, C. A. (1992) *High Noon in Southern Africa: Making peace in a rough neighbourhood* (Norton: New York/London).

Crocker, C. A. (1999) 'Peacemaking in Southern Africa: The Namibia–Angola settlement of 1988', in C. A. Crocker, F. O. Hampson and P. R. Aall (eds), *Herding Cats: Multiparty mediation in a complex world* (USIP: Washington, DC).

Crocker, C. A., F. O. Hampson and P. Aall (eds) (1999) *Herding Cats: Multiparty mediation in a complex world* (USIP: Washington, DC).

Cross, C. T. (1999) *Born a Foreigner: A memoir of the American presence in Asia* (Rowman & Littlefield: Lanham, MD).

Cull, Nicholas J. (2006a) ' "The Perfect War": US public diplomacy and international broadcasting during Desert Shield and Desert Storm, 1990/1991', *Transnational Broadcasting Studies*, 15, Fall/Winter [www].

Cull, Nicholas J. (2006b) ' "Public Diplomacy" before Gullion: the evolution of a phrase', USC Center on Public Diplomacy [www].

Cull, Nicholas J. (2007) 'Public diplomacy: seven lessons for its future from its past' [www].

Deeks, Ashley S. (2008) 'Avoiding transfers to torture', *Council on Foreign Relations Special Report*, 35, June.

Denza, E. (1998) *Diplomatic Law: A commentary on the Vienna Convention on Diplomatic Relations*, 2nd edn (Clarendon Press: Oxford).

De Soto, A. (1999) 'Ending violent conflict in El Salvador', in C. A. Crocker, F. O. Hampson and P. Aall (eds), *Herding Cats: Multiparty mediation in a complex world* (USIP: Washington, DC).

Dickie, J. (1992) *Inside the Foreign Office* (Chapman & Hall: London).

Dimbleby, D. and D. Reynolds (1988) *An Ocean Apart: The relationship between Britain and America in the twentieth century* (Hodder & Stoughton: London).

Dinstein, Yoram (2005) *War, Aggression and Self-Defence*, 4th edn (Cambridge University Press: Cambridge).

Dixon, Peter and Mark Simmons (2006) *The role of track two initiatives in Sudanese peace processes* (Conciliation Resources) [www].

Dunham, Lawrence, [US] Assistant Chief of Protocol (2002) Remarks by, at the Consular Corps General Meeting, Las Vegas, 14 March [www].

Dunn, D. H. (ed.) (1996) *Diplomacy at the Highest Level: The evolution of international summitry* (Macmillan – now Palgrave Macmillan: Basingstoke).

Eagleton, W. L., Jr (1990) 'Evolution of the U.S. Interests Sections in Algiers and Baghdad', in D. D. Newsom (ed.), *Diplomacy under a Foreign Flag* (Hurst: London; St Martin's Press – now Palgrave Macmillan: New York).

Edwards, R. D. (1994) *True Brits: Inside the Foreign Office* (BBC Books: London).

FAC (2001) *Minutes of evidence*, 24 April [www].

FCO (2007) *Delivering Change Together: The consular strategy, 2007–2010* [www].

FCO Historians, 'Slavery in Diplomacy: The Foreign Office and the suppression of the transatlantic slave trade', *History Note*, 17 [www].

Fennessy, J. G. (1976) 'The 1975 Convention on the Representation of States in their Relations with International Organizations of a Universal Character', *American Journal of International Law*, 70(1).

Foreign Service Journal (2007a) 'Embassies as command posts in the war on terror', March 2007 [www].

Foreign Service Journal (2007b) 'Focus on country team management', December [www].

Franck, T. M. and E. Weisband (1979) *Foreign Policy by Congress* (Oxford University Press: New York/Oxford).

Frey, Linda S. and Marsha L. Frey (1999) *The History of Diplomatic Immunity* (Ohio State University Press: Columbus, OH).

FRUS (1986) *1955–1957, Volume 11, China* (US Government Printing Office: Washington, DC), Robert Murphy, memorandum of 29 April 1955.

Fullilove, M. (2005) 'All the presidents' men', *Foreign Affairs*, March/April: 13–18.

Geldenhuys, D. (1984) *The Diplomacy of Isolation: South African foreign policy making* (Macmillan: Johannesburg).

Glennon, M. J. (1983) 'The Senate role in treaty ratification', *American Journal of International Law*, 77.

Gore-Booth, P. (1974) *With Great Truth and Respect* (Constable: London).

Gore-Booth, Lord (ed.) (1979) *Satow's Guide to Diplomatic Practice*, 5th edn (Longman: London/New York).

Gotlieb, A. (1991) *I'll be with you in a minute, Mr. Ambassador: The education of a Canadian diplomat in Washington* (University of Toronto Press: Toronto).

Greene, Graham (1974) *The Honorary Consul* (Penguin Books: Harmondsworth).

Grenville, J. A. S. and B. Wasserstein (1987) *The Major International Treaties since 1945: A history and guide with texts* (Methuen: London/New York).

Guicciardini, Francesco (1890) *Counsels and Reflections*, trsl. by N. H. Thomson (Kegan Paul: London), first published ca. 1530.

Haass, R. N. and M. Indyk (2009) 'Beyond Iraq: A new U.S. strategy for the Middle East', *Foreign Affairs*, January/February.

Hale, J. B. (1957) 'International relations in the West: diplomacy and war', in G. R. Potter (ed.), *The New Cambridge Modern History*, Volume I (Cambridge University Press: Cambridge).

Hall, W. E. (1917) *A Treatise on International Law*, 7th edn (Clarendon Press: Oxford).

Hamilton, Keith (1999) 'Historical diplomacy: foreign ministries and the management of the past', in J. Kurbalija (ed.), *Knowledge and Diplomacy* (DiploFoundation: Malta).

Hammer, A. with N. Lyndon (1987) *Hammer: Witness to history* (Simon & Schuster: London).

Hankey, Lord (1946) *Diplomacy by Conference: Studies in public affairs, 1920–1946* (Benn: London).

Hansard (2001) House of Commons, Written Answers for 5 February 2001 (pt 9), col. 389W [www].

Harrison, S. (1988) 'Inside the Afghan talks', *Foreign Policy*, Fall.

HCPP (1858): *Report from the Select Committee on Consular Service and Appointments; together with the Proceedings of the Committee, Minutes of Evidence, Appendix and Index*, 27 July (482).

HCPP (1872): *Report from the Select Committee on Diplomatic and Consular Services; together with the Proceedings of the Committee, Minutes of Evidence, Appendix and Index*, 16 July (314).

HCPP (1943): *Proposals for the Reform of the Foreign Service*, Cmd. 6420.

HCPP (1954): *Summary of the Report of the Independent Committee of Enquiry into the Overseas Information Services*, April, Cmd. 9138 ['Drogheda Report'].

HCPP (1964): *Miscellaneous No. 5 (1964). Report of the Committee on Representational Services Overseas appointed by The Prime Minister under the Chairmanship of Lord Plowden 1962–63*, February, Cmnd. 2276 ['Plowden Report'].

HCPP (1969): *Miscellaneous No. 24 (1969). Report of the Review Committee on Overseas Representation 1968–1969. Chairman: Sir Val Duncan*, July, Cmnd. 4107 ['Duncan Report'].

HCPP (1993): *Memorandum by the FCO: Taiwan. FAC, Relations between the UK and China in the period up to and beyond 1997: Mins. of Evidence*, 14 July, 842-i.

Heikal, M. (1984) *Autumn of Fury: The assassination of Sadat* (Corgi: London).

Henderson, N. (1994) *Mandarin: The diaries of an ambassador, 1969–1982* (Weidenfeld & Nicolson: London).

Henkin, L. (1979) *How Nations Behave: Law and foreign policy*, 2nd edn (Columbia University Press: New York).

Hersh, S. M. (1983) *Kissinger: The price of power* (Faber: London).

Hoare, J. E. (2007) 'Diplomacy in the East', in P. Sharp and G. Wiseman (eds), *The Diplomatic Corps as an Institution of International Society* (Palgrave Macmillan: Basingstoke/New York).

Hocking, B. and D. Spence (eds) (2002) *Foreign Ministries in the European Union: Integrating diplomats* (Palgrave Macmillan: Basingstoke/New York).

Hoffmann, S. (1978) *Primacy or World Order: American foreign policy since the Cold War* (McGraw-Hill: New York).

Horn, D. B. (1961) *The British Diplomatic Service 1689–1789* (Clarendon Press: Oxford).

House of Representatives (1989) *Hearing before the Subcommittee on Asian and Pacific Affairs of the Committee on Foreign Affairs, House of Representatives, 28 July, 1988: The implications of establishing reciprocal interests sections with Vietnam*, (US Government Printing Office: Washington, DC).

ILC (1956) *Yearbook of the International Law Commission*, Volume II (United Nations Publications).

ILC (1957) *Yearbook of the International Law Commission*, Volumes I and II (United Nations Publications).

ILC (1958) *Yearbook of the International Law Commission*, Volumes I and II (United Nations Publications).

ILC (1960) *Yearbook of the International Law Commission*, Volumes I and II (United Nations Publications).

ILC (1961) *Yearbook of the International Law Commission*, Volume I (United Nations Publications).

ILC (no date) 'Consular Intercourse and Immunities' [ch. 2], in *Report...to the General Assembly on its work, 1 May–7 July 1961* [www].

Inman Report (1985) Report of the Secretary of State's Advisory Panel on Overseas Security [www].

IO (1999) *Yearbook of International Organizations, Edition 36, 1999/2000*, Volume 1B (K. G. Saur: Munich).

Jackson, G. (1981) *Concorde Diplomacy: The ambassador's role in the world today* (Hamilton: London).

James, A. M. (1980) 'Diplomacy and international society', *International Relations*, 6(6).

James, A. M. (1992) 'Diplomatic relations and contacts', *British Yearbook of International Law 1991* (Clarendon Press: Oxford).

Jenkins, R. (1989) *European Diary, 1977–1981* (Collins: London).

Johnson, Chalmers (1986) 'The patterns of Japanese relations with China, 1952–1982', *Pacific Affairs*, 59(3), Autumn.

Kear, S. (1999) 'The British Consulate-General in Hanoi, 1954–73', *Diplomacy and Statecraft*, 10(1), March.

Kear, S. (2001) 'Diplomatic innovation: Nasser and the origins of the interests section', *Diplomacy and Statecraft*, 12(3), September.

Keeley, R. V. (1995) 'Crisis avoidance: shutting down Embassy Kampala, 1973', in J. G. Sullivan (ed.), *Embassies under Siege* (Brassey's for the Institute for the Study of Diplomacy: Washington, DC).

Keens-Soper, M. (1985) 'The General Assembly re-considered', in G. R. Berridge and A. Jennings (eds), *Diplomacy at the UN* (Macmillan – now Palgrave Macmillan: Basingstoke).

Kennan, G. F. (1967) *Memoirs, 1925–1950* (Hutchinson: London).

Kerley, E. L. (1962) 'Some aspects of the Vienna Conference on Diplomatic Intercourse and Immunities', *American Journal of International Law*, 56.

Kissinger, H. A. (1979) *The White House Years* (Weidenfeld & Nicolson/Michael Joseph: London).

Kissinger, H. A. (1982) *Years of Upheaval* (Weidenfeld & Nicolson/Michael Joseph: London).

Klieman, A. (1988) *Statecraft in the Dark: Israel's practice of quiet diplomacy* (Jaffee Center for International Studies: Tel Aviv).

Lakoff, G. and M. Johnson (1980) *Metaphors We Live By* (University of Chicago Press: Chicago/London).

Lee, Luke T. and John Quigley (2008) *Consular Law and Practice*, 3rd edn (Oxford University Press: Oxford).

Lim Dong-won (2008) *Peacemaker: South–North relations and the North Korea nuclear issue over the past twenty years* (JoongAng Books: Seoul), extract in English trsl. in 'Korea Focus' [www].

Liverani, Mario (2001) *International Relations in the Ancient Near East* (Palgrave: Basingstoke).

Lord, Winston (1995) *Statement on U.S. Policy toward Vietnam, Laos and Cambodia and the POW/MIA Issues before the House Committee on National Security, Subcommittee on Military Personnel*, December 14 (Electronic Research Collection East Asia and Pacific Bureau) [www].

Lowe, V. (1990) 'Diplomatic law: protecting powers', *International and Comparative Law Quarterly*, 39(2), April.

McDougall, B. (1999) 'Haiti: Canada's role in the OAS', in C. A. Crocker, F. O. Hampson and P. R. Aall (eds), *Herding Cats: Multiparty mediation in a complex world* (USIP: Washington, DC).

Macmillan, Margaret (2006) *Seize the Hour: When Nixon met Mao* (John Murray: London).

McNair, Lord (1961) *The Law of Treaties* (Clarendon Press: Oxford).

Mattingly, G. (1965) *Renaissance Diplomacy* (Penguin Books: Harmondsworth).

Meier, S. A. (1988) *The Messenger in the Ancient Semitic World* (Scholars Press: Atlanta).

Miller, M. (1976) *Plain Speaking: An oral biography of Harry S Truman* (Coronet: London).

Mitchell, George J. (1999) *Making Peace* (Heinemann: London).

Mitrany, David (1943) *A Working Peace System: An argument for the functional development of international organization* (RIIA: London).

Monroe, E. (1963) *Britain's Moment in the Middle East, 1914–1956* (Methuen: London).

Morgenthau, Hans J. (1978) *Politics Among Nations: The struggle for power and peace*, 5th edn (Knopf: New York).

Munn-Rankin, J. M. (1956) 'Diplomacy in Western Asia in the early second millennium B.C.', *Iraq*, 18.

National Archives, London (1952) PM's personal minute, 1 August, PREM 11/691.

National Audit Office (2005) *Consular services to British Nationals: The Foreign and Commonwealth Office* (Stationery Office: London) [www].

Newhouse, John (2009) 'Diplomacy, Inc.: the influence of lobbies on US foreign policy', *Foreign Affairs*, May/June.

Nicol, D. (1982) *The United Nations Security Council: Towards greater effectiveness* (UNITAR: New York).

Nicholas, H. G. (1975) *The United Nations as a Political Institution*, 2nd edn (Oxford University Press: London/New York).

Nicolson, H. (1937) *Peacemaking 1919* (Constable: London).

Nicolson, H. (1954) *The Evolution of Diplomatic Method* (Constable: London).

Nicolson, H. (1963) *Diplomacy*, 3rd edn (Oxford University Press: London).

Nixon, R. M. (1979) *The Memoirs of Richard Nixon* (Arrow: London).

O'Brien, Conor Cruise (1996) *The Long Affair: Thomas Jefferson and the French revolution* (Sinclair-Stevenson: London).

OIG (2006) *Memorandum Report: Impact of Department of Homeland Security Expansion Overseas on Chief of Mission Authorities*, ISP-1–06-26, May [www].

OIG (2007) *Report of Inspection: U.S. Interests Section Havana, Cuba*, July [www].

Parsons, A. (1984) *The Pride and the Fall: Iran 1974–1979* (Cape: London).

Patterson, Jr, Bradley H. (2000) *The White House Staff: Inside the West Wing and beyond* (Brookings: Washington, DC).

Peters, J. (1994) *Building Bridges: The Arab–Israeli multilateral talks* (RIIA: London).

Peterson, M. J. (1986) *The General Assembly in World Politics* (Allen & Unwin: Boston).

Peterson, M. J. (1997) *Recognition of Governments: Legal doctrine and state practice, 1815–1995* (Macmillan – now Palgrave Macmillan: Basingstoke).

Peyrefitte, A. (1993) trans. by J. Rothschild, *The Collision of Two Civilizations: The British expedition to China in 1792–4* (Harvill: London).

Picavet, C.-G. (1930) *La Diplomatie Française au Temps de Louis XIV (1661–1715): Institutions, mœurs et coutumes* (Librairie Félix Alcan : Paris).

Platt, D. C. M. (1968) *Finance, Trade and Politics in British Foreign Policy, 1815–1914* (Clarendon Press: Oxford).

Platt, D. C. M. (1971) *The Cinderella Service: British consuls since 1825* (Longman: London).

Plischke, E. (1967) *Conduct of American Diplomacy*, 3rd edn (Van Nostrand: Princeton, NJ).

Princen, T. (1992) *Intermediaries in International Conflict* (Princeton University Press: Princeton, NJ).

Putnam, R. (1984) 'The Western Economic Summits: a political interpretation', in C. Merlini (ed.) *Economic Summits and Western Decision-making* (Croom Helm: London; St. Martin's Press – now Palgrave Macmillan: New York).

Quandt, W. B. (1986) *Camp David: Peacemaking and politics* (Brookings Institution: Washington, DC).

Queller, D. E. (1967) *The Office of Ambassador in the Middle Ages* (Princeton University Press: Princeton, NJ).

Ragsdale, L. (1993) *Presidential Politics* (Houghton Mifflin: Boston).

Rana, Kishan (2000) *Inside Diplomacy* (Manas: New Delhi).

Rana, Kishan (2004) *The 21st Century Ambassador* (DiploFoundation: Malta/ Geneva).

Randle, R. F. (1969) *Geneva 1954: The settlement of the Indochinese war* (Princeton University Press: Princeton, NJ).

Reagan, R. (1990) *An American Life* (Hutchinson: London).

Report of the Special Group established for entries into Iraqi presidential sites (1998), UN Doc. S/1998/326, 15 April [www].

Reynolds, David (2007) *Summits: Six meetings that shaped the twentieth century* (Allen Lane: London).

Rhoodie, E. (1983) *The Real Information Scandal* (Orbis: Pretoria).

Roberts, Andrew (1999) *Salisbury: Victorian titan* (Weidenfeld & Nicolson: London).

Rona, Gabor (2004) 'The ICRC's status: in a class of its own', 17 February [www].

Ross, Dennis (2007) *Statecraft: And how to restore America's standing in the world* (Farrar, Straus & Giroux: New York).

Rozental, A. (1999) 'Mexico', in B. Hocking (ed.), *Foreign Ministries: Change and adaptation* (Macmillan – now Palgrave Macmillan: Basingstoke).

Rubin, B., J. Ginat, and M. Ma'oz (eds) (1994) *From War to Peace: Arab–Israeli relations, 1973–1993* (Sussex Academic Press: Brighton).

Rubin, J. Z. (1991) 'The timing of ripeness and the ripeness of timing', in L. Kriesberg and S. J. Thorson (eds), *Timing the De-escalation of International Conflicts* (Syracuse University Press: Syracuse, NY).

Safire, W. (1975) *Before the Fall: An inside view of the pre-Watergate White House* (Doubleday: New York).

Satow, Sir E. (1922) *A Guide to Diplomatic Practice*, 2nd edn (Longman: London).

Saunders, H. (1985) 'We need a larger theory of negotiation: the importance of pre-negotiating phases', *Negotiation Journal*, 1.

Schlesinger, A. M. Jr (1965) *A Thousand Days: John F. Kennedy in the White House* (Deutsch: London).

Segev, S. (1988) *The Iranian Triangle: The untold story of Israel's role in the Iran-Contra affair* (Free Press: New York).

Sharp, Paul and Geoffrey Wiseman (eds) (2007) *The Diplomatic Corps as an Institution of International Society* (Palgrave Macmillan: Basingstoke/New York).

Shaw, Malcolm N. (2008) *International Law*, 6th edn (Cambridge University Press: Cambridge/New York).

Shlaim, Avi (1990) *The Politics of Partition: King Abdullah, the Zionists and Palestine, 1921–1951* (Oxford University Press: Oxford).

Shultz, G. P. (1993) *Turmoil and Triumph: My years as secretary of state* (Scribner's: New York).

Shultz, G. P. (1997) 'Diplomacy in the Information Age', Keynote address at the Virtual Diplomacy Conference, Apr. [www].

SIAC, Appeal No.: SC/02/05, Date of Judgement: 8 February 2007. [All open judgements of the Special Immigration Appeals Commission, which provide extremely interesting diplomatic background information, can be accessed via the SIAC website (click on 'Outcomes').]

SIAC, Appeal No.: SC/15/2005, Date of Judgement: 26 February 2007.

SIAC, Appeal No.: SC/42 and 50/2005, Date of Judgement: 27 April 2007.

SIAC, Appeal No.: SC/32/2005, Date of Judgement: 14 May 2007.

SIAC, Appeal No.: SC/59/2006, Date of Judgement: 2 November 2007.

Simpson, S. (1967) *Anatomy of the State Department* (Houghton Mifflin: Boston).

Smith, G. S. (1999) *Reinventing Diplomacy: A virtual necessity* [www].

Smith, L. P. (1907) *The Life and Letters of Sir Henry Wotton*, Volume 1 (Clarendon Press: Oxford).

Stadler, K. R. (1981) 'The Kreisky phenomenon', *West European Politics*, 4(1).

Stearns, M. (1996) *Talking to Strangers: Improving American diplomacy at home and abroad* (Princeton University Press: Princeton, NJ).

Stein, J. G. (1989) 'Getting to the table: the triggers, stages, functions, and consequences of pre-negotiations', *International Journal*, 44(2).

Strang, Lord (1955) *The Foreign Office* (Allen & Unwin: London).

Sullivan, W. H. (1981) *Mission to Iran* (Norton: New York).

Summary Report of the 4th Review Meeting of the Contracting Parties to the Convention on Nuclear Safety, 14–25 April 2008, Vienna, Austria [www].

Taylor, P. M. (1992) *War and the Media: Propaganda and persuasion in the Gulf War* (Manchester University Press: Manchester/New York).

Thatcher, M. (1993) 'The Downing Street Years', *Booknotes Transcript* [www].

Thatcher, M. (1995) *The Downing Street Years* (HarperCollins: London).

Touval, S. (1982) *The Peace Brokers: Mediators in the Arab–Israeli Conflict, 1948–1979* (Princeton University Press: Princeton, NJ).

Touval, S. (1989) 'Multilateral negotiation: an analytic approach', *Negotiation Journal*, 5(2).

Tower Commission Report (1987) (Bantam Books/Times Books: New York).

Trevelyan, H. (1971) *Living with the Communists* (Gambit: Boston).

Trevelyan, H. (1973) *Diplomatic Channels* (Macmillan – now Palgrave Macmillan: Basingstoke).

UN Treaty Collection (Status of Treaties) in connection with ICC arrest warrant for Sudan's president, March 2009 [www].

United Nations (1997) *The Status of Jerusalem* (United Nations: New York).

US Advisory Commission on Public Diplomacy (2008) *Getting the People Part Right: A report on the human resources dimension of public diplomacy* [www].

US Department of State (1991) *Dispatch*, 2(19), 13 May.

Vance, C. (1983) *Hard Choices: Critical years in America's foreign policy* (Simon & Schuster: New York).

Vattel, Emmerich de (1758) *Le Droit des Gens* (Neuchâtel) [English trsl. www].

Walden, George (1999) *Lucky George: Memoirs of an anti-politician* (Allen Lane: London).

Ware, R. (1990) 'Treaties and the House of Commons', *Factsheet*, FS.57 (Public Information Office, House of Commons: London).

Watson, A. (1982) *Diplomacy: The dialogue between states* (Eyre Methuen: London).

Webster, Sir C. (1961) *The Art and Practice of Diplomacy* (Chatto & Windus: London).

Weinberg, S. (1989) *Armand Hammer: The untold story* (Little, Brown: Boston).

Weizman, E. (1981) *The Battle for Peace* (Bantam: Toronto/New York/London).

Werts, J. (1992) *The European Council* (North-Holland: Amsterdam).

Whelan, J. G. (1990) *The Moscow Summit 1988* (Westview Press: Boulder, CO).

Wilton, Christopher, J. Griffin and A. Fotheringham (2002) *Changing Perceptions: Review of public diplomacy* ['Wilton Review'], [www].

Wolfe, R. (1998) 'Still lying abroad? On the institution of the resident ambassador', *Diplomacy and Statecraft*, 9(2), July.

Wood, J. R. and J. Serres (1970) *Diplomatic Ceremonial and Protocol: Principles, procedures and practices* (Macmillan – now Palgrave Macmillan: London).

Wriston, H. M. (1960) 'The special envoy', *Foreign Affairs*, 38(2).

Wylie, Neville (2006) 'Protecting powers in a changing world', *Politorbis*, 40(1) [www].

Xiaohong Liu (2001) *Chinese Ambassadors: The rise of diplomatic professionalism since 1949* (University of Washington Press: Seattle/London).

Young, E. (1966) 'The development of the law of diplomatic relations', *British Yearbook of International Law 1964*, Volume 40 (Oxford University Press: London/New York).

Young, J. W. (1986) 'Churchill, the Russians and the Western Alliance: the three-power conference at Bermuda, December 1953', *English Historical Review*, 101(401).

Young, J. W. (2008) *Twentieth-Century Diplomacy: A case study of British practice, 1963–1976* (Cambridge University Press: Cambridge).

Young, Kenneth T. (1968) *Negotiating with the Chinese Communists: The United States experience, 1953–1967* (McGraw-Hill: New York).

Zartman, I. W. and Berman, M. (1982) *The Practical Negotiator* (Yale University Press: New Haven/London).

Newspaper publications

Al Arabiya (2009) 6 March.

Financial Times (1994) 20 September.

Guardian, The: (2000) 18 January; (2001a) 4 April; (2001b) 31 July; (2008) 5 July; (2009) 9 January.

Haaretz (2007) 23 January.

Independent, The: (1988) 17 November; (1994) 11 February.

Mail Online (2007) 4 January.

New York Times: (1991) 12 February; (2009) 31 January.

Sudan Tribune, in connection with ICC arrest warrant for Sudan's president, March 2009.

Times, The: (1951) 18 April; (1954) 31 August; (1981) 3 July; (1983) 4 November.

Washington Post, The: (2003) 20 February; (2004) 6 May; (2007) 15 March.

Index

Abkhazia 207
Acheson, Dean 14, 164–5
Adaleh Centre 92
Adelman, Kenneth 39
ad hoc conferences 142–53 *passim*
  see also summitry
ad hoc envoys, *see* special missions
Afghanistan 150
  Geneva Accords on (1988)
    79–80, 81
  Taliban consulate of in Karachi 134
African Union 163, 168, 241
agendas 31–3, 47
agreements 70–82
  see also under individual agreements
agrément 112, 212, 224
Aix-la-Chapelle, Treaty of (1748) 85
al-Assad, Bashar 175
al-Assad, Hafez 172, 198
al-Bashir, Omar 162, 163, 233
Albright, Madeleine 195
Algeria 91, 93, 213
  Iran hostages mediation and 77,
    237–41 *passim*
ambassadors 104
  conferences of 119
  consuls and 135–6
  full representative character of 105
  mediation and 238
  public diplomacy and 186–8
  see also representation, resident
    embassy, roving ambassadors
ambassadors-at-large, *see* roving
  ambassadors
Amnesty International 88, 92
ancient Near East 1–2, 13
Anglo-Taiwan Education Centre 220
Anglo-Taiwan Trade Committee 220
Angola/Namibia talks (1988)
  deadlines in 59–63 *passim*
  details stage of 49, 51
  linkage in 48, 82
  metaphors of movement in 64

packaging of agreement and 78, 82
parties excluded from 150
publicity and 67
US mediation of 61, 67, 247, 248
venues of 38, 38–9, 237
Ankara 120
Annan, Kofi 87
apostolic delegate 220
Arabic broadcasting, Western 184, 185
Arab-Israeli conflict 28, 29
  UNSCR 242 (1967) and 45
  see also Arab-Israeli 'multilaterals',
    Camp David talks, Geneva
    Conference on Middle East
    (1973), Israel, Kissinger (Middle
    East and), Madrid Conference,
    PLO
Arab-Israeli 'multilaterals' 150, 155
Arab League summit 61, 163, 168, 169
Arafat, Yasser 62, 68
  see also PLO
arbitration 236, 242
archives, diplomatic mission 111, 210
archives, MFA 6, 13, 185
Argentina 143, 241
  see also Beagle Channel, Falkland
    Islands
aristocracy 7–8, 11, 108, 127
Arms Control and Disarmament
  Agency 17
arms control talks 48, 49, 51, 68, 75
  see also monitoring of agreements,
    SALT I, SALT II
ASEAN summit 168, 176
Atlantic Charter (1941) 71, 73
Australia 9, 136, 143
Austria 9, 37, 127
  mediation and 240
  protecting power role of 210,
    212, 240
  see also Kreisky
'automobile' metaphor 63–4
Aziz, Tariq 231